T0342051

Heuristics
in Analytics

Wiley & SAS Business Series

The Wiley & SAS Business Series presents books that help senior-level managers with their critical management decisions.

Titles in the Wiley & SAS Business Series include:

Activity-Based Management for Financial Institutions: Driving Bottom-Line Results by Brent Bahnub

Big Data Analytics: Turning Big Data into Big Money by Frank Ohlhorst

Branded! How Retailers Engage Consumers with Social Media and Mobility by Bernie Brennan and Lori Schafer

Business Analytics for Customer Intelligence by Gert Laursen

Business Analytics for Managers: Taking Business Intelligence beyond Reporting by Gert Laursen and Jesper Thorlund

The Business Forecasting Deal: Exposing Bad Practices and Providing Practical Solutions by Michael Gilliland

Business Intelligence Success Factors: Tools for Aligning Your Business in the Global Economy by Olivia Parr Rud

CIO Best Practices: Enabling Strategic Value with Information Technology, second edition by Joe Stenzel

Connecting Organizational Silos: Taking Knowledge Flow Management to the Next Level with Social Media by Frank Leistner

Credit Risk Assessment: The New Lending System for Borrowers, Lenders, and Investors by Clark Abrahams and Mingyuan Zhang

Credit Risk Scorecards: Developing and Implementing Intelligent Credit Scoring by Naeem Siddiqi

The Data Asset: How Smart Companies Govern Their Data for Business Success by Tony Fisher

Delivering Business Analytics: Practical Guidelines for Best Practice by Evan Stubbs

Demand-Driven Forecasting: A Structured Approach to Forecasting, Second Edition by Charles Chase

Demand-Driven Inventory Optimization and Replenishment: Creating a More Efficient Supply Chain by Robert A. Davis

The Executive's Guide to Enterprise Social Media Strategy: How Social Networks Are Radically Transforming Your Business by David Thomas and Mike Barlow

Economic and Business Forecasting: Analyzing and Interpreting Econometric Results by John Silvia, Azhar Iqbal, Kaylyn Swankoski, Sarah Watt, and Sam Bullard

Executive's Guide to Solvency II by David Buckham, Jason Wahl, and Stuart Rose

Fair Lending Compliance: Intelligence and Implications for Credit Risk Management by Clark R. Abrahams and Mingyuan Zhang

Foreign Currency Financial Reporting from Euros to Yen to Yuan: A Guide to Fundamental Concepts and Practical Applications by Robert Rowan

Health Analytics: Gaining the Insights to Transform Health Care by Jason Burke

Heuristics in Analytics: A Practical Perspective of What Influences Our Analytical World by Carlos Andre Reis Pinheiro and Fiona McNeill

Human Capital Analytics: How to Harness the Potential of Your Organization's Greatest Asset by Gene Pease, Boyce Byerly, and Jac Fitz-enz

Information Revolution: Using the Information Evolution Model to Grow Your Business by Jim Davis, Gloria J. Miller, and Allan Russell

Manufacturing Best Practices: Optimizing Productivity and Product Quality by Bobby Hull

Marketing Automation: Practical Steps to More Effective Direct Marketing by Jeff LeSueur

Mastering Organizational Knowledge Flow: How to Make Knowledge Sharing Work by Frank Leistner

The New Know: Innovation Powered by Analytics by Thornton May

Performance Management: Integrating Strategy Execution, Methodologies, Risk, and Analytics by Gary Cokins

Retail Analytics: The Secret Weapon by Emmett Cox

Social Network Analysis in Telecommunications by Carlos Andre Reis Pinheiro

Statistical Thinking: Improving Business Performance, second edition by Roger W. Hoerl and Ronald D. Snee

Taming the Big Data Tidal Wave: Finding Opportunities in Huge Data Streams with Advanced Analytics by Bill Franks

Too Big to Ignore: The Business Case for Big Data by Phil Simon

The Value of Business Analytics: Identifying the Path to Profitability by Evan Stubbs

Visual Six Sigma: Making Data Analysis Lean by Ian Cox, Marie A. Gaudard, Philip J. Ramsey, Mia L. Stephens, and Leo Wright

Win with Advanced Business Analytics: Creating Business Value from Your Data by Jean Paul Isson and Jesse Harriott

For more information on any of the above titles, please visit www.wiley.com.

Heuristics in Analytics

*A Practical Perspective
of What Influences
Our Analytical World*

Carlos Andre Reis Pinheiro
Fiona McNeill

WILEY

Library of Congress Cataloging-in-Publication Data:

Reis Pinheiro, Carlos Andre, 1940-
    Heuristics in analytics : a practical perspective of what influences our analytical world / Carlos Andre Reis Pinheiro, Fiona McNeill.
    1 online resource. — (Wiley & SAS business series)
    Includes bibliographical references and index.
    Description based on print version record and CIP data provided by publisher; resource not viewed.
    ISBN 978-1-118-42022-5 (pdf) — ISBN 978-1-118-41674-7 (epub) — ISBN 978-1-118-34760-7 (cloth)
    1. Management—Statistical methods.   2. Decision making—Statistical methods.   3. Business planning—Statistical methods.   4. Heuristic algorithms.   5. System analysis.   I. Title.
HD30.215
658.4'033—dc23

                                                                    2013043850

*No matter how heuristic our world is, we
always have some certainties in life.*

*This book is dedicated to our certainties, family.
Regardless how much we try, and how many mistakes
we make, nothing would be possible without family.*

*This book is totally dedicated to Daniele,
Lucas, and Maitê.*

And Jerry, Glo, and Emily.

Contents

Preface

Suppose you have a magical black box. You put a huge amount of data into it, from everywhere you can find. And say that each of these inputs are in different formats and each format, in turn, represents several distinct time periods, frequencies, and seasons, as well as different characteristics. Imagine that you can then push a button and voilà! Out pops new knowledge from that hodgepodge of input. You now know the likelihood that the next event will occur, you can predict behavior; you have quantified risk, the propensity to act, and well-defined emerging patterns. And all this magically produced output would be ready to use—in the format needed to take action. This is amazing, isn't? You just fill some box with lots of different stuff and get results that are easy to understand and that can immediately be put into use.

That black box is *analytics*. And it isn't a brand-new discipline but is heavily used in most industries these days. Analytics combines mathematics, statistics, probability, and heuristics theories. So now, after this brief description, we all understand that analytics is easy, right?

Mathematical disciplines, including statistics, probability, and others, have always been assigned to practical applications in some form or another, including those of business. Sometimes the relationship between the method and the application is quite clear, and sometimes it is not. As human beings, we have used trade since we started to relate to each other. Because of a need to interact we'd exchange goods. Mathematics was, and still is, a wonderful tool to support exchanges and business purposes—used to address issues from the simple to the complex.

The word *mathematics* comes from the Greek word *máthema*, which means learning, study, science. This word has always related to describing quantities, to depicting structures of distinct types and shapes, and to portraying spaces. Pattern recognition is forever an elusive topic for mathematicians. Recognizing patterns, whatever it is they represent and from whatever source they emerge, people hope to better understand the past, and as a rule, understand the past to foresee the future.

History (the study of past social and human perspectives) is often used as a way to understand former events, learn from them to explain the present, and possibly help understand and even predict the future. We document how societies, governments, groups of people, ghettos, all clusters of some sort, behave prior to a particular event. By understanding and describing these sorts of scenarios (like documenting them), historians try to explain events that took place to provide context of what happens in the future.

Historians and mathematicians are quite similar that way. For mathematicians, past events and their associated facts are gathered together and analyzed in order to describe some set of data. If the attributes describing those past events are not too large in terms of size or scope, a mental correlation might be done. This is what social and human researchers often do. Given some attributes along with a description of a particular scenario in relation to a past event, they correlate distinct aspects of the event itself to explain what happened. And, based on the description and the strength of correlation between event attributes associated with the past event, they also try to foresee what might happen next.

Although the methods may differ, this isn't far removed from what mathematicians do. We may use different terms (in fact, that is one of the plaguing realities of every discipline), but we analysts do the same thing. Mathematics is just another way to map what human beings do, think, understand, act, explain, and so on. What is a mathematical formula in the end? It is a way to describe the future by understanding past observations (well, at least one branch of mathematics does this). We used to do this in the past, when mathematics was used to count things for trade. Today, we examine scenarios with specific conditions and particular constraints, calculating outcomes for use in operations and decisions.

As with any other discipline, mathematics has evolved over time. In addition to counting physical objects, early uses of mathematics involved quantifying time, defining values for trade (bartering of goods lead to the use of currency), measuring land, measuring goods, and many other areas. As time passed, arithmetic, algebra, and geometry were used for taxation and financial calculations, for building and construction, and for astronomy. As uses continued to evolve, so did mathematical theory. Mathematics became a tool to support different scientific disciplines such as physics, chemistry, and biology, among others. And it is likely that mathematics will be used as a tool for disciplines that haven't even been defined yet.

In order to play this important role and support science, mathematics must be quite rigorous. One of the rigors of mathematics is proofs. Mathematical proof is a method that turns theorems into axioms by following a particular set of laws, rules, constraints, meanings, and reasons. The level of rigor needed to prove theorems has varied over time, changed in different cultures, and certainly extended to satisfy distinct scenarios for political, economic, and social applications.

But a crucial truth of mathematical proofs is that they are often simply a heuristic process. The procedures used to prove a particular theorem are often derived by trial and error. Heuristic characteristics might be present in the entire theorem scenario, or just at the inception. But in reality, heuristics is often involved in one or more stages of proof. Heuristics can support the definition of the proof from simple observation of an event (therefore helping to recognize a pattern), or heuristics may govern the entire mathematical proof by exception or induction.

Most mathematical models have some limits in relation to the set of equations that portray a particular scenario. These limits indicate that the equations work properly given specific conditions and particular constraints. Consider standard conditions for temperature and pressure in chemistry. Some formulas work pretty well if temperature and pressure are in a specific range of values, otherwise, they don't. Is the formula wrong? Or could it be that at other times in history, the formula was valid, but not now? The answer is no, on both counts. It just means that this particular formula works pretty well under some specific conditions, but not others. Remember that formulas are built to model a particular event, based on a set of observations and, therefore, this formula will work fine when the constraints of the model scenario are true.

This is a perfect example of why mathematical models can describe a particular scenario using one or more equations. Although these equations may properly depict a specific scenario, the methods work properly if, and usually just if, a particular set of conditions are satisfied. There are boundary conditions limiting accuracy of equations, and therefore, a model simply represents some specific scenario. These boundary conditions are sometimes just a specific range of possible values assigned to constants or variables.

Think about physics. The classical mechanical physics of Isaac Newton describe regular movements considering regular bodies (not too small and not too big), traveling at regular speeds (not too slow and not too fast). However, once we start to consider very high speeds, such as the speed of light, the classical Newtonian theories no longer describe the movements. This doesn't mean the formulas are wrong; it just means that the particular scenario Newton wished to describe using those formulas requires a particular set of condition and constraints. To describe regular bodies at very high velocity we need to use Einstein's formulas. Einstein's theory of relativity (and his corresponding formulas) describes the movement of regular bodies at very high speeds. His theory doesn't conflict with Newton's; it simply explains a different scenario. Eventually, very small bodies at very high speeds also needed a distinct theory to describe their movement, and quantum physics was born. As we continue to learn, and delve even more specifically into areas of physics (and the authors would argue, any discipline), the need for different methods will continue— a story like this one never ends.

And so, we are not that different from historians. As mathematicians, statisticians, data miners, data scientists, analysts (whatever name we call ourselves), we too take into consideration a set of attributes used to represent/describe a particular scenario, and analyze the available data to try to describe and explain patterns or predict (which is, as a matter of fact, a particular type of pattern).

Once upon a time, a mathematician named Edward Lorenz was quite focused on predicting weather. At that time, this sort of work was largely based on educated guesses and heuristics. Is it so different today? Maybe (guesses are still fundamental and the heuristic process is undoubtedly still present). Back in Edward Lorenz's day, weather prediction included assumptions, observations, and lots of guesswork—in spite of the scientific instruments available at the time. When computers came onto the scene, Lorenz foresaw the possibility to combine mathematics with meteorology. He started to build a computer mathematical model, using differential equations, to forecast changes in temperature and pressure. Lorenz had created a dozen differential equations and managed to run some simulations and estimate virtual weather conditions. This was certainly a dramatic improvement over historical guesswork. During the winter of 1961, Edward Lorenz was examining a sequence of numbers. At the time, computers used a total of six decimals for all observations. However, in order to save space on the printout, Lorenz decided to use three decimals instead of six to define the sequence. Lorenz assumed that the difference in one part in a thousand wouldn't really make any difference at all.

This assumption seemed to be quite reasonable. Scientists accept that small noises in initial conditions will lead to small changes in the onward behavior. But Lorenz was using a deterministic system of equations, which required a particular starting point. Initial conditions, being well determined and described, are quite important to deterministic processes. When Lorenz had suppressed three decimals in his set of equations, he found a completely unexpected result. Instead of finding results similar to those of previous runs, the derived virtual weather patterns substantially diverged from previous patterns. In only a few months of iterations, the three-decimal and the six-decimal forecasts held no similarity at all.

Lorenz thought that small numerical variation in the initial conditions was similar to a small puff of wind, and unlikely to represent an important impact on the large-scale features of weather systems. However, the virtual puff of wind led to a catastrophically different outcome.

This puff of wind phenomenon is known as sensitivity dependence of initial conditions. Lorenz called his observation the *butterfly effect*. Nonlinear equations that explain weather are incredibly sensitivity to initial conditions, so much so that a butterfly flapping its wings in Brazil could set off a tornado in Canada.

Finally, imagine yourself quite alone, settled down at the bar, with no one to chat with. I know, in a regular pub (particular in the Irish ones), you can always find yourself in a chat, eventually. But stay with us, this is just an assumption, a hypothetical approach if you will—as we love to postulate. Anyway, suppose you're alone and looking at your pint and begin to watch the bubbles dancing, in a somewhat disorderly fashion, up to the top of the glass. If you are familiar with Guinness you see an even more beautiful scene unfold—with liquid and foam scrambling up to the top. In either beer selection, if you really pay attention to the process (don't worry, in a situation like this we understand if you don't), you might observe that there isn't a pattern of bubble collisions, nor is there a pattern of liquid and foam interfusion. And even more importantly, past bubbles collisions don't help foresee the next ones. The past behavior of the liquid and foam interfusion doesn't help establish the next path of mixing. The past events don't give you a clue about the overall pattern of the events and, therefore, about future events.

When past events don't help forecast eventual occurrences, we usually call this phenomenon a stochastic process. This means that past events are a sequence of random steps, making it impossible to predict the next step by studying the historical behavior (also known as a random walk). Imagine yourself once again, still at the pub watching bubble collisions. When you decide to go home, your way out could be very unpredictable (okay, it was a very, very late night at the pub). You can take a path outside the pub and walk a sequence of indecipherable steps. Your past steps in this (shall we even say) stumble won't help any mathematician predict what your next step should be.

We aren't the first to notice this—in addition to the classic notions of random walks, this pub-induced phenomenon is also (officially) known as the drunkard's walk. It explains all notions of pubs and Guinness. If a drunkard is at the end of the night and there is a combination of pubs each with Guinness, what is the fastest way to consume . . . sorry, we digress. The important thing here is that there are events in business, science, and many other environments where knowledge about the past doesn't in fact give us appropriate knowledge about the future.

The drunkard's walk phenomenon refers to the element of randomness assigned to this particular process. And if we decide to be totally comprehensive, this randomness is assigned to most processes we experience in life. It is similar to optimization problems. We always want to consider the problem as linear, but if we look deep inside it, it is most often a nonlinear problem. But this is par for the course. In order to make it easier to solve problems, we accept approximations. And these approximations don't significantly change the results. Given that, we feel better and more confident in using them.

So, after all that, analytics is quite easy, isn't it?

Sorry, but that magical box still doesn't exist. Analytics isn't that easy after all. The truth is that analytics can be quite hard, precisely because there are heuristic processes at work. Taking into account the heuristic factors of analytics, wherein trial and error processes are used to discover useful knowledge, or when past events don't lead to future forecasts, and when small noises in the initial conditions can dramatically change final results, we can easily assume that analytics is not easy at all.

In the development of analytical models we need to consider how heuristic the business scenario is. We need to examine past occurrences to understand if the scenario is governed by stochastic process or not. We also have to properly define initial conditions for the model being created.

For each situation there is a particular technique employed. Sometimes, even for the same situation, considering exactly the same scenario, there is more than one technique to be used. Comparison and assessment processes are needed in order to select the model representation of the available data. Data mining models are based on the patterns in data, and so accuracy and performance are highly influenced by the data being studied.

We have a plethora of techniques, methods, and types of analytical models to choose from for a specific business objective. On the other hand, we have a huge amount of data to process. The only way to move forward is by using the proper tool or set of tools. Analytics is no longer mathematics, statistics, or probability. Analytics has become computer science. Analytics involves all those theories (math and stats, etc.) via the right computer program. The appropriate set of computer programs that are grounded in theory, but that can also handle huge amounts of data is the new pen and paper.

This book focuses on analytic processes and how they fit into our heuristic world.

In spite of the strong heuristic characteristic inherent in analytical processes, this book emphasizes the need to have the proper tools and approach to analytical problem solving. Randomness has a valid impact on virtually everything we do, on everything that happens, and on business events. Nevertheless, this fact makes it even more important to put in place analytics to assess the randomness, and to understand business events, marketplace scenarios, and behavior.

Competitive marketplaces are compelled to use analytics. To perform better, organizations need to understand not just the market and those within it but how consumers behave when they have options. By understanding customer behavior, companies are able to take business actions in an attempt to encourage different behavior—like enhancing service usage, improving product adoption, extending customer lifetimes, reducing insolvency issues, and more. The effectiveness odds improve when companies act in the marketplace based on the knowledge generated by analytical models. Why? Because they are placing their bets more wisely—investing in customer-focused strategies that they have some evidence will work, and measured expectations regarding what the results are likely to be. Increasing customer spending and service adoption and reducing losses from fraud, for example, change the portfolio of behavior of the customer base. If it didn't, then the strategies employed wouldn't be effective. So if you are effective, then the behavior of customers will change, as will the associated data describing them. The only real constant, in fact, is change.

This book is in praise of analytics, no matter how heuristic our world is.

CARLOS ANDRE REIS PINHEIRO
AND FIONA MCNEILL
JULY, 2013

Acknowledgments

I started writing this book in 2011, first in Dublin as a visiting researcher, and then with Oi Communication in Brazil. During the commute from Niteroi to Rio de Janeiro (usually by bus or ferry), I read three books. Actually I read more than three, but these three impacted the desire to write this book. The first one was *The New Know: Innovation Powered by Analytics*.[1] Thornton May brilliantly explored the power of analytics to solve business problems, allowing companies to innovate. The book really gives us a sense of how important analytics is and how crucial it is to companies nowadays. However, as most of the books do, it describes what goes right. As with a formula, if we properly select the variables, we may get the expected result. Unfortunately, analytics is not a science. It is based on science, but it is also an art. Maybe analytics is really about the art of how to use science to solve problems. But anyway, this book was an inspiration. So, my first acknowledgment is to Thornton May.

The second book was *Blink: The Power of Thinking without Thinking*, by Malcolm Gladwell.[2] This book sticks to you. I missed my bus stop many times because of it. It shows how often we make decisions without thinking. Let me rephrase that: How often we make decisions thinking we are thinking about these decisions. In a flash, when required, we capture information in our brain, we gather it appropriately, weighing the pros and cons, and just then—we make the decision. Sometimes right, sometimes wrong. But the interesting thing in here is all these happen in a blink of an eye. This book showed me how heuristic the process of thinking truly is, particularly when

---

[1] May, Thorton. *The New Know: Innovation Powered by Analytics* Hoboken, New Jersey, John Wiley & Sons, 2009.
[2] Gladwell, M. *Blink: The Power of Thinking without Thinking.*, New York, Little Brown and Company, Time Warner Book Group, 2005.

we consider time. We also learn from the process itself and eventually we make better decisions. And I thought to myself, these books are seemingly opposite, but they aren't, not really. They are complements. Analytics really helps solve most of the business problems we currently face. But the process to solve these problems sometimes is far from being exact, as it is in science (actually in many times science is not like this as well). Very often we do analytics thinking without thinking. And most of the times, it works. So my second acknowledgment is to Malcolm Gladwell.

Finally, the third book that was a catalyst for this book, and has driven many studies in Heuristics, is *The Drunkard's Walk: How Randomness Rules Our Lives*, by Leonard Mlodinow.[3] In this book Mlodinow explores a series of random events that touch our lives on a daily basis. He describes historical mathematic stories, including experiments covering probability, demographic and economic data, statistics, logic, regression, and prediction. The book illustrates how our lives are profoundly impacted by change and randomness, and how everything from wine rating and corporate success to school grades and political polls are less reliable than we believe.

The sum of how analytics can solve real problems, how important it is to believe in your feelings and in your way of thinking, and given that, in the end, everything is biased by chance—found in these three books formed the essence of this work.

Unfortunately, I never met any of these brilliant authors. But even so, I also want to thank the people I actually do know. And for that, I'll do this chronologically. I begin with my former boss, Bruno Martins, who created an effective environment for me and the other members of the Oi team, for being brave in embracing the idea of an Analytics Lab at Oi. Also thanks to my peers Herivelton Pereira, Jair Carvalho, Flávio Sebastião, Rodrigo Telles, and Rosane Lisboa. Other Oi colleagues who helped create the encouraging atmosphere that began this endeavor are Bruno Kitsuta, Ana Sidreira, Daniella Alfaya, Vitor Cordeiro, Nivaldo de Moraes, Adriana Ferreira, Michelle dos Santos, Larissa Borges, and Ana Paula Cohen.

---

[3] Mlodinow, Leonard. *The Drunkard's Walk: How Randomness Rules Our Lives.* New York, Vintage Books, 2009.

Other industry colleagues that deserve special mention include Luis Francisco de Campos Henriques from Brasil Telecom and Karl Langan from SAS Ireland.

A special thanks to Fiona McNeill who honored me by coauthoring this book. Fiona gave me new perspectives for my own ideas, organizing them, putting them into a more understandable shape, and then creating a perfect atmosphere for sharing innovative thoughts about analytics. Because of her, this is a brand new book, quite different than the one I started. And I am so proud of this one!

▧　▧　▧

Indeed Carlos, it has been my honor working with you! Frankly, when I was first introduced to some of the initial concepts of the text, Carlos won me over with butterflies and beer. His openness, responsiveness, and dedication, even as he moved across the globe, were inspirational. I'd like to thank Carlos for his gracious sharing of time, thoughts, and talents in coauthoring this book. I'm pretty proud of it too.

I'd like to also thank Buffie Silva because, if it wasn't for her, I'd never have had the opportunity to work on this project. She got the ball rolling, all the necessary wheels on the bus, cheering along the way. I sincerely appreciate your faith.

▧　▧　▧

In addition to the inspiration I was gifted from Carlos, I'd like to acknowledge four key people who, over the years, inspired me and encouraged me to go outside the box, teaching me things in my career that I drew on to complete this book. So, to Tony Lea, Greg Breen, Joel Grosh, and Don Goodland—I extend my sincerest gratitude. Your words, deeds, and mentorship continue to echo within me.

▧　▧　▧

And finally, to Stacey Hamilton, who had the challenge of reviewing the book. Stacey you are more than a reviewer, guiding us along the exhausting process of writing the book (and poking us from time to time too). Your expertise as editor and patience as a colleague made this book real. Thank you so much Stacey (once again)!

About the
Authors

Carlos Andre Reis Pinheiro

Dr. Pinheiro began his business career in analytics in 1996 for a Brazilian worldwide shipping company, now called CSAV. Working at some of the largest telecommunications providers since the market privatized in 1998, he has examined business problems in database marketing, data warehousing, data mining, and social networks analysis across a wide range of departments including IT, marketing, sales, revenue assurance, and finance.

Dr. Pinheiro holds a PhD in engineering from the Federal University of Rio de Janeiro where he focused on high performance computing methods for topology generation in neural networks to prevent insolvency; a MSc. in computer science from Fluminense Federal University; and a B.Sc. in mathematics and computer science.

He has also completed three postdoctoral research terms, in optimization at IMPA[4] (2006–2007); in social network analysis at Dublin City University, Ireland (2008–2009); and in human mobility and complex networks at Université de Savoie, France (2012). He is currently a visiting professor at KU Leuven, Belgium, and a lecturer at FGV, Brazil, investigating human mobility in urban areas.

Dr. Pinheiro authored *Social Network Analysis in Telecommunications*, John Wiley Sons Inc. in 2011. Today, he is in Leuven, Belgium,

---

[4] A world renowned mathematical sciences research institute that leads research in both Brazil and Latin America.

or Niteroi, Brazil, with his wife and two children. And when not researching, teaching, or writing you'll find him on the soccer field with his son or playing with his daughter.

Fiona McNeill

Ms. McNeill has applied analytics to business problems since she began her career in 1992. Having worked with some of the largest financial, retail, manufacturing, communications, transportation, education, services, and government agencies in North America, McNeill has consistently helped companies benefit from strategic use of data and analytics.

Throughout her career, she has been affiliated with data and technology companies, information and survey providers, IBM Global Services, and—for the past 15 years—at SAS.

Ms. McNeill holds an M.A. in behavioral geography from McMaster University where she examined time and space in stochastic models of consumer behavior; and a B.Sc. in bio-physical systems from the University of Toronto.

Today, you'll find her with her daughter in Lunenburg, Canada. When she's not working and writing, she'll be dory rowing or sailing on the Atlantic Ocean.

The Heuristics of Analytics is their first collaborative volume.

Heuristics in Analytics

CHAPTER 1

Introduction

Analytics is used to address many different types of business problems. It is used to understand customer behavior and how consumers may be adopting new products and services. It is used to describe different marketplace scenarios and their impacts. It is also used to decipher competitor's movements and patterns. And it is used for predicting potential future revenue, detecting risk, uncovering fraud, minimizing bad debt, optimizing operational processes, and more. Analytics is used in all of these business applications.

In most cases, and in particular in customer scenarios, there are many factors that cause misunderstanding of what is currently happing within a market, or even what is happing with a specific customer within a particular market.

It is always important to bear in mind that consumers present different types of behaviors and in accordance with the market they are interacting with. As a customer, I can be very aggressive in terms of purchasing high-tech products, often buying cutting-edge gadgets. However, I am quite conservative in terms of investing, putting my money into low-risk accounts. There is no one, overall general behavior for any customer. We each behave in different ways depending upon the situation in which we find ourselves. Essentially, we wear different hats, having distinct behaviors that are observable—each in relation to the distinct roles we play. And sometimes, even in similar scenarios, we may play different roles and exhibit different behaviors, depending on the other scenario actors that are involved.

All analytical models, whether they are supervised (classification), semi-supervised, or unsupervised (segmentation), take into consideration most of the structured information that companies currently hold in their databases. They include information about customer characteristics, the products and services that they offer, and how customers interact with them. They include financial inputs such as credit rating, payment history, late payment durations, and so forth. All of this information, however, describes only a limited part of the end-consumer's behavior. In other words, we really can't say too much about an individual customer's profile, but we can describe how they behave in a single scenario, like when using the company's products and services.

You could say that, based on my historical data, I am an aggressive buyer of high-tech gadgets. And it is just as possible to state, based on my buying history, that I work hard to purchase high-tech products in advance. But this behavior doesn't replicate to other situations, like my conservative financial investment behavior. I also might be very price sensitive regarding telecommunications services, but on the other hand, I may not be sensitive to aspects such as quality when it comes to hotel rooms. The important thing to keep in mind is that there isn't an overall understanding of behavior. Instead, behavior is always in relation to something, to hotels, financial investments, or telecommunication preferences.

Consider for a moment, understanding and even predicting behavior in a telecommunications scenario. Most analytical models consider call frequency and duration, demographic information about the consumer, billing and payment history, and—when available and in reasonable quality—historical contacts with customer care channels. Based on such data, companies are able to build the majority of the analytical models used to examine common business issues such as product/service cross-sell or up-sell, churn, revenue leakage, risk specification, or fraud detection. Furthermore, for classification problems (that is, the ones that use a target class for training), historical information is quite crucial in that it teaches the model which behavior is most highly relevant to that particular event. What are the main characteristics for all customers who bought some particular product? How do they behave before this purchasing event? Which variables were most relevant to describe the business event or triggered it? Historical data, when it is in relation to a particular business event, teaches the analytical model to foresee the likelihood for each customer to perform when exposed to a similar event.

However, this is a purely mathematical approach. Even more specifically, it is a purely statistical approach. The analytical model teaching, also called the *training process*, is based on the average customer's behavior. However all customers with similar past behavior will not proceed in the same way, will not purchase the same product, will not consume the same service in the same way, and so on.

For example, according to my past behavior, and as represented in my historical data, I might be about to purchase a particular bundle of telecommunications services because customers who have been behaving like me have bought this bundle in the past, after a similar sequence of events. So, it is quite reasonable for any company to think that now is my turn. Then, the week that I'm going to buy that bundle approaches. Most unfortunately, one special Sunday afternoon, my soccer team lost the derby. It was the final match of the championship, and we lost to our biggest rival. So instead, my forthcoming week is a sequence of five long days of frustration from the loss, and I'm certainly not in the mood to buy anything. Instead, I hide myself and simply wait for time to move on. This completely external event was not considered by the model and yet has changed everything to do with the accuracy of my predicted behavior. Statistically I should have purchased the bundle that week, and the likelihood of it would be around 87 percent. Unfortunately, the analytical model didn't take into account that possible result for the final match. And with great sadness, this particular variable—the result of the final match—was indeed most relevant in my actualized behavior. It is the single factor that made all difference in my buying something or not.

These external influences happen all the time in our lives. Very often they impact analytical models, especially those that are defined for business purposes. It is not possible to consider all variables, all attributes, all information required to create a particular inference. Everything in modeling is about an approximation. As my historical behavior was quite similar to other customers who did buy that particular bundle, my likelihood of purchasing the same bundle might also be very high. But it isn't a definite or a sure thing that I will buy it at all. It is just an approximation. It might be a highly accurate approximation, but in the end, it is just a simple approximation. The likelihood assigned to each customer is simply an approximation of how they might eventually behave in relation to a particular business event.

This fact shouldn't push us to give up on analytical endeavors. As a matter of fact, it should do just the opposite. It hopefully brings us even closer to understanding the true value of analytics. Unexpected events will always take place, and they will always affect predicted outcomes. Analytical models work well for the majority of cases, for most of the observations, and in most applications. Unexpected or uncontrolled events will always occur and typically affect a few observations within the entire modeling scenario. However, there are some events that will impact the entire analysis population, like a war, an earthquake, or a hurricane, and as such, a new historical behavior is built.

Analytical methods that understand the past and that are prepared to explain present circumstances do provide forecasts into the future that improve business decisions. Other books describe the value that analytics provides.[1] This book is different. It examines the unimagined and unforeseen events that impact analytic results, describing the art of analytics, which is founded in the science of mathematics and statistics.

The formula to predict a particular event works a lot like the standard conditions for temperature and pressure in chemistry. If everything is right, if the temperature is in the expected range, as well as the pressure, then the formula forecasts the outcome quite well. While we certainly can have exceptions, the formula is just a way to model a particular scenario and be aware of what is coming next, and what could be expected in certain conditions. Likewise in science, and several other disciplines, this approach is the closest we can get to being in touch with reality. It is much more enlightened than doing nothing. The key is to properly understand what is happening in order to dramatically increase your model's usefulness.

---

[1] See for example, Stubbs, E. *The Value of Business Analytics: Identifying the Path to Profitability,* (Hoboken, New Jersey) Wiley & Sons, 2011.

THE MONTY HALL PROBLEM

The Monty Hall Problem is a very good example of how important it is to be well aware of activities in the marketplace, the corporate environment, and other factors that can influence consumer behavior. And equally important, it illustrates how critical it is to understand the modeling scenario in order to predict activities and events. In order to increase your chances, particularly from a corporate perspective, it is important to understand the equations that, at least with reasonable accuracy, explain the scenario under investigation—even if that scenario is largely composed of a situation that is dependent on chance. It is then possible to at least create an expected outcome of a particular scenario, whether it be probabilistic (based on historical information of past events) or stochastic (as would be with a sequence of random activities). Breaking this down, if you are going to flip a coin, and you are about to bet based on it, you should know your chances of winning the toss are about 50-50, no matter whether you choose heads or tails. Although this sounds quite simple and straightforward, companies don't do this very often. Companies typically do not prepare themselves for upcoming events—gambling even more than they should. The Monty Hall Problem is a case that illustrates this notion, that the knowledge about the scenario and the chances involved make all the difference between winning and losing.

Let's Make a Deal is a television game show originally produced in the United States and thereafter popularized throughout the world. The show's premise is to have members of the audience accept or reject deals offered to them by the host of the show. The members of the audience who participate in the game usually have to analyze and weigh all the possibilities assigned to a particular offer described by the host. This offer could be a valuable prize or a totally useless item. Monty Hall was the famous actor and producer who served as the host for this game show for many years.

The Monty Hall Problem is in fact a probability puzzle, considered to be a paradox because although the result seems implausible it is statistically observed to be true. This problem was first proposed by Steve Selvin, in a letter to the *American Statistician* in 1975.[2] This

---

[2] *American Statistician*, Vol. 29, No. 1 – 1975 "Letters to the Editor": http://www.jstor.org/stable/2683689

problem was published again in *Parade Magazine* in September 9th, 1990, within the Sunday "Ask Marilyn" column, on page 16.

> "Suppose you're on a game show, and you're given the
> choice of three doors: Behind one door is a car; behind
> the others, goats. You pick a door, say no. 1, and the host,
> who knows what's behind the doors, opens another door,
> say no. 3, which has a goat. He then says to you, "Do you
> want to pick door no. 2?" The question is: Is it to your
> advantage to switch your choice?

In her response, Marilyn vos Savant said that the contestant should always switch to the other door and by doing so, she explained, that the contestant was going to double his or her chances. She was flooded with more than ten thousand letters from all over the country, including letters from five hundred PhDs, mathematicians, and statisticians associated with revered and prestigious universities and institutions. The majority of the letters expressed concerned with Savant's mistake, and some of them even asked her to confess her error in the name of math. Intuitively, the game concept leads us to believe that each door has a one-in-three chance to have the car behind of it, and the fact that one of the doors has been opened does change the probability of the other two. Once one door is opened, the chances of having a car behind one of the other two doors are one in two for each one left. When one door is opened it is like we have essentially changed the original scenario, from three doors to just two. But in reality, there is no changing the probabilities for each door, either before or after the first door has been opened. All doors keep the same one-in-three chance of having a car behind of it, both in the occasion of the first question (three doors closed) and on the occasion of the second one (two doors closed and on opened).

Marilyn vos Savant stated that if the car is equally likely to be behind each door, a player who picked door number one and doesn't switch, has a one-in-three chance of winning the car, while a player who picks door number one and does switch has a two-out of-three chance. In this way, the players must switch the door to double their chances. It is quite simple, isn't it?

The Monty Hall Problem demands some assumptions. The first one is about fairness. The car should have an equally likely possibility of being behind any of those three doors, and the contestant can initially choose any door. Monty will always open another door, giving the contestant the opportunity to switch from their initial door choice. And finally, and mostly important, Monty knows what is behind the doors—and will always open a door that reveals a goat. If Monty revealed the car the game would otherwise be over. By revealing the goat behind the door, Monty doesn't alter the chances of the remaining doors to 50-50. Actually, and from the beginning, each one of the other two doors not chosen has a one-in-three chance and, therefore, the sum of the remaining doors is two out of three. The fact that Monty opens a door he knows has a goat behind it puts all two thirds of the chances to win in the door not yet picked by the contestant.

You can also understand this problem by calculating the probability of losing. Switching the door makes you lose only if you have previously picked the door with the car behind. And initially, you have one in three chances to pick the car. Hence, if you switch the door, you have a two in three chance to not lose (1/3 for each remaining door).

To finish this up, let's think about the details of this problem illustrated in a table showing all possible arrangements of one car and two goats behind a total of three doors, as shown in Table 1.1. Suppose you pick door no. 1. In the first row of the table, you can see that if you switch you lose and if you stay you win. In the second row, if you switch you win and if you stay with your original choice, you lose. Finally, in the third arrangement, if you switch you win and if you stay you lose. By choosing door no. 1, if you keep the door and stay with that choice, you win one time. But if you switch you have a chance to win two times. Analogous calculus can be made for doors 2 and 3. At the end, by switching the door you should double your chances to win. Table 1.1 shows the options and the chances in keeping or switching the doors.

Table 1.1 Itemized Choices in the Monty Hall Problem

Door 1	Door 2	Door 3	Switch	Stay
Car	Goat	Goat	Goat	Car
Goat	Car	Goat	Car	Goat
Goat	Goat	Car	Car	Goat

The point is that in spite of this particular problem being about gambling, by knowing the proper theory and by understanding the correct way to calculate and model in the scenario, you can double your chances of winning. The same thing happens with analytics. In spite of the heuristic influence over real-world events, such as the loss of my soccer team on that awful Sunday, by knowing the proper way to model the business scenario you can substantially increase the chances of applied model success. In theory, if a company offers a particular product to a customer, the chances that he or she will get that product should be 50-50. But if the company knows about this particular customer, their past behavior, the current behavior for similar profiles, products, and services held by similar customers, and so on, then the company could substantially increase the chance of succeeding in this selling process.

EVOLVING ANALYTICS

Over the past few years, analytics has evolved into a major discipline for many corporations, particularly those exposed to a highly competitive marketplace. Analytics is composed of a set of distinctive approaches that use technologies and methods to describe business processes, to support decision making, to solve issues, and to help with improving performance.

Analytics can involve simple business intelligence applications, such as predefined multidimensional databases that are queried, to more advanced interactive visualizations of data across different dimensions, allowing analysts to glean insight from large volumes of data. These types of business analytics tools can be applied to single, built-to-purpose applications all the way up to large data marts that are used to examine questions in particular department(s). They can also be associated with a corporate data warehouse—as either a collection of multidimensional databases or as a single, high-performance business intelligence platform from which multipurpose tools are used to examine business problems across the whole company. Typically, these types of applications are associated with raw data collected from transactional systems, aggregated based on a particular business perspective, and examined through a user friendly front-end—allowing analysts to execute several types of queries in a short period of time. Business insights very often come from such multidimensional examinations of data as deep inquiries of operational inputs—formatted in a digestible, managed layout.

Analytics also goes a step further to include statistical and mathematical analyses. These types of analytic endeavors are often completed on a more ad hoc basis, demanding timely examination associated with a particular business purpose. And usually, this type of analysis is not periodic nor does it demand frequent reprocessing of the task. It oftentimes does, however, require output monitoring to foresee if changes are occurring that require adjustments to the model over time. Such a model could be developed to examine the overall marketplace, a snapshot inquiry about customer behavior, or a forecast study in relation to costs, sales, or market growth, for example. This sort of analysis is often performed by using statistical and/or mathematical procedures and is commonly done in a stand-alone environment. As an ad hoc process it usually does not require the same infrastructure of a production environment. It is a set of tasks and procedures that are used to understand a particular business question and, once deployed, raise useful knowledge that can change operations and activities.

Finally, there is a third layer of analytics that is composed of data mining models. The data mining discipline includes artificial intelligence algorithms such as neural networks, decision trees, association rules, and genetic algorithms, among others. These artificial intelligence methods often use a more mathematical approach and are well suited to specific business issues, like predicting a particular business event from large volumes of inputs. Association rules, also known as induction rules, are very good at describing particular subject relationships, such as in retail. They are used to understand how products are selling together, highlighting the correlations between products to identify grouping, or sell with relationships. Consumers who buy bread, cheese, and ham usually buy butter as well. Consumers who buy red wine and Grana Padano cheese commonly also buy honey and cinnamon. These rules highlight product correlations, some of which might be quite useful, others not. Two metrics affiliated with association rules help us understand how relevant and strong the rule is—namely support and confidence. However, if you run an association algorithm over a hospital database, particularly using data from the obstetric department, a rule would probably emerge that women have babies, with both a high level of support and confidence. Of course, that rule has no business value—and although true, is not useful to any particular business decision.

This brings to light a very common phenomenon in analytics— you have to build a bridge between the technical procedure and the business results. Outcomes from analytics should raise the knowledge about the market, the customers, the products, and so forth, enabling companies to deploy practical, well-informed actions that improve their businesses. The results are beneficial associations and rules are that are not only informative but can also be applied to business actions. Validation of the value to the business derived from analytics-based knowledge should always be performed and encompasses the measured effect that analytics has on activities, events, and processes.

Artificial intelligence (AI) techniques are often assigned to methods that focus on classification or prediction. Commonly, the predictive AI methods are referred to as supervised learning models, given that they demand historical data and a target variable. The target variable is what the model is trying to predict and the historical information is used to train the model in order to predict the target variable. This historic information drives the model's learning process, correlating the past behavior to the target. This learning process allows the model to foresee possible values for the target variable in the future. Artificial neural networks, decision trees, and regression equations are the most commonly used data mining techniques. These types of models usually require less business knowledge validation because they are trained in recognizing patterns in the data. So, once this type of model has its premise, which is the target variable, the outcome results are based on the pattern recognized in the historical information, rather than by some particular type of business knowledge itself. AI tasks are more about the training process and the pattern recognition rather than an overall analysis in traditional statistics (the latter of which doesn't have previous history or a historical premise).

AI classification methods are also pattern recognition procedures— that, instead of predicting a target variable, focus on delineating patterns that describe the data. This type of modeling includes clustering, k-means and self-organizing map methods—all of which require business validation because there is no premise in relation to the model training; that is, no target variable. Therefore, business expertise validation determines if the results are sound—demonstrating that bridge between the technical process and the business knowledge. A classification model essentially looks at the past, learns from it (creating a pattern), and uses it to apply that pattern to data not involved in the model training process. A clustering model usually requires a calculation that identifies the correlation between the main characteristics of the clusters found and the business threats and opportunities. Each cluster holds some set of characteristics which describes the cluster and which lead to business actions, like protecting the company from threats or exploring some hidden opportunities. Customers can also be stimulated to migrate from one cluster to another, say from a medium-value cluster to a high-value cluster, or from a disloyal cluster to a loyal one.

Many business actions can benefit from the insight gleaned from clustering techniques, particularly those that involve understanding groups of customers, products, and services. Distinct marketing campaigns can be based on the characteristics associated with individual clusters giving different incentives and alternate messages to each. A cluster, in and of itself, highlights some trend, type of behavior, or a particular need—some specific grouping driven by the data itself. Identified trends can be used to create a new product, the type of behavior can be used to establish an incentive, and the need can be used to adjust a service. There are many interactions companies can deploy and benefit from by using the subjective and descriptive information emanating from the clustering process.

The Business Relevance of Analytics

Analytical modeling plays a key role in distinguishing companies within any marketplace by driving opportunities for competitive advancement. This competitive advantage enables companies to be more innovative, helping them stand above the others in their market. Analytics helps identify when and what products to launch, informs which services will maintain customer loyalty, and optimizes product and service price, quality, and turnover. But perhaps even more important than being innovative is to maintain innovation—and where analytics becomes crucial. Innovation means solving problems with simple solutions rather than complex ones, in an appropriate amount of time, and using a feasible replication process. In order to sustain innovation companies need to create a suitable environment to identify problems, threats, and opportunities; to create quick solutions that address the issues; and to deploy these solutions into the production chain. If the solution is too complex to be readily understood, too expensive to be deployed into a production process, or if it takes too long to be developed, then this solution certainly isn't innovative. It is just a solution, not feasible, not touchable, and not applicable to the company.

Be simple. Be fast. Be innovative.

Although easy to say, it isn't as easy to do. Companies around the world are trying to do exactly this, although many aren't succeeding. What's the secret? Unfortunately, there is no secret. It's like they say in the cartoon movie *Kung Fu Panda*. The secret of the amazing noodles was . . . there is no secret at all. It was all about the passion, love, and care put into making the noodles. The secret is in each one of us, who work with passion, love, respect, and who put all effort and energy into doing our best. The secret is to look at the past, to observe the present, and to try to foresee the future. So the secret is all about us, is it? Is it just a matter of looking at the past, observing the present, and foreseeing the future? Then why doesn't this approach always work? It doesn't always work because of the heuristic factor. Even though we may proceed on a well-trodden path and follow a typical pattern, there are so many unpredictable variables in our world, each with so many attributes to be considered that even a small change in the overall environment might alter everything.

You can do everything exactly the right way, but perhaps not in the right time. You could do it in exactly the right time and the right way, but perhaps not considering all the variables involved. You can even do everything in the proper way, in the right time, but by not taking into account some small external factor (which is unknowingly completely relevant to the entire model) that may be unmapped, unpredictable, and untracked. This one factor may be something you would never consider being important to your model—it could be a natural event, a political fact, a social change, or an economic disruption. The same approach, by taking the same steps, performing exactly the same routines, would thrive perfectly if done a bit earlier, or even a bit later, but not right now. This is the imponderable! This is something you cannot predict. So what do you do? How can you manage this heuristic world? We have no other tip—but to keep trying to model the scenario at hand.

Organizations need to use the best tools they have available in order to adapt themselves to the scenarios, to both current and future business environments and to both current and pending changes. Analytics will help you to understand all these changes, all these business scenarios, for all corporate environments. And, even when an analytical model fails, the analysis of that failure will help you understand why it happened, why your prediction didn't materialize as expected, and, hopefully, what you would need to do to different next time. Even the failures help you reroute your strategy and drive your company toward the proper trail.

Being innovative is not the destination; it is the journey. In order to be innovative, companies need to steady themselves into this analytical path by monitoring modeled outcomes and improving models over time. Increasing the usage of these models and by converting this whole analytic environment into an operational process that exists across the enterprise drives access to innovation. The organization's strategy should totally direct the analytical environment, and in turn, the analytical environment should totally support the company's strategy.

This relationship between organizational strategy and the analytical environment can be envisioned as three distinct steps. These steps may be performed at different stages of analytics maturity—or may even occur simultaneously. Irrespective of timing, each of these steps resonates with different stages of applied analytic procedures, each of which are aimed at addressing specific business issues, and with particular goals.

1. **Stage One Analytics**. This first layer of analytics provides long-term informational insight, helping organizations analyze trends and forecast business scenarios. Data warehouse,

data marts, multidimensional applications (OLAP—On Line Analytical Processing), and interactive visual analysis usually support this stage one purpose. These inputs support analyses geared toward identifying trends, historical event patterns, and business scenarios. This analysis is concerned with presenting information about past sales by region, branches, products, and, of course, changes that have occurred over time. You can easily replace sales by any other business issue such as churn, subscription, claims, investments, accounts, and so on. Also, you can replace the dimensions region, branch, and product by any business factor you may be interest in analyzing. However, you can't replace the dimension time, which should be always a consideration in this exploratory analytical approach. Often there is a production environment available that readily provides this kind of analytical information in a pre-defined environment, usually through a web portal.

2. **Stage Two Analytics**. A second layer of analytics maps out the internal and external environments that impact the question at hand. This can include market considerations, the customers' behavior and the competitor's actions, as well as details about the products and services that the organization offers. Questions that are explored in this stage include: How profitable are my products/services? How well have they been adopted by the target audience? How well do they suit the customer's need? Statistical analyses support these tasks, with correlations, topic identification, and association statistics methods. Usually in these cases there is an analytical environment available to perform such queries and analyses. However, further distinguishing it from the first stage, there is typically no production environment that provides real-time answers, nor a predefined web portal or any other interface for rapid response to such questions. This stage of analysis is performed on demand, when business departments request deep information about a particular business issue.

3. **Stage Three Analytics**. Finally, the third layer of analytics is driven by to the company's strategy. Model development

is directed by core business issues such as cross sell, up sell, churn, fraud, and risk, and models are also deployed and used once the results are derived. Data mining models that use artificial intelligence or statistics commonly support these types of endeavors, deploying supervised and unsupervised models to classify and predict some particular event and to recognize groups of similar behavior within the customer base for subscribed business change.

For example, let's consider what analyses are required when a company decides to launch a new product. Before establishing the proper packaging or price, the company may decide to run a deep study about the marketplace, the competitors, and the consumers. This study should take into consideration current customer needs: Are customers willing to adopt the product? What price might they be willing to pay for it? Do competitors have similar products in the market? If so, how much do they charge? Does the company have pre-existing products that compete with this new one? All these questions might be addressed by using the second layer of analytics. This task is completely on demand, and it would be required to support the product launch.

A more in-depth analysis regarding how customers consume similar products, taking into account historical information about sales, might lead to a predictive model that establishes the likelihood of customers purchasing this new product. This predictive model would support sales campaigns, by defining target customers who have higher likelihoods of purchase, for example. This type of procedure would be associated with the third layer of analytics.

And finally, once that product has been launched, the company could monitor the sales success over the time. Business analysts might have a clear view about how well sales for the product occur in relation to different customer segments, different types of promotions, how profitable the product is in different branches, regions, sales channel, and so forth. This type of task is associated with the first layer of analytics, by delivering readily available insights through a web portal, published reports, interactive visualizations, and other ad hoc queries about that product across different business dimensions.

The entire analytical environment, including applications that support the three stages of analytics, should all relate to the organization's strategy, cover all business issues, and be aligned with the company's priorities. For a new company just starting out, a key objective might be to acquire as many customers as possible. In this scenario a customer acquisition dashboard should be deployed as part of the first stage of analytics, in order to monitor the changing size of the customer base. A market analysis that describes customers' needs should be performed in the second stage, to understand which products and services must be launched. And a predictive model that targets acquisition strategies to the most appropriate prospects should be developed in the third stage of analytics.

On the other hand, if this company is well established and there are several other players emerging in their market, similar applications should be put in place but would be focused on monitoring different activities and events. In this situation the organization would want to monitor, understand, and predict churn (i.e., the rate at which customers leave the company), as well as develop predictive models that target cross and up-sell marketing activities. Nevertheless, the same three layers of analytics are used to adequately cover all the relevant business issues and organizational priorities.

The Role of Analytics in Innovation

Analytics plays a crucial role in modern corporate innovation. The outcomes from analytical models are used to drive new sales processes, to change customer experiences in order to avoid churn, and to identify triggers detecting fraud, risk, or any sort of corporate threat, as well as many other business issues. The knowledge from analytical models is commonly assigned to recognize customer behavior, to predict an event, or to assess the relationship between events, impacting company actions and activities.

The three layers of analytics provide a foundation for data-driven innovation, both creating and delivering new knowledge and accessible information. Each one of these layers might support insights and decisions for different members of the organization, based on their role and responsibility, however, in innovative organizations, access to analytically based answers is fundamental throughout the company. Data is seen as a corporate asset and analytical methods become intellectual property.

Innovation is a wonderful process. It continually evolves, allowing companies to remain ahead of competitors, ahead in the market, and ahead of its time. However, innovation has a price. Perhaps it is an intangible price—and maybe even a higher price than we could imagine. Innovation demands companies stay at the pinnacle of available technology and be on the leading edge of new business actions. But even more than this, innovation requires people to change their minds.

We've all heard that innovation is, at least in part, about thinking outside the box. To ourselves, we often wonder: Which box is that? The proverbial box is really the virtual hedge that each one of us creates and that confines our own ideas. This is a box that we all have to some degree, and many fear it will be criticized, it needs to be argued, and may be interrogated by something new. It is a box composed of our shield against the new and all associated consequences that new can bring forth. By instinct we are afraid of the unknown, the new, and the changing. We can be quite confident in our comfort zone or existing box, but quite unsteady outside of it.

Innovation demands change. It means we must take a chance and address a particular situation and put into place something that may never have been tried before. It means to pursue an idea, check if it is true, and examine if it is valid, feasible, consistent, understandable, comprehensive, and applicable. And in this respect, innovation means to try, and sometimes get it right and make things better, and sometimes not. Therefore, innovation is a trial-and-error process, and as such it is also a heuristic process.

Innovation in a Changing World

Everything changes. The market changes, the consumer changes, the technology changes, and thus products and services must change as well. Analytical models raise the business knowledge regarding what has changed and what needs to change. The new knowledge delivered by analytics is about the company itself, the competitive environment, and the market, but mostly it is about the consumers/ constituents that the company serves.

Change is also dynamic. Consumer behaviors change, sometimes for no clear reason and sometimes in response to other events and stimuli. We, as consumers, leave behind a trail of behavior, the way we buy, use, complain, inquire, and so on. By our very behavior we create history for all companies that care about acquiring or retaining our share of wallet to use and to foresee what we might do in the future. However, keep in mind that the unforeseen exists, and someone's team loses the final match of the national championship, or someone's girlfriend decides to split up, someone's son gets ill, or someone is fired. From this day to the next week, month, or perhaps even quarter, consumers can completely change their behavior, putting themselves out of the confidence intervals of the expected curve of behavior, thereby increasing false-positive occurrences.

Analytics is geared toward understanding the average, to accurately forecast for the majority, to target most of the population at hand. What companies, analysts, and data miners need to bear in mind is how heuristic this process can be and, as a result, how they need to monitor and maintain all analytical models to reflect changing conditions.

In the end, because of the dynamic condition, it becomes even more important to accurately frame business questions, and in order to do that well, analytics becomes even more important and essential, helping identify both the known and the unknown. And in many forward-thinking, highly competitive marketplaces, such as banking, telecommunications, and online retail, the use of analytics has become a mandatory corporate strategy.

SUMMARY

This chapter introduced the concepts and foundation of the analytics process, presenting its main purposes: how to apply analytics to solve real-world business problems, how the production and operational environments need to support it, and the heuristic characteristics assigned to the development of most analytical models.

The Monty Hall problem was used to exemplify the importance of theoretical grounding and fundamentals of mathematical science, including statistics and probability, and how such fundamentals are critical to appropriately framing an analytic problem, and hence a solution. The foundation of any analytical model is the rigorousness of the underlying theory assigned to the technique chosen to address the business issue at hand.

The evolution of the analytical processes was also covered in this chapter, describing the different stages involved in business analytics, what the goals are for each stage, and the most common types of insight derived from each one. And while these stages can be chronological it is really a cycle, which improves upon itself with iterations in the process. The distinct stages are typically geared toward a particular purpose and audience, composed of a different set of tools and techniques for each stage in the process.

The relevance of analytics to innovation was also presented, making quite clear how crucial the knowledge stemming from analytical models is to companies who wish to thrive in their marketplaces.

The rest of the book examines different aspects of analytical endeavors, the lifecycle of analytic processes, and the many factors, both internal and external, that influence the definition of the problem, the description of the scenario, the choice of the attributes, the technique, and ultimately the outcome.

Chapter 2 describes how randomness impacts both model development and the results that can be expected. Regardless of how precisely we try to define a particular problem, or how well we describe the problem situation and the variables used to describe it—it all becomes an approximation. The randomness associated with most business problems that organizations are trying to solve influences the results and can make model training more difficult, increase the model error, and affect the overall accuracy and value. In particular, when we are talking about human behavior, we are depicting all scenarios as an approximation of their reality. We are prescribing the general or average behavior to an individual and due to this approach, the expected results might change in the end.

Chapter 3 details the heuristic approach, how we use it (consciously or not) during the model definition, the development phase, and particularly in the adjustment steps, done to ensure the outcomes achieved satisfy the objectives established. This chapter describes how heuristics are present in most of the analytical tasks we perform—in the definition/selection of attributes used to explain a particular problem, in the approximation we chose to describe the boundaries of the problem scenario, and in the parameters used to develop the analytical model (including the techniques used). Many aspects of this analytical cycle are actually a set of choices we have to make as analysts, some based on previous experience, others based on trial and error. These choices define the rationale as to why we chose an artificial neural network instead of a decision tree or regression and answer questions regarding why, by selecting an artificial neural networks, we chose the particular topology, error propagation technique, and particular type of activation function.

Chapter 4 presents the analytical approach to develop and deploy analytical models, considering some of the more common techniques applied to solve real-world business problems. Most of the statistical approaches in and of themselves are not that difficult to implement. The challenge of making them successful lies in the reasonableness of the interpretation. This translation of model outcomes to business rules is one of the most important aspects governing the success of statistical models in both operational and production environments. We focus in this chapter on the analytical approach based on data mining, mostly artificial intelligence and mathematical models. Techniques such as artificial neural networks, decision trees, and genetic algorithms, as well as optimization models such as social network analysis, are described. The competitive cycle is used to describe practical application steps for analytical modeling. We show how and where each type of model might be used in order to improve the business performance and competitiveness. This cycle covers steps from data analysis to persistence, including data mining and outcomes application, and the chapter is generally focused on data mining.

Chapter 5 complements Chapter 4 with a description of practical case studies. Real-world examples that illustrate data mining methods in knowledge discovery are described. In practice, such analysis is used to understand customer behavior—highlighting the most likely customer to purchase (acquisition), to consume (cross and up selling), and to churn (retention). The analytical models described include clustering techniques, predictive models for collection—including insolvency segmentation and bad debt prediction—and fraud detection.

Chapter 6 describes a very special type of optimization models, known as graph analysis (aka network analysis). We discuss the fundamental concepts, types of the graph structures, the network metrics, and some analyses approaches.

Chapter 7 illustrates the use of graph analysis by way of three real-world business cases. Social networks are a particular case of graph analysis being used by some organizations driven by the desire to understand big data relationships. Two of the case studies are associated with the telecommunications industry: one associated with churn and sales diffusion, the other describing a fraud scenario. Exaggeration of claims in insurance, and how to identify potential suspicious actors, is also discussed.

Chapter 8 explores a newer technique in the analytical world, that of transforming unstructured text data into one that is structured. Unstructured text data is, by definition, descriptive and includes commentaries contained in call centers memos, log notes from servicing events, and reports from claims or interviews. Such text data can be verbose, such as in research papers, patent applications, and even books, or terse, like that from social media tweets. Regardless of the source, analysis of text data can provide deep insight as to why customers behave as they do, what they say they will do, and how they perceive what they are doing. Given this method is based on the meaning of words, the analysis of text requires interpretation, thereby making it heuristic by its very definition.

This book illustrates the overall customer lifecycle and how analytics can be successfully deployed in order to improve each and every step of this cycle. Regardless of the lifecycle phase, analytics can be used to solve a wide range of business issues. To the uninitiated, analytics might look like very complex, mystical science, heavily based in mathematics, statistics, or linguistics, composed of formulas and countless algorithms. And perhaps, behind the scenes, it is indeed like that. But when analytical tools hold the promise of making our life easier and our organizations more successful, it is better to dive in and begin to derive value from analytic methods. Most of the good tools, such as SAS, contain a substantial range of algorithms and techniques that are user ready—and oftentimes require minimal configuration effort. This book aims to describe how analytics can solve business problems in practice, and perhaps even more important, how these outcomes might be translated into successful business actions. A marketing perspective is used to depict a variety of possible analytics usage in companies, considering distinct industries, including telecommunications, banking, insurance, retail, entertainment, and others. Common to all industries, this overview considers practical examples, covering analytical models to acquire customers, to improve sales, avoid turnover (aka churn), as well as to detect fraud, bad debt, payment risk, and collection. By using a suite of analytical models, organizations are better prepared to appropriately serve customers and more accurately comprehend the marketplaces they are involved with, the competitors they face, and how they can boost their business strength.

Throughout the book, many examples are presented to illustrate analytical processes for all three stages described in this chapter. All of these examples were developed with SAS software, including products such as Base SAS®, SAS® Enterprise Miner™, SAS/STAT®, SAS/GRAPH®, SAS/OR®, and SAS® Customer Link Analytics. Most of these examples of analytical implementations were really developed in practice, and mostly in larger organizations.

CHAPTER 2

Unplanned Events, Heuristics, and the Randomness in Our World

One of the features of the heuristic method is to deal with unexpected scenarios or random events. When business scenarios change—and they do quite often—analytical models need to adjust to the new boundaries and constraints. The heuristic method of problem solving addresses this by providing a framework to test distinct solutions that can be examined in accordance with the range of possible solutions.

Unplanned events are often described as randomness in modeling and encapsulate how business situations can change unexpectedly, altering perspectives about the marketplace and the pattern of behavior assigned to consumers, products, and services. This chapter introduces overall concepts associated with seemingly arbitrary processes, including mathematical approaches to handling random events.

The basis for these notions is that everything is connected. Changes in one aspect of the system can lead to other changes, sometimes even very small initial changes. Popularly known as the butterfly effect, slight alterations in inputs, conditions, and events can impact analytical model development, as will be described in this chapter. Random walks are another phenomena used to describe the unsystematic processes operating in real world environments. And lastly, the drunkard's walk, a particular case of random walks, is described. All of these different effects illustrate that while we can neither control nor predict everything, a forecast or predictive model essentially represents a defined series of chances, which sometimes are very high and sometimes are quite low. The drunkard's walk also presents the belief that traditional methods using historical data to predict a target variable are not always appropriate, particularly when a subset of information in the past cannot represent future phenomena.

We will see that the what-if concept is extremely relevant to assessing problem scenarios, providing a vehicle to include heuristic methods. Even in exact sciences, such as mathematics and statistics, where we are able to produce models that predict some particular class or event in the future, there is always a bias and error involved. And this error, no matter the size, is intrinsic to these types of models. We cannot guarantee that something will really happen. We can simply indicate and infer with some degree of likelihood that something has a chance to happen or not. We can assign probabilities to a particular target variable, classifying the eventuality of an occurrence, but it is just a probability. That customer, according to his or her past behavior, may have a calculated 82 percent likelihood of purchasing a broadband service, but that also means we can be wrong 18 percent of the time. Similarly a sales forecast might predict that next month's sales will be 15 percent higher than the current month. This future forecast has an 88 percent likelihood of happening, which also means that there is a 12 percent chance that this forecasted increase is wrong. Although probability error is intrinsic in predictive models, they provide us with a degree of confidence that we are in charge and, in business terms, helping steer the company toward success. Knowing that a particular customer has an 82 percent chance of purchasing a broadband service is much better than having no sense of their possible behavior. With quantified understanding we can create a promotional campaign for customers we know are more likely to buy, and expect better campaign results than if no models were developed. Without models we'd be relying on the notion that all customers would have the same chance of buying a product, leaving the company, or consuming a particular service.

It's like gambling—tossing a coin and betting on what might happen—and investing dollars based on random chance. Instead, if we calculate the likelihood of buying, leaving, or consuming, we can target investments to customers more effectively. We can do more than simply flip a coin or throw the dice. By using analytics, we are really stacking the cards and ruling the dice. We know, with a quantified degree of certainty on which customers we should spend time, effort, and/or money in order to retain them. We know which customers we have to target in order to sell more products and services because they are more likely than others to buy and consume those products and services. We know, in advance, which customers are likely to not pay their bills, thereby customizing collection strategies to mitigate the problem.

The strategic benefit is to know, in advance, what business events may occur in order to devise effective strategies and competitive actions. Note that we refer to devising effective strategies, rather than creating strategies. Analytical models provide knowledge, insight as to what (and sometimes when, how, and why) needs to be done. Companies must take this knowledge and turn it into action in order to derive benefit. This is the difference between analytics and business analytics, the insight/knowledge and the application of that knowledge to operations, planning, and tactics. The marketing team, sales, and finance departments need to define business actions based on the knowledge raised by analytics. Analytics supports business actions—making them informed, fact-based, traceable, and understood, creating the environment for sound tactical and strategic decisions. By using analytics, even in our heuristic world, we are able to define more effective business actions and consider different scenarios in the market for consumers, products, and services. Just like what-if decision trees, with branches of choices defining successive selections, companies are able to establish distinct actions for each range of analytically derived probabilities. And by doing this, companies are empowered to knowingly define the actions required to improve corporate performance.

HEURISTICS CONCEPTS

The term *heuristic* refers to the technique of solving problems based on experience and includes actions associated with finding, learning, discovering, testing, erring, and correcting. Heuristics aim to find a good enough solution in a space of possibilities. And while it may not be the best or optimal solution (but only a good one), it can address a particular business issue in the right time and in a feasible way. Typically the quest for the optimal solution demands more time, effort, technology, accurate data, and so on than is available in practice. And so chasing the best solution gives rise to hunting for a solution, the good enough solution that can address the business problem at hand.

You may have heard the expressions that "the perfect is the enemy of the good," and while you may not agree, in the pursuit of analytics, you must know when to stop. In this pursuit of the best solution ever, you might miss the opportune time for analytic-based action—dispatching it at the wrong time, when that knowledge is no longer required or as impactful. Business, in particular, has a timeframe of effectiveness, after which the opportunity may no longer exist, or it is simply too late to do something about it.

Time to insight can be delayed by pursuit of the optimal solution, either in terms of business modeling or in terms of complex algorithm computation. Sometimes we chase the best solution by testing (which is much of the heuristic process of analytics) new variables, different weights, distinct models, different techniques, and so forth. These tasks can be very time consuming and might postpone delivery. While you may be a fan of artificial neural networks for creating a classification model to predict bad debt, for instance using it instead of decision tress or logistic regression, very often, artificial neural networks take substantially more computation time than do either of the other methods. Moreover, their results are not directly interpretable, which can make this model difficult to explain to business managers. So, even if you are a big fan of it, if the different models have achieved similar accuracy, from a practical perspective you'd really need to leave the complex neural network model behind.

You can't compromise total performance because of a few decimals of precision. That being said, a few decimals, in some business environments such as banking, insurance, and telecommunications, may represent a huge amount of money. However, keep in mind the inherent unplanned characteristics involved in developing analytical models, the possible randomness involved in most processes and about the intrinsic error that all predictive models can hold.

The point of developing analytical models in business is to deploy them in some way—say into a production environment—so time to delivery needs to be as fast as possible in order to dispatch the appropriate knowledge in the right time. The opportunity timeframe is crucial and should be satisfied. Less than half a percentage point can't be the determining factor for selecting an artificial neural network over a decision tree or logistic regression. Which is faster and has enough accuracy should define the appropriate business solution.[1]

In analytics, heuristics can refer to a particular solution that has computational time processing gains. It also refers to a solution that can solve a real problem effectively even if it isn't mathematically proven. Sometimes, when developing analytical models you have to test new attributes, change their weights, create ranges and buckets, transform original variables into new ones, filter factors, and many other techniques in order to adjust the model toward a good business solution. This adjusting process is heuristics in analytics; it is trial and error.

The heuristic approach is quite suitable when a range of possible solutions is available, and this indeed reflects the majority of business cases. Analysts don't necessarily need to explore all possible branches to find an optimal solution. Instead they can move forward by selecting a particular path(s) and iteratively find a good solution to the problem. In business, we often face problems with a wide range of possible solutions, particularly because different business scenarios can describe the same issue. Additionally, any new perspective on the business scenario, any new variable considered, any new information regarding the problem (say, decrease churn or increase sales), or

---

[1] High-performance analytic environments can significantly improve the time to model delivery, supporting faster execution of analytically derived knowledge. The complexity, rigor, and palatability of any model for the intended audience will always be a consideration, regardless of the speed of the analytic results.

the product/service, and consumption patterns or even information about the customer, might change the scenario and/or its description.

New information might also change the model's outcome. Different descriptions can define different development methods for the model. Implicit knowledge about the marketplace, about product or service consumptions, about the customer groups can be utilized during model development. Unstructured information held in commentaries, conversation notes, and logs would lead to model development using different techniques, create distinct variables, or even create derivative attributes. Any of these conditions, circumstances, and sources could cause the model to reach a distinctly different outcome. As analysts and data miners, we have to focus on the problem and not on the solution. In that way we can develop the good enough solution that allows business departments to use this new knowledge and create effective actions. All of this is occurring in a marketplace that is constantly changing—so finding a good solution, one that can be developed and deployed while still relevant, is key. This becomes a recursive process in which the analyst needs to know when to stop developing the model and when to deliver a good solution, one that is perhaps not the best, but one that will work well enough to achieve the desired results. In a way, this is quite similar to writing a book. You need to know the time to stop writing; otherwise, the book never ends. Everything can always be improved and work can expand to fill the time. But, as mentioned before, business opportunities hold a specific timeframe and because of this limitation, the solution pursued should be the one that addresses the particular business issue in a timely fashion. The optimal solution is completely worthless in the wrong time. A good enough solution, in the right time, is much better.

Heuristics in Operations

Companies have been using analytics to understand historical behavior in order to define specific business actions to change the future. Past behaviors might refer to usage, financial trends, past sales, old shipments, previous loans, ongoing traffic, and so forth. Any kind of market, industry, organization, and even individual can be associated with historical information. This information is used to build classification models used to predict a particular class, attribute, or value. The historical data is used to train the model, teaching it mathematically or statistically how these past attributes and values are related to a target being estimated.

Using analytics is about changing the future. While this may sound quite dramatic, it is undeniably the purpose of predictive analytics. If a company is continuously losing customers, and no action is put in place to avoid it, that company will eventually no longer exist. Every company needs customers or constituents of some kind, no matter the industry or the market. Every organization demands someone or something to consume what is being produced or offered. And if that company wants to take some action to change its future, such as avoiding customer churn, a success would be equal to curbing the defections and minimizing them in the future. If this company doesn't do anything in relation to the churn being experienced, or does it incorrectly, it could eventually cease to exist. If the company does something properly to reduce churn it would persevere. Analytics can dramatically help direct what actions would best address the problem.

Monitoring trends is often done to foresee when desired levels of activity require intervention. Trends themselves can also be easily understood by using analytics. Sales rates can be monitored, for example, and according to past purchasing behavior of customer business actions, could be seen to affect the environment—say by increasing the purchase rate. By first understanding the sales process and inspecting the historical patterns of sales, alternatives for different sales methods can be identified. And analogous to the churn scenario, analytic examination of past customer purchasing behavior can also be used to identify the customer profiles associated with the highest spending rates. Similar characteristics are then sought in the population to target sales promotions.

Business actions can change the future. By understanding customer behavior a company might improve product/service diffusion, encouraging consumers to change their purchasing patterns. And if this company succeeds in its business actions, the purchasing and sales trends would correspondingly change, and the rate of sales would be different than previously expected. These are real changes that occur downstream of analytics implementation. The future can be changed and monitored with analytics. Vigilance in the operational effectiveness resulting from analytics is required to see if in fact business situations are improved, thereby identifying the need to replicate similar approaches for other product/service lines. Just as important, monitoring to see if analytically based actions didn't improve the situation can identify the need to create a different business question.

THE BUTTERFLY EFFECT

Chaos theory is a concept that refers to how final results (or expected outcomes) hold a high degree of dependence on the initial conditions. This theory is also assigned to scenarios where any small change in the initial conditions of a complex system can have a large effect on the entire environment. For instance, a ball placed at the cusp of a hill can roll down in several different directions according to its initial position. Any slight change on this initial position could vary the direction that it rolls. Other conditions in the environment, such as the wind, the weight of the ball, its material, the type of surface, the geomorphology of the land, in fact any sort of detail will impact how it rolls. And of course, conditions can change. A sudden gust of wind at the moment the ball is released might change the direction of the movement.

Theoretically, and in perfect conditions, once all of the variables are set the result is clearly expected. However, in a physical experiment, if a ball is dropped several times at the top of a hill, it would take a different direction each time. Even if you try to simulate the exact same conditions as the previous dropping, the ball can still take a different direction each time. These distinct directions may be very subtle, obvious, or a combination of both. The point is that even those small changes in the initial conditions, such as the sudden wind gust, demonstrate the butterfly effect.

The phrase *Butterfly Effect* gained popularity based on the work of Edward Lorenz's[2] weather experiment in which decimal values

---

[2] Lorenz, Edward, N., 1963, "Deterministic Nonperiodic Flow", *Journal of Atmospheric Science* vol. 20, page. 130–141: http://journals.ametsoc.org/doi/abs/10.1175/1520-0469%281963%29020%3C0130%3ADNF%3E2.0.CO%3B2

were truncated when typed into a particular formula. Lacking the additional decimal points completely changed the atmospheric model outcome, producing a different result compared to when the decimals weren't removed. This phenomenon, a minor change in initial conditions leading to different results, became analogous to how a simple flap of a butterfly's wings in Brazil could create a tornado in Texas. The butterfly's flapping wings represent a change in the initial conditions within the complex system. The same metaphor applies to analytics. Anything, no matter how small it is, can change the entire scenario of observation, thereby altering the space of possible solutions that address a particular problem. In a business context these wings include any uncounted attribute, variable, information, source, and more that change the way the problem is described, and thus its resultant solution.

For this reason, any analytical model developed to address a particular business problem may change according to the initial conditions specified. These conditions may entail information about the company, the competitors, the customers, the products, service usage, payment behavior, and so on. Due to different possible descriptions of the business scenario, different models might be built and lead to distinct final results.

In the end, everything is an approximation. Analytic results are rough, general solutions that are based on the attributes used to describe a particular business environment, at a specific point in time. Any additional information amended to the problem's initial description may lead to a distinctly different solution. Thus, for the same business issue, according to the distinct descriptions of the problem, it is possible to reach different solutions and hence different business outcomes. Analytics is basically a heuristic discipline. The outcome specified by a model is completely victim to the initial conditions: the variables used and the information available to describe the business problem. A change in any of these inputs could change all of them. Furthermore, all business actions that result from analytics initiatives change the environment somehow. It is the goal of analytics to take action that is different from what occurs without the application of analytics. So no matter how effective business action can be from applying analytics, be it dramatic impact (substantially changing the former churn rate or sales, for instance) or moderate (only slightly changing those rates), the fact remains that the business action alters the business environment.

Add to this the fact that the environment also continues to change, oftentimes due to circumstances beyond the organization's control. Suppose your predictive model to anticipate churn is a complete success. The model is quite accurate and the business actions created by the marketing department are reasonable and appropriate to affect the behavior of customers believed to be at risk of leaving. The company might contact the at-risk customers, offering them a compelling promotion. In this way the company could change the current churn scenario, (hopefully) substantially decreasing the trended rate, and commit customers to stay longer with the company, retaining them to continue to use the organization's products. By applying the insight gleaned from the analytic model, the company has realized a change in the business scenario. In turn, this changes the marketplace, for example, by not having customers move to a competitor. Now suppose your predictive churn model is terrible. And the model's accuracy is not good at all. In spite of that, the marketing department goes ahead and creates business actions based on it. As a result, the company will probably contact the wrong customers, even if they are offering them the appropriate churn prevention promotion. The target group for the promotion isn't addressed and so customers would keep leaving company—possibly causing bankruptcy. The business environment also changed in this case—taking this company out of the marketplace. And finally, suppose your predictive model to anticipate churn is quite good, with high accuracy of classifying the target variable. But now suppose the business actions defined by the marketing department are a mess. The company will still contact the right customers, but the promotional offering fails to resonate with this audience. Just as in the second case, customers would probably continue to leave the company, and an eventual bankruptcy may happen. This also results in a change in the business scenario, both in marketplace, and most significantly, for that particular company.

These three different descriptions for the same business problem illustrate that no matter what the combination of the predictive model and the business actions are, the market environment will always change. No matter how good the analytical model is or how good the business actions are, the business scenario will eventually change. And given this change, analytical models developed in relation to the initial business conditions cease to be valid—as the conditions have changed. A new analytical model needs to be created which represents this new business scenario, the very scenario that you have changed by implementing your model, regardless of how good the model was. This is another heuristic rule in analytics. Everything you currently do will eventually change the way you will do things in the future.

This heuristic rule impacts model development even when you do things right. If the exact same approach is performed at another point in time, following the same steps, but simply in a different timeframe, the outcomes might be different. Even within the same timeframe, if a different seed or sample is used to train a particular model, the outcomes reached might be different as well. Certainly, if the approach is different and the timeframe is distinct, the outcomes would be different indeed. Given this, continuity associated with analytical modeling becomes one of the most important considerations. As long as an organization is deploying analytics and applying the outcomes as business actions, a monitoring process needs to be enacted to ensure they are on the correct path to produce analytic results that are aligned with business goals.

Tracking changes in models once they are deployed and monitoring happenings in the environment are critical to evaluations of model effectiveness and appropriateness to the ever-changing conditions. Monitoring business scenarios empowers companies to perceive all changes that occur and which will naturally happen no matter actions the company has performed, including those originating from the deployment of analytically based business actions. Regardless of the reason, we've seen that even a small change in the environment can make the analytical model invalid. An invalid model no longer describes, represents, or reflects the current business scenarios, and for this reason, it needs to be revised, remodeled, and ultimately redeployed. This is a continuous cycle. Once a company starts to implement analytics, the analytical monitoring and modeling process never stops—that is, at least while the company stays in business.

Consider the consumer electronic company Apple for example. By analyzing customer behavior and consumer needs and desires, Apple launched electronic gadgets. Recent commercial success of the company, however, was based on its evaluation of the marketplace and realization of a market gap based on what the majority of companies were offering to consumers. By looking at historical activity, and understanding the present gap, Apple foretold a new future, launching the popular iPods, and soon after converted iPhones and then iPads. All these technologies were delivered at a point in time and altered customer behavior. Indeed Apple went beyond competitive equivalence, envisioned more than what customers wanted, and it delivered on what customers would want in the future. By doing this Apple completely changed the marketplace. Correspondingly, consumers have become more tightly connected to multimedia content, more invested in application mobility, and more passionate about entertainment.

Apple's innovation shocked the market into a new realm of consumer expectation and need, shaking up competitors along the way. Who could have successfully commercialized tablets prior to the iPad? What rationale or use would have existed for a normal, everyday person to want to carry a gadget similar to a notebook but with less power? Why would someone want to carry something similar to a smart phone but which is just a bit bigger? Perhaps eventually consumers would have stated the desire to carry something a bit lighter than a notebook but that did almost the same thing, or something a bit bigger than a smart phone that did a bit more to stay connected, up-to-date, and entertained. The innovation lesson is that while consumers may have been about to require this, they didn't state it. Apple was faster than the market and launched before they were asked, and perhaps even before we realized we needed or wanted it.

This tipping point completely changed the consumer electronic marketplace, and not just the behavior of consumers but the market itself. After Apple many vendors started to produce and deliver smart devices like iPhones, multimedia players, and tablets. This has effectively changed the competitive landscape and the manner in which companies operate in this particular business scenario.

So, if everything has changed, including consumer behavior, the market, corporate procedures, the competition, and the business scenarios, is the analytical model still valid? No, certainly not. Analytics may have helped Apple glimpse potential new opportunities resulting in the launch of innovative products. But those analytic models were no longer valid once Apple succeeded. New analytics were required to monitor and understand the changed market trends and new consumer behavior—and so the analytic cycle repeats (perhaps most fortunately for analysts and data miners). Everything we do somehow changes what we are going to do next.

Extreme market shifts from innovation, or tipping points, don't happen all the time. They've notably happened in the transportation market (with the automobile and airplane), in household electronics (with microwave ovens), computing (home computers), mobile telecommunications, and within a few other industries. Perhaps none of these new things were expected, particularly when they first showed up. This is apparent when we revisit quotes by leaders in the respective markets from the time when these innovations first surfaced. All of them illustrate how unexpected these things were.

"Airplanes are interesting toys but of no military value," said Marshal Ferdinand Foch, a French military strategist, around 1911.

"There is no reason for any individual to have a computer in his home," said Ken Olsen, the founder and CEO of DEC, in 1977!

"The horse is here to stay, but the automobile is only a novelty, a fad," said the president of the Michigan Savings Bank in 1901 to Horace Rackman, Henry Ford's lawyer.

Many bad predictions were made with respect to these new innovations, but today our societies can't live without them. It is hard to perceive of a world without cars, in spite of what the president of Michigan Savings Bank said; a world without airplanes, in spite of Marshal Ferdinand Foch's misgivings; and a world without computers (particularly in our homes), in spite of Ken Olsen's beliefs.

There are many quotes about innovation disbelief for phones, the Internet, and perhaps, even iPods, iPhones, and iPads. In searching the Internet you'll find them. And speaking about the Internet, a read worth finding is associated with Paul Krugman, a renowned

New York Times economist, who in 1998 wrote an article: "Why most economist's predictions are wrong,"[3] predicting that by 2005 or so, "it will become clear that the Internet's impact on the economy will be no greater than the fax machine's." Our world is continuously evolving—and there is more change to come. All of this dramatically impacts analytics work, including the tasks involved in analytical model development. And as long as the world evolves, analytics will evolve with it, reinventing, recreating, and redefining itself. Unlike Charles Duell, an official at the U.S. Patent office, who said: "Everything that can be invented has been invented" in 1899—we know, with certainty, that new innovations have occurred and will continue to shape our modern world. As much we know, we realize that there is much more to be known. A single discovery triggers a chain of new discoveries, progressively increasing knowledge. This is our world. This is analytics.

Tipping points do happen, albeit not so frequently. You may wonder: Why don't innovations happen more often? There are probably a number of reasons but one relevant reason is certainly because of randomness—the randomness in the heuristic world we live.

Randomness is present in almost everything in our lives. It may be quite obvious in some cases and hidden in others. But randomness, whether implicit or explicit, affects the course of our lives and how we interact in our world. There are many explanations for why Pelé became the best football[4] player in history. Perhaps there was another boy in his time who could have been a better player than him. Why didn't he become the best player ever? Why didn't that boy have the career of Pelé? Analogously, why did Robert De Niro become an amazing actor? Weren't there other good actors in the era he began his work? Why did he surpass the others? How did Tom Hanks become a wonderful director, even with his initial foray in lighthearted comedy movies? How did Obama become President of the United States? Why did my neighbor win the lottery instead of

---

[3] Krugman, Paul, June 1998; 'Why most economist's predictions are wrong', *Red Herring* Magazine: http://web.archive.org/web/19990417224527/http://www.redherring.com/mag/issue55/economics.html

[4] Also known as soccer within North America, Edison Arantes do Nascimento, commonly called Pelé, was voted Football Player of the Century by the International Federation of Football History & Statistics.

me? There are so many questions that we have, and we really don't have any clue about the answers.

RANDOM WALKS

A random walk is a formal description of a particular trajectory made up of successively occurring random steps. The path traced by the froth within a pint of Guinness (We didn't mean to insist on this theme) illustrates random walks. After pouring the pint, the foam travels up from the bottom to the top of the glass. Guinness is ready to drink after all the foam reaches the top, creating the well-known creamy head. Any pint pulled presents a unique path for this upward migration of foam and is so unique that Guinness advertises the beer saying, "it's alive inside." Probably each foam path has unique upward movement. Perhaps ordering as many pints of Guinness as you can afford and watching the foam move will be the only way to prove it. In theory, anyway, each path has its trajectory to move, just like bubbles in a glass of Coca-Cola. Foam and bubbles are both good examples of random walks, in addition to several other examples in nature and society, most of them more formalized than beer or soda, like the crash of molecules within chemical fluid reactions.

The fluctuating prices of stocks in the stock market considered over time is an example of a random walk and is a choice problem in analytics. Sometimes they increase and sometimes they decrease, without inherent periodicity or seasonality patterns. Mathematical and statistical models have been developed to understand patterns in relation to stock price variations. But once again, randomness is always present. External factors, usually in politics, international relations, and sometimes even in the private lives of the stakeholders can substantially impact price fluctuations. The stock price of a large corporation can be easily affected by a private scandal involving the CEO. Without changes in relation to company health, to its financial situation, or its performance in the marketplace, the stock price can be affected just because of a private scandal. How could an analytical model predict this external fact? It simply can't. And while there are several graphing techniques that are used to analyze historical fluctuation of stock prices and both mathematical and statistical models to understand and predict stock price, they are focused on the majority of the cases.

It is the outliers, the rare and unpredictable events like a private scandal that can, out of the blue, impact the stock situation. Analytics is still a crucial tool used to help keep companies abreast and growing in this market—at a minimum to help understand the impact of what is occurring, even if it can't be predicted. There are other examples of events that can't be predicted by history. The paths of animals when they hunt or search for food can also be considered a random walk. Ultimately, there are so many variables to consider, the available prey, the geographic location, weather, season, and, perhaps mostly important, the character of each animal involved. It is almost impossible to use the past events of hunting and historical animal behavior to foresee how the next chase would proceed.

Gambling also reflects random walks. Roulette and card games are based on probabilities. And for this, the historical path of the cards revealed, or the numbers that have been previously picked in roulette spins, reveals little to show about what will happen next. If you watch roulette for hours, and observe that red numbers come up more times than black, you cannot surmise that red will come up next. Analysis of the historical events of reds and blacks doesn't precisely define the next color in roulette. Your predictions would be strictly a matter of chances.

Random walks also happen in business. The way customers behave in response to marketing campaigns or products/service launches could also be modeled as random walks. There can be no predictable sequence of events in relation to customer behavior. Consumers might respond better to some campaigns than others, not because of individual preferences per se, but because of when they receive the call, the voice of the call center attendant, the script used, the mood they are in, what happened five minutes or five days before the call, and many other possible reasons. The same offering, attendant, script, and date might be effective five minutes later, say after a loved one's call, or ineffective five minutes earlier after a difficult conversation with a boss. What can occur five minutes before the call center agent calls is unpredictable and yet, it may change everything. It could change the customer's response from a yes to no. The historical events that impact the result might fit a random walk simply because what happens five minutes prior is unknown and can control the outcome. There can be no clear reason as to the response outcome. And in fact, the most significant factor influencing the result can be completely random to the analysis driving the business activity.

Similarly, customers may be seen to rapidly adopt some products/ services over others, with unclear reasons as to why. Consider the Newton and the iPad. Do we clearly understand why the first one wasn't adopted and the second one was? Was the first one launched too early, simply to a market that wasn't ready? Were they ready for iPad? One can certainly speculate about the reason, but we can't confirm the exact reason. At least from an analytical perspective, it appears to be unknown and random.

With all the uncertainty governing outcomes, what can an organization do? Giving up and riding with the seemingly random market tide will not result in a more profitable, innovative, or effective business. What may be a comfort is that particular events, which could completely alter outcomes, don't happen to all observations (such as consumers) at the same time. In business processes, we can assume that these are extraordinary events that rarely affect all customers simultaneously. Organizations need to build their analytical models as usual knowing that there will be cases that won't behave as expected. This may be due to intrinsic error assigned to the mathematical or statistical model or according to a random occurrence that relates, in some unforeseen way, to the business event. If we work with the majority who tend to behave as predicted, we will still likely see the desired outcomes. For business events, the majority becomes the focus and the rare, exceptions, and outliers are not. Naturally, there are some events, like fraud, that are modeled by focusing on the rare, the outlier. Even still, you expect the model to predict as per expectations for the majority of the observations. Given that random walks can happen in nature, societies, and business, heuristics plays a role in analytical models associated with any of these topics. And this fact emphasizes the stated need to continuously monitor all analytical-based processes so as to bring awareness when changes to modeling efforts need to occur, including when seemingly random activity changes the business environment.

The Drunkard's Walk

Leonard Mlodinow wrote a best-selling book, *The Drunkard's Walk: How Randomness Rules Our Lives*.[5] It is a wonderful and intuitive guide that describes how random our lives really are, and how personal, natural, and business events take place that are completely beyond our control. Each one of these events could be directed, in their natural course, toward very different endings. The drunkard's walk is used to describe a particular random motion. A typical example could start with a point beginning at the origin of a Euclidian plane. This point might moves a distance of one unit for each unit of time, for example. However, the direction of this unit of motion is random each time. The problem of the drunkard's walk is to find, after some fixed timeframe, the possible location of a point subjected to random motions. This possible location is given by the probabilities of moving some distance in some direction. However, in the end, this prediction is driven by probabilities and cannot be calculated based on the history of previous motions.

With random motion we are not able to predict movement based upon past occurrences and this can be particularly true in business scenarios when there can be many variable factors involved in an analysis or similarly when there is no history available. We can address these types of situations in business analytics as Markovian processes, which assume that future behavior is independent of the past history. Markov processes vary randomly over time according to Markov properties, as there is an absence of memory in the stochastic (i.e., random) process. The main feature of such processes is the effect of a particular condition on the present state of the system and so both the past and the future are independent.

This absence of memory and the independent conditions between past and future events is very helpful to analysis of consumer behavior. In this situation, it is important to monitor and track customer behavior and how they interact with your organization, regardless of the market, product, service, geography, and so on, in order to

---

[5] Mlodinow, L. *The Drunkard's Walk: How Randomness Rules our Lives*, Vintage Books, New York. Random House, 2009.

understand what the existing conditions actually are. Different types of techniques can be put into place in order to track changes in the marketplace (applicable to all segments and industries). A mathematical system, called a Markov Chain, can be a suitable approach to measure transitions from one state to another (i.e., changes in conditions), within a finite number of states and assuming a random selection of any particular state. The Markov property stipulates that the next state depends only on the current state, and not on the past history of states. This becomes a very different approach to predictive analytics than we may be accustomed to. Typically, we use analytic methods that foresee new business events based on past events, predicting the derived pattern into future time periods. However, with random processes, such as many real-world business scenarios, historical dependence on future events is not a valid assumption to begin with. As such, a Markovian, or similar framework is needed to model the business scenario. When problem scenarios arise in which the past can't help us to foresee the future, such as with random walks, alternate analytic methods become crucial tools in order to accurately model the business scenario and to meaningfully define the question at hand. In business, no matter the industry or segment, random walks take place quite often, and although they are governed by randomness, it doesn't mean we can't use analytics to understand and predict the future. On the contrary, we need to extend our use of analytics, using new and alternate methods. Monitoring what is happening in the market continues to be key to knowing if, and to what extent, the activities and actions of your customers require methods that intrinsically account for randomness.

Probability and Chance

Randomness describes an event that doesn't follow any particular pattern or holds no specific aim or purpose. It isn't guided toward a specific direction. It has no order. Randomness is closely related to the notion of chance and has been examined in probability-related disciplines. When a particular event could fall into a number of categories and we don't have any sense, history, or formula that can enlighten what could occur, then it is a random event.

Using probability theory, we might determine the chances of event occurrence for any number of options. However, each probability, each option if you will, is still a matter of chance.

Say, for example, you have a basket containing 50 plastic balls, 30 blue and 20 red. Probabilistically, if you close your eyes and take any ball from the basket (assuming each ball has an equal chance of being selected), you have a 60 percent chance of picking a blue ball and a 40 percent chance of picking a red ball. And although you have propensities assigned to each color (60/40), the event of your picking up any particular ball from that basket is a matter of chance, it is random. In other words, you have a 50 percent chance of picking a blue ball 60 percent of the time, and a 50 percent chance of picking a red ball, 40 percent of the time. In fact, you could pick up three red balls sequentially, in spite of the lower probability of this really happening. Factors that affect the choice include the way the balls were placed in the basket, their weights, surfaces, or any other ball/basket factor (or even external factor) that might make you pick one color over the other more times than determined by the formal probabilities.

The same frequently occurs in our world. Going back to our roulette example, there may in fact be something other than a 50-50 chance of black and red coming up when the wheel is spun. The inclination of the wheel, its weight, the weight of the ball, its surface, the material, the size of the cavity for each number on the wheel, and so on could impact one color being selected over another. Each might influence the chances of a red or a black number being chosen. So while these conditions might change the formal and expected probabilities, the actual event remains to be random.

This lack of order and absence of aim or purpose means that random events are not predictable. A random process, on the other hand, is a repeated sequence of events that produces outcomes that cannot be described in a deterministic pattern. In other words, it is something that is recurrently unpredictable. It can be quite frustrating to be aware that something shall happen but you cannot predict what it is, how it will play out, and the impact the outcome could have on a scenario or environment.

The marketplace can also behave this way. No matter how close companies track and monitor the market, customers, and competitors, some events can happen that change everything. Natural disasters can completely modify the current market status and often change consumption patterns, with people buying less and saving more. This, in turn, can cause a change in company strategies. Social disorders such as conflicts, wars, and acts of terrorism might drive the marketplace to totally unexpected paths. People might become more conscious and less enthusiastic, emotionally drained from horrific events leading to diminished consumption from a financial perspective. Political activities, like elections or sporting events like the World Cup or Olympic Games, might bring out nationalistic enthusiasm that could lead to increased consumer consumption. If an event isn't predictable or can't be foretold and even if there are tendencies based on past behavior (even human behavior), the resultant outcome to any particular event might still be unpredictable—or at least unprecedented. You may become highly nationalistic in World Cup season, at least until your national team is sent off home in the first round. In this case, you may barely leave the house because it seems as though the world has collapsed. Something you expect can change dramatically in as little as 90 minutes. This is a perfect example of randomness. Like with gambling, you aren't able to predict the next steps. A much better team might be beaten by a worse one. Mathematically we can translate this as the end result, no matter the initial chances of both teams going into the game—and so it also seems random.

Regardless of probability, randomness means you can't determine what comes next. Organizations can use probability models to at least establish different strategies for different business options. It is no different than if a national team completes the World Cup tournament and becomes the world champion, companies can explore elements that may have led to success in order to replicate them in the future. However, just as if the national team dashes the nation's hopes, companies can also learn from failures in an effort to avoid similar outcomes in the future. Again, a specific strategy should be defined to accomplish whatever the goal (no pun intended). A probabilistic approach is quite useful to prepare companies for the possible events that may take place in the marketplace, perhaps not predicting the eventual outcomes per se, but in support of distinct strategies and action plans that are at the ready as different options for whenever the chance avails itself.

SUMMARY

In this chapter we exposed how random personal and business events can be. We described how random walks indicate that past events can't drive us to forecast the future. We also described how the butterfly effect can completely change expected outcomes and eventual scenarios based on small changes in the initial conditions.

In spite of the unknown and randomness in our lives, both personally and professionally, analytics does offer companies the opportunity to better their chances, particularly in highly competitive markets. Analytics is the most appropriate way to monitor and track business environments, to identify events in the past—which can, in many cases be very helpful in predicting the future—and also aid in identifying changes in existing conditions. And even with the impact of randomness on results, analytics keeps companies closer to the truth, and supports the development of business strategies based on facts, regardless of the number of possible options. Analytics is the most effective way to monitor the usage and behavior of customers. It is also the most effective means we have to forecast their next steps, or at a minimum define a set of possible scenarios of the next possible movements they may take. Even with random events, analytics can help identify eventual business scenarios, computing all possible outcomes.

In the end, and even though it is a heuristic world, within a set of possibilities analytics provides a framework to understand the marketplace, customers, and the organization itself.

As famously stated by General Sun Tzu[6]:

> If you know the enemy and know yourself, you need not fear the result of a hundred battles. If you know yourself but not the enemy, for every victory gained you will suffer a defeat. If you know neither the enemy nor yourself, you will succumb in every battle.

Analytics can help you to know yourself, as a company and your competitive enemies, so you don't need to fear any battle or competition in a business scenario.

---

[6] Tzu, Sun. *The Art of War*, Vintage Books, Wilder Publications, LCC, Radford VA, 2008.

CHAPTER 3

The Heuristic Approach and Why We Use It

euristic comes from the Greek's word heurísko, which means discovering or finding. It is tightly coupled with experimental methods including what if scenarios as well as simple trial and error. Heuristics is commonly assigned to the science (and art) of discovery, a discipline based on the investigative process. The Greek word *eureka*, used by Archimedes when he found out how to measure the volume of an irregular object by using water, has the same etymology of heuristic (heurísko).

Heuristics is part of the scientific method that strives to achieve new developments or empirical discoveries. More formally, the heuristic procedure is an approximation method to develop ideal solutions when faced with different kind of problems. The heuristic method assumes a solution close to the ideal is possible and is functionally based on an assessment of the result. However, the solution from a heuristic method is not necessary the optimal one. In other words, finding a solution using heuristic methods is like exploring different paths and possibilities that are each evaluated based on a theory. That theory is known as a progressive theory, one that is capable of guaranteeing a particular empirical development, foreseeing new facts not previously observed at the moment of the heuristic theory's construction.

For many centuries the heuristic method was misrepresented as a means to justify (or explain) the empirical discoveries. From the work of Sir Francis Bacon we know that the development of a theory can survive without experiments.[1] This was a revolutionary concept because prior to that it was believed that any scientific theory produces hypotheses that are confirmed or rejected through experiments. The concept of heuristics provided a method to justify new discoveries *a posteriori*, but it didn't stipulate direct paths to materialize the findings. As a result, some scientists disclaimed the existence of a unique heuristic theory for many years. In time, however, the scientific community came to accept that in the development of science there are many different and viable approaches due to the evolution of unique characteristics, and different scenarios, hypothesis, experiments, cultures, ages, and many other factors.

Nowadays, studies regarding heuristics processes focus on core aspects associated with each discipline, such as the heuristic in mathematics, chemistry, biology, and so on. For the field of science in general, the heuristic approach retains the theoretical premise that it is quite difficult to formulate general principles for complete processes. In other words, a general heuristic method is less effective if one considers the entire field of science. On the other hand, particular to a specific field in the discipline (such as mathematics), heuristic processes are highly effective for describing alternate situations.

Heuristics was popularized in George Pólya's book *How to Solve It: A New Aspect of Mathematical Method*.[2] Pólya examined ways to solve problems of all kinds, not just mathematical ones, attempting to figure out how solutions are reached. This seminal work established guiding principles which define a heuristic approach, including:

---

[1] For example, within *Novum organum scientiarum*, F., Bacon, 1620, Venetiis, Typis G. Girardi Publisher, http://archive.org/details/1762novumorganum00baco.

[2] The book, G. Pólya, *How to Solve It: A New Aspect of Mathematical Method*, 1945, New Jersey: Princeton University Press continues to be available: http://www.amazon.com/How-Solve-Mathematical-Princeton-Science/dp/069111966X#._

- If you cannot understand a particular problem, build a schema.
- If you cannot find a solution, try to proceed in an inverse approach in order to reach a possible solution. (This is similar to the concept of reverse engineering.)
- If the problem is not abstract, try to formulate the same problem in a concrete example.
- Try to first approach a more general problem. (This is the paradox of the inventor; the most ambitious proposal is the one with more chances to possibly succeed.)

The heuristic method is not a scientifically proven concept, meaning it doesn't have a formal mathematical proof associated with it. In fact, any heuristic solution, or possible assumption, is based on experience, intuition, common sense, or any other type of procedure that doesn't require a mathematical proof. In spite of this, the heuristic method is commonly used in decision-making processes, especially in analytical model developments, even though the concept doesn't have much appreciation in exact sciences (such as mathematics, physics, and engineering). We actually use heuristics in our lives, typically on a daily basis as we make decisions. Most often we base our decisions on our past experiences, on those of our friends and parents experiences, by using our common sense, or our intuition that a particular path is the right one. When formulating business problems as analytical ones, we quite often overlay heuristic methods guiding the development and definition of the problem at hand. And when we realize we've made a mistake, we just redefine the problem description and we try again. This trial-and-error method is how the heuristic method is most commonly known.

HEURISTICS IN COMPUTING

The heuristic method is often used in production systems as an approach to finding the best scenario for a production environment. Optimizing supply chains is related to the way in which a production cycle evolves, and as such, it needs to be trained and adjusted while in operation. The production cycle relies upon distinct programming, machinery capacity, human resources, and time, among other factors.

All these components can change over time, so the overall process of learning and training the system needs to be revisited from time to time. In this situation, the heuristic method conceptually mimics the development of optimization models, both in terms of how the problem is defined and in the definition of the variables—some dependent and others independent.

Behind the scenes of most Enterprise Resource Planning (ERP) systems, heuristic methods are encoded in the software, working to define the most practical solution for allocating resources as close to optimally as possible. Often there aren't too complex algorithms driving solutions in ERP systems. Procedures are developed by trial and error, and simple techniques are encoded into the system that is developed as users and the software learn from each other throughout the specification process.

In computer science, the heuristic method is widely used to find algorithmic solutions to problems using exploratory analysis. In this case, each possible solution is evaluated and the progress toward finding the optimal solution is measured. These successive approximations are developed iteratively, and the process ends when no better outcome in the space of possible solutions is found. Exploratory and heuristic approaches used in computing use algorithms that are defined in a sequence of computing procedures. The progress toward the best solution is reached via empirical evaluation of each of the outcomes produced in the process.

Mathematical optimization programs are commonly developed in a similar fashion, and heuristics can be quite useful in this area. Take the situation of a solution that becomes increasingly complex, as measured by an exponential function of a particular parameter. In other words, when the value of the parameter increases, the problem becomes more complex, at an exponentially increasing rate. In this case, the heuristic method provides an alternative approach to this problem so that a possible optimal solution may be found even if that parameter increases. In this case, a feasible solution is found *due to* the exponential growth rate of the solution's complexity. The heuristic method does not guarantee the best solution, only valid solutions— often approximated—that reflect consideration in the space of all possible solutions. Moreover, the heuristic method frequently cannot formally justify the validity of the result. However, in most traditional business problems, a possible solution (even cheaper and sometimes not as good) is better than an unfeasible, optimal solution.

As a reflection of the algorithmic, procedural nature of computing, there are basically three types of ways to apply heuristic methods:

1. The blind search—randomly chooses where to search in the search space of possible solutions.

2. The heuristic search—based on previous experience to determine where to search in the search space of possible solutions, and

3. The rational search—based on a defined reasoning method to instruct where to search in the search space of possible solutions.

In all three approaches the goal isn't an optimal solution, which is perhaps incongruent to these being methods for mathematical optimization solving. In fact, based on the problem and its complexity, a sequence of possible and valid solutions is iteratively evaluated until a good solution is found. So although this is under the guise of optimization, these heuristic optimization methods address common business scenarios in which the perfect solution might be too expensive and provide little incremental benefit over a valid solution—a good solution—which could be cheaper and the gain the desired results.

This subjectivity (or lack of precision) assigned to heuristic approaches is not to be considered a shortcoming of the method at all. It is a peculiarity of the method itself, which happens to also be a peculiarity of human beings. Our minds don't require complete, precise information about a problem in order to determine a feasible solution. Take parking, for example. We don't need to get out of the car, measure the space between the two cars we want to park between, return to the car, and then proceed to park. We also don't need to measure the angle of the curve if we are parallel parking. We just stop (or at least slow down) a bit beside the space between those two cars, take a rough look at the space, mentally measure the available room, and park the car. We don't look at the steering wheel, calculating the angles when we turn right or left, and seldom even look at the steering wheel at all. We look behind us to check how well we are backing the car into the available space, allowing us to quickly adjust the angle and/or the speed in order to park. And true, many of us may have to adjust the parking solution, moving forward and backward a few times. The valid solution in the space of possible solutions is simply parking. The car actually doesn't need to stay completely parallel and 10 centimeters away from the curb. It just needs to be parked.

I recall a friend of mine, who, when asked how many drops of sweetener he wanted in his coffee would very often say: "Lots!" He didn't need to measure how much liquid went into the cup, or know in advance if the coffee is strong or weak, or hot or warm. Those parameters didn't matter. You'd just start dropping in the sweetener and eventually he would say "Stop!" That is it. It would be done. Now you could name this a heuristic search method, based on his experience about how many drops he needed to sweeten his coffee. Or you could call this a rational search, as he had his own reasoning algorithm that assessed the amount of liquid, surmised the strength of the coffee provided, and therefore readily established the proper amount sweetener needed. Regardless the method, his approach was totally heuristic, and worked well to find a good and valid solution.

You could also think about the heuristic method as the problem of finding the highest mountain on earth. Suppose you are in charge of conducting this research. You might find you have some constraints, such as other people to help or tools to help you do it (i.e., human and material resources), or time, budget, and so forth. You could begin your research by choosing a random location as the first local optimum and proceed with the search outward from there. As your search progresses, the first mountain randomly chosen becomes the highest peak on earth at that moment. Then the searching continues and eventually you might find higher mountains, changing the local optimum, and therefore the solution for that particular time. The search goes on until no higher mountains are found, or perhaps there are some peaks that remain, but cannot be measured due to other constraints, like time, safety, or budget. By exploring the search space this way, a local optimum solution is found and while higher mountains on earth may not be found by this particular research, you did find a solution. As in business, problem-solving methods can always be improved as research continues to extend toward a global optimum solution.

HEURISTIC PROBLEM-SOLVING METHODS

There are several approaches to solving problems, particularly business problems. Some of these reflect heuristic methods to define the issue, describe it, and discover the mechanism to solve it.

Heuristics methods include approaches like trial and error; breaking down issues to solve simpler problems; describing and addressing similar or analogous problems; simplifying to tables, diagrams, or schemas; exploring for patterns or standard models that explain the issue, focusing in on special cases, formulating a equation to generalize the issue; reversing the problem and examining the outcome, and retracing the initial conditions (i.e., reverse engineering), among others. Most of these approaches serve as a guide to finding good or possible solutions to a particular problem. The application of the method may work progressively, finding successively better solutions each time.

Heuristic reasoning is essentially a flexible and temporary process used to solve problems. And although problem definition may be quite strict, the process to solve it can be very flexible in terms of finding reasonable solutions over time, incrementally improving results. Within heuristic methods the sequence of procedures doesn't need to be fixed. The steps can be changed or reordered to decrease the time needed to find an answer, or even as a way to improve result quality. Strictly following predefined steps established for problem solving doesn't guarantee success.

George Pólya[3] defined four stages describing how to find solutions to a problem. Each includes a set of suggestions and questions that are used to articulate and identify characteristics of the problem.

The first stage is the *problem comprehension*. To understand the problem and portray it as a problem the following questions are posed:

■ Can you describe the problem in your own words?

■ What are you looking for? What is the outcome you want to achieve?

---

[3] Pólya, G. *How to Solve It*, 2nd ed., New Jersey: Princeton University Press, 1957.

▪ What kind of information could you gain from solving the problem?

▪ What information is available about the problem?

▪ Is the information about the problem enough? Is something missing? Do you need additional information to define the problem?

▪ Could you simulate an answer to this problem?

The second stage relates to how to *define a plan* to solve the problem once it is established. Questions such as the following are formulated:

▪ Have you solved a similar problem before?

▪ Have you see an analogous problem that can work as a guide to this one?

▪ Could you organize all available information into tables, graphs, diagrams, or schemas?

▪ Does a standard model exist that relates to your problem?

▪ Can you split your problem in parts and work on each part separately?

▪ Is there a simpler problem to start with?

▪ Could you write a mathematical sentence that would describe and/or solve the problem?

▪ Could you iterate a trial-and-error method to solve this problem?

The third stage is associated with defining the *execution* path and consists of some simple procedures like:

▪ Executing your resolution plan, checking at each step.

▪ Solve the mathematical sentence previously formulated, if possible.

▪ Complete your table, graph, diagram, or schema according to the problem definition, looking for possible and feasible solutions.

▪ Perform all necessary computation assigned to solving the problem, supporting the heuristic method by searching for possible resolutions.

The last and fourth stage is the *retrospective* procedure. It is used to identify any areas of improvement by examining a reverse proof for the current solution. The following guidelines can be used:

- Evaluate and check all results and conclusions made/found in the solving process, considering the original problem definition at each step.
- Are there any other solutions to this particular problem?
- Are there any other approaches that could find similar results to this particular problem?
- Could you solve similar problems using the method deployed?
- Can you further generalize the problem and the solution found?
- Could you elaborate analogous problems from the problem you just solved? Is there a way to make them easier problems?
- Could you use the definition and the resolution for this particular problem to formulate some mathematical theory?

These questions at each stage of the problem-solving process provide discipline toward improving not just on the way to solve the problem at hand but also understanding the scope of a larger suite of issues that may be at play. And looking back to the problem during the retrospective stages can often lead to a revision of the results, evaluation, and improvement of the resources used, analysis of the arguments and parameters assigned, assessment of the methods deployed, and perhaps most important, as a deliberate way to continue learning. The learning process is quite often informed by such hindsight—looking back to the overall steps performed, from the initial problem definition right through to the resolution. And yet while we instinctively know this to be true, often we don't apply the discipline of doing it, and simply take the solution and run with it. However, when we do evaluate each phase accomplished in the light of the result, we might be able to better understand the most important steps, the key inputs, the necessary outputs, and any other possible improvements that can be made the next time this problem arises. Often in business applications, there will be a next time.

The what-if approach can also be helpful to this retrospective evaluation task. Very often, the solution to a particular problem needs to satisfy some conditions, constraints, or boundaries. But what if some of those parameters change? What if you can draw upon more resources to find a better solution? What if you identify additional constraints to finding a possible solution? Typically, problem resolution is quite sensitive to these different characteristics. Where possible, generalizing both the problem and the resolution increases the knowledge about it and increases the potential to solve similar problems. Of key importance to what-if testing is to examine all results, both those that are right and those that are wrong. The good outcomes can lead you to improve the problem-solving paths, whereas the bad outcomes can help you avoid taking the wrong paths to problem resolution in the future. In other words, all experiences achieved throughout the process are relevant and should be continued somehow, just as in our everyday lives we often learn more from our mistakes than from our successes.

GENETIC ALGORITHMS: A FORMAL HEURISTIC APPROACH

Genetic algorithms are a heuristic method used to optimize a specific scenario and solve real-world problems. Genetic algorithms are a class of heuristic methods and perhaps are most popularly known in their application to DNA sequence investigations. So although an approach to optimizing a scenario, genetic algorithms will find a solution, even where traditional optimization models may not. Another common method associated with this approach is more typically known as survival analysis—used in business scenarios, these method study individuals (aka observations) wherein one particular event (a default) takes place after a period of time (a default period). The survival approach is utilized in different fields, each with their own naming convention. If the event and default period is associated with engineering equipment or structures, this approach might be called reliability analysis. When examined to reflect economic activity it can be cited as duration analysis. And in geography and sociology, this approach is known as event history analysis. Although the term *survival analysis* stems from bio-medical and disease applications (i.e., affiliated with the length of time before a subject dies), it has become standard terminology used to define this type of problem-solving approach in business applications. There is a set of main characteristics assigned to any survival analysis problem, namely the response (i.e., target) variable is nonnegative, it is univariate (modeling of only one variable), the time horizon is continuous, and observations can be censored (i.e., unknown).[4]

One possible outcome of survival analysis is a score, a value that can be used in business applications to drive bundles of products and services as well as specific marketing and sales campaigns associated with individual customers or customer groups. And while perhaps not the traditional method to derive a survival score, genetic algorithms can successfully be used to identify the survival outcome. Using these algorithms, the best or optimal population can be identified for marketing-, sales-, and retention-related initiatives. Before we describe such an example, let's examine how the broader classes of genetic algorithms are constructed and how they resolve problems.

Foundation of Genetic Algorithms

Genetic algorithms embody a search technique used in computing to find approximate solutions within a class of optimization and search problems. Genetic algorithms are categorized as global search heuristics and can be associated with evolutionary computation, a specific class of evolutionary algorithms. The naming convention associated with this method illustrates the linkage of this technique to evolutionary biology, and includes notions of inheritance, mutation, selection, and crossover. Successfully implemented as a computing simulation process, genetic algorithms can be applied to questions in fields including biogenetics, computer science, engineering, economics, chemistry, manufacturing, mathematics, physics, and others.

In a nutshell, a population of candidate solutions to a particular optimization problem is evolved toward better solutions. The process is quite interactive, and many intermediate solutions are evaluated before the best (local optima) is reached. Solutions based on genetic

---

[4] In fact, observations can be both left and right censored—either before (left) and/or after (right) the event.

algorithms are traditionally expressed as a string of binary values composed of zeros and ones, and the evaluation process starts with an initial population. This initial population can be created randomly by selecting individuals from different generations. Therefore, for each generation the fitness of all individuals in that particular subpopulation is evaluated. Based on this assessed fitness, a subset of individuals is selected and used to create a new population. This creation of a new population follows evolutionary methods in biology, with the observations recombining and mutating in a random way. This modified population (modified by the evolutionary process) is then input to the next iteration of the algorithm—which continues to computationally repeat the process until a pre-defined maximum number of generations are produced, or when a prescribed fitness level for the population is reached. If the computation ends because the desired fitness level for the population is reached, then a satisfactory solution may be found. However, when the algorithm stops because the maximum number of generations is reached, a satisfactory solution may not be found since the population may not have achieved the desired outcome (i.e., fitness level) but simply, reproductively speaking, run out of time.

A typical genetic algorithm basically requires a good definition for the representation of the solution space and a fitness function to evaluate the solution. The normal representation of the solution found by a genetic algorithm is an array of bits, containing zeros and ones as possible values. Usually these arrays are fixed in size that allows the component parts to be equally aligned. These aligned arrays enable the fundamental operations for genetic computing to be performed, such as the crossover between two arrays. The fitness function is defined based on a genetic representation and is used to evaluate the quality of the solution reached over multiple iterations. Normally, the fitness function depends on the problem definition.

Take for example the knapsack problem, one that anyone with school age children might relate to. In this problem, the objective is to maximize the number of objects that can be put into a knapsack, considering the bag has a fixed capacity. A possible solution can be represented as an array of bits, wherein each bit represents a different object, and the value of the bit (0 or 1) represents whether or not the object is in the knapsack. During an iterative process, some solutions might not be valid, particularly once the size of the objects exceeds the knapsack's capacity. A fitness function would then summarize all the values for all objects in the knapsack. If the representation for the solution is valid, then the fitness function value would be one; otherwise it is zero.

The first step to define a genetic representation is identifying the fitness function. From there, the genetic algorithm can randomly initialize a particular population of possible solutions. Through an iterative process, the population is evolved by employing repetitive applications of mutation, crossover, inversion, and selection operations.

Initialization

Once the fitness function is identified, a set of individual solutions is randomly generated in order to create the initial population. The size of this population depends on the type of problem. It may contain several hundred or even several thousands of possible solutions. Very often the initial population of solutions is created by using a random process which tries to address the full range of possible solutions, also called the search space, that are used to initialize the optimization problem.

Selection

The selection phase is an iterative process used to create the desired population. Each iteration produces a subset of the existing population, breeding a new generation (an improved population). Once a new generation is defined, a second process occurs, using the fitness function to select individual solutions that produce the best measures yielded in the fitness function. A more fit (i.e., more appropriate) solution is more likely to be selected at the end of each iteration. Some selection methods rate each possible solution for fitness, selecting the best one at the end, while other methods rate the fitness of a random sample of the population and select the best one from all those available. This, as you can imagine, can be a computation-intensive exercise. Fitness functions are mostly stochastic and may select a small proportion of less-fit solutions in order to keep the diversity of the population as large as possible, in an attempt to prevent premature convergence on poor solutions.

Reproduction

The reproduction phase aims to create a second-generation population of solutions from the initial selection. This creation is based on genetic operators, such as crossover and mutation, applied to the original population of solutions.

Each new population of solutions produced by the genetic operators is defined as a pair of solutions. These solutions become the parent solution and are used as breeders for new solutions. A child solution (using operators like crossover and mutation) shares characteristics from the parent solution pair, just as a child would inherit characteristics from both parents. In turn, each child generated in this process becomes one parent in a paired solution and breeds again, continuing the process until an entirely new population of solutions is created.

This iterative process creates a new generation population that is different from the original one due to the combinations and mutations performed during the process. Usually this new generation has higher average fitness values than the original population, given that are the fittest individual solutions from the first generation were retained. These fit solutions were used to breed the succeeding generations, reaching in the end what may contain a small proportion of less-fit solutions.

Termination

Termination decides whether or not an iteration that is searching for the best solution will stop. Each criterion assigned to the termination specification is checked after every new generation of solutions is identified, ending the process if conditions are met. The following describes some common criterion used to establish the termination process:

- The solution found satisfies the minimum criteria.
- The iterative process reached the fixed number of previously established generations.
- The iterative process maximized the available allocated resources.
- The new generation of solutions is no longer producing better results.
- The iterative process ended because of manual inspection.
- The iterative process terminated due to a combination of the aforementioned criteria.

Pseudo-Code Algorithm

The following steps outline the computational tasks that would be encoded to implement a genetic algorithm:

1. Define a fitness function.
2. Randomly select the initial population.
3. Evaluate the fitness of each individual in the population.
4. Repeat steps 2 and 3.
5. Select best-ranking individuals to reproduce.
6. Breed a new generation through crossover and mutation (genetic operations) and give birth to offspring.
7. Evaluate the individual fitness of the offspring.
8. Replace the worst-ranked part of the population with offspring.
9. Repeat until termination conditions are met.

As mentioned, genetic algorithms can be applied to a variety of problems, like those involving time-tabling and scheduling as well as engineering problems, and are often used to solve local and global optimization problems. In general, genetic algorithms are quite useful when techniques based on calculus do not work well. For example, when the objective function has many local optima, when the fitness function is not continuous, or when the population solution is limited to integers or sequences.

Benefits of Genetic Algorithms

Genetic algorithms address a particular set of optimization problems and can also be used to compare relative performance of different solutions. Genetic algorithms demand basically two main features: a good representation of the problem and a meaningful fitness evaluation process. Both of these features make it possible for the model to reach an optimal population solution. The greatest attraction of genetic algorithms is probably their simplicity as a robust search method to good solutions, typically in a reasonable amount of time, even with high-dimensional problems.

Genetic algorithms are also quite effective when the search space is large, complex, or difficult to understand. They also perform efficiently when the expert knowledge is barely encoded into the search space. Some optimization problems are established in such a way that mathematical analysis is simply not possible. In these cases, genetic algorithms perform quite nicely. Genetic algorithms can be applied in global and local search optimization when the other traditional methods fail.

Even when arbitrary types of constraints and objectives are in place, genetic algorithms can handle searching for an optimal solution. By using weighted components and fitness functions, genetic algorithms can adapt to continue to evaluate the search space to find the best solution.

For these reasons, genetic algorithms have been used as a solid problem-solving approach in many different types of industries and scenarios, such as:

- *Optimization*: used in a wide variety of optimization tasks, such as numerical and combinatorial optimization problems that aim to examine problems like the traveling salesman problem, circuit design, and job shop scheduling.

- *Automatic programming*: used to evolve computer programs for specific tasks such as sorting networks.

- *Machine and robot learning*: used for machine-learning applications, such as classification and prediction or to design rules for a learning classifier in neural networks.

- *Economic models*: used to model processes of innovation, the development of bidding strategies, and the emergence of economic markets.

- *Immune system models*: used to model aspects of the immune system, including somatic mutation over an individual's lifetime, as well as the discovery of multigene families during evolutionary timeframes.

- *Ecological models*: used to model ecological scenarios such as biological arms races, host-parasite co-evolutions, symbiosis, and resource flow in ecologies.

- *Population genetics models*: used to answer questions such as "Under what conditions will a gene for recombination be evolutionarily viable?"

- *Interactions between evolution and learning*: used to examine how individual learning processes and species evolution phases affect each other.

- *Models of social systems*: used to study evolutionary aspects of social systems such as the evolution of cooperation and communication.

It has been mentioned that genetic algorithms can be computationally intensive. Outside of a high-performance analytic environment, this can be assisted by controlling parameters to speed up the convergence process. In particular problems, it is highly recommended to use a *hybrid algorithm*, taking advantage of both traditional optimizations along with the genetic algorithms. To address a high number of variables (say a large population with a high number of generations to cover the solution space), the computational cost of a genetic algorithm could be quite high. The use of a hybrid model may diminish this cost effect and define a more optimal result. In large corporations, however, computational costs can often be outweighed by the potential returns associated with deployed genetic algorithms.

Influences in Competitive Industries

Competition is all around, more in some industries and less in others, but every kind of market has its competition. And telecommunications is no different. In fact, telecommunications may be considered one of the more competitive industries in business today. Once communication services were commoditized, the same types of service bundles were often offered by all market providers (with minimal distinctions). This industry is also plagued with new entrants to the marketplace offering similar products and services. In addition to the traditional operators offering mobile, landline, broadband, and sometimes television, you may also see companies such as pay television services offering broadband service, Skype and MSN offering long-distance calls (nowadays even mobile services), and specialized mobile radio companies offering mobile communications services. In the end, you have different companies from distinct industries all offering similar services, each one perhaps with its own specialization. This helps make the communications industry an incredibly competitive market. The effect of this degree of competition compels companies to be more effective in their operational processes. In order to achieve operational excellence, companies must improve their analytical culture to provide superior decision-making support.

One straightforward way to distinguish your company in such a competitive landscape and maintain a reasonable level of profitability is to better understand (and hence service) the customer lifecycle. What do customers need in the beginning, when they first subscribe to the company? What do they need when they are consuming products and using services? What do they need to remain a loyal customer, extending their relationship for as long as possible? Understanding all these stages of the customer lifecycle with analytics is a good approach to improving the business activities, because you are empowered to make fact-based decisions for each individual customer, what makes sense to offer them when, and under what conditions, for example.

It therefore becomes fundamental and, in highly competitive industries, mandatory to know the behavior and needs of customers. Making corporate processes more efficient in the strategic, tactical, and operational activities to acquire qualified prospects and offer desired products and services to retain the most profitable customers—rather than those that drain organizational resources —some typical objectives. By focusing on profit over revenue and deploying an optimized suite of activities, organizations can better manage the customer life cycle, making their experiences better and hence generating quantifiable success.

Now, in order to achieve such efficiencies, it is necessary to do more than just simple manipulation and analysis over huge amounts of data related to operational and productive processes. This means going beyond the traditional business intelligence environments and even outside of data warehouse and/or data marts (i.e., independent data stores), or even database marketing. If it was that easy, everybody would do it, and it would simply be another competitive equivalence. What is required to go beyond the competition is to adopt a business analytics environment that creates new knowledge about customers and products/services and can be used to study the efficiencies of operational and tactical processes. This new knowledge, as previously described, continues to incrementally grow and translates into business action and measured results. It also relies on analytic applications like statistics, data mining, and optimization. Predictive models are commonly used to foresee future scenarios events such as potential credit risk, fraud, and bad debt. These inform revenue assurance requirements, churn prevention strategies, product adoption and promotion activities, and cross-selling and up-selling sales potential to name a few. These should differ for each company, thereby leading to competitive differentiators given that the data assets are different (i.e., customers that have identified with your company), the intellectual property developed within algorithms address unique, company-specific scenarios, and the pragmatic wherewithal of the organization to test ideas experiment, and execute based on insights.

Data-mining techniques are a feasible method within an analytical intelligence environment and can be further extended with genetic algorithms to help companies further optimize the processes associated with decision making. Actions can then be made with even more confidence, as once optimized the analytic results can assert what to offer, to whom, when, and through which channel.

Within the customers' lifecycle, optimization models can be built to improve business results. In the acquisition period, such models can improve efficiencies. During consumption of products and services, optimization can increase sales. And in the predicted event of churn (whether voluntary or not), these models can be used to assign customers to the most effective prevention strategies.

Improvement processes throughout the customers' lifecycle that include optimization models, such as those based on genetic algorithms, use target variables like profitability and independent factors, such as value, tenure of relationship, payment forecast, or credit risk, and so on as maximization or minimization functions. Using optimization models in this context can identify the best populations for acquisition campaigns, cross-sell/up-sell actions, and even for retention strategies.

Genetic Algorithms Solving Business Problems

If we consider customers as individuals contained within a particular species, (i.e., the species of consumers), genetic algorithms allow us to foresee how long they would live (as a customer of a particular company), and under which conditions (measured, for example, by how much they would consume). As such, the customer lifecycle can be adapted to a species evolution perspective for an individual. How long might customers last, since they were born (acquired)? How much are they able to spend on product/service consumption (how strong/weak are they) until they stop consuming (i.e., they die)? Genetic algorithms are an ideal method to assess the overall customer lifecycle evolution process.

We can use genetic algorithms to compute a new and distinctive value score, indicating how long they would last as a customer and how much they would spend over their lifetimes. Note that factors such as time and strength are in relation to the company and not specific to the individual's life, so attributes used in this value score are mostly assigned to the relationship between consumers and the company itself. As a result, the lifetime and the quality of life (or strength of living) is in reference to the company portfolio and it isn't possible to know, at least not given the described attributes, how those consumers will behave as individuals in their general lifetimes, nor long they would biologically live. If a key aspect of the customer lifecycle is to better understand how long the customers will continue to consume and how much they might consume over their cycle lifetime, this customer-derived value is quite sufficient to describe how the portfolio will evolve.

In fact, combining and mutating the best individuals (i.e., the best customers) over time could lead to an optimal consumer species (i.e., customer portfolio). Each specific customer could then be measured in terms of their distance from the derived optimal standard. In turn, this score can then be included in a matrix along with associated time period and consumption strength. This result is an analytically informed strategy that can be used to help direct contact communications for marketing campaigns, given that it provides a measured assessment of consumer value in relation to their desirability to the portfolio. If the company realizes that a particular customer has reached its maximum capacity of consumption, it is of no use to continue to contact them for new offerings. Similarly, if the company realizes that the lifetime for a particular customer is coming to an end, a directed retention communication could be used in anticipation of the churn event, attempting to keep the customer alive and spending money with the company.

Marketing efforts can be optimized using the heuristic method of genetic algorithms at each stage of the customer lifecycle, as depicted in Figure 3.1.

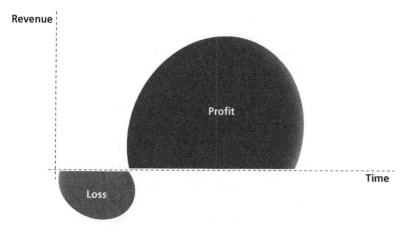

Figure 3.1 The Customer Lifecycle

Typically, actions related to the customer lifecycle are the responsibility of marketing, customer relationship, or customer engagement/operation departments. Most often these teams have defined objectives to profitably acquire customers, increase the wallet share composition of the customer portfolio with cross-sell and up-sell campaigns, and employ strategies to minimize customer churn.

Genetic algorithms create an individual customer-value metric that could describe some of the business dimensions such as profile and usage attributes. And according to this distinctive customer value a company can identify the products and services most suitable to the customer, their capacity to consume these products and services, and the possible time period that they will consume them.

This customer value operates like a predictive score, although in this situation it is assigned to multiple business events. The higher the score, the more likely it is for a particular event to occur. In a sense, the score is similar to those derived from clustering models. For instance, when analyzing overall cluster characteristics, we usually describe a particular cluster by the overall average behavior of all customers contained in that cluster membership. Based on the distance between clusters from their centroid (i.e., averaged central measure), we can then measure the distance between distinct customer groups. Therefore, each customer has a score that describes the degree to which they fit into a particular cluster. The closer a particular customer is to the centroid, the higher the chance that they behave like the cluster's average. In the same way, the distance from the optimal population identified by a genetic algorithm represents how close that customer is to behaving as an optimal customer. One can then determine the likelihood of a customer to purchase products or consume services based upon the capacity of the optimal customers to spend money, or to churn, as measured by the distance from the optimal.

During acquisition, the main objective is to present the most suitable products/services to a prospect. The value for a particular customer, derived from the genetic algorithm (GA), can indicate the correlation between the prospect's behavior and the products/services to be offered. Similarly, during the consumption phase, the GA value could indicate the propensity of fit for a particular product/service in addition to a projected expectation of the capacity to pay or consume.

In this way the GA value helps identify specific customers that are good targets for upsell/cross-sell offers.

And finally, the GA value determined by this heuristic model provides a sense of possible customer lifetime/tenure. With this, the company might decide to contact them in advance of a churn event as an attempt to keep them. Distinct offerings such as bonuses, discounts, and free upgrades might be viable strategies to extend the projected customers' lifetime.

Given the dynamic nature of customer lifecycles it is important to apply a strict maintenance process to the optimization models. If the customer(s) change their behavior (perhaps reflecting new entrants to the market or new offerings), the heuristic models should also be adjusted, fitting them to the new characteristics associated with customers.

Maintaining analytic models is a critical part of deriving value from them. When data changes over time, models need to be revisited in order to assess the relevance of initial attributes or if new coefficients or even entirely new variables are now more important to describe the behavior and patterns. This is no different with data mining, forecasting,[5] optimization, or any type of model, heuristic or not. Monitoring model degradation over time and refitting to current conditions are standard parts of an effective analytic process. There are many other possible business actions that can be put in place that are important to the customer lifecycle, some of which are described in later chapters. The set of possible actions described in this chapter were used to describe the usage of the heuristic model—an optimization model—based on genetic algorithms.

SUMMARY

The notion that a computer algorithm based on evolutionary concepts can be successfully applied in business scenarios might be surprising. As described within this chapter, genetic algorithms encompass a

---

[5] Forecasting is not described at length in this text, as there are many books already available that address heuristic notions in forecasting. One such volume is Gilliland, M. *The Business Forecasting Deal: Exposing Myths, Eliminating Bad Practices, Providing Practical,* Hoboken: John Wiley & Sons, Inc., 2010.

flexible methodology that has been applied in many fields, including those that are commercial, educational, and scientific. Genetic algorithms have begun to increase in popularity due to their ability to discover optimal solutions in large search spaces. They are also quite effective in solving complex optimization problems, particular when these problems involve several variables within a high-dimensioned solution space. Genetic algorithms are also attractive because they have the ability to extract knowledge from the problem's domain, learning and evolving within the particular field over the time.

This chapter presented the heuristic approach to business problems solving, and examined genetic algorithms in more detail as a particular analytical approach that exemplifies heuristic modeling. Genetic algorithms are often applied in optimization, engineering, and human sciences problems. Intrinsic to this modeling method is the notion of natural selection with each genetic evolution. Analogous to species evolution is the notion of a genetic constitution of a population that evolves over time, answering questions such as how long they will last and what the quality of living conditions will be over that time. Genetic algorithms can therefore compute a type of probability for customer value, including how long they might remain with the company and under which conditions they will be strong (or weak) consuming customers during their lifecycle.

CHAPTER **4**

The Analytical
Approach

Several methods are available to apply analytics to solving business problems, the oldest of which are based on mathematical approaches. There are some indications that the oldest mathematical objects are from 35,000 BC—from the mountains of Swaziland (currently known as Kingdom of Swaziland), bordered by South Africa and Mozambique—used as an early attempt to quantify time. The history of mathematics spreads out from these roots, and there are suggestions that formal mathematical models were deployed by the Babylonians, Egyptians, and Greeks at different time periods and mostly for arithmetics and geometry. Mathematics was basically a method used to describe natural phenomena, sometimes based on observations and at other times used to develop formulas to predict results. Chinese, Indian, and Islamic developments also contributed to the field of mathematical science, particularly further developing geometry, trigonometry, and algebraic disciplines. Since those early times, we have been using mathematics in virtually every field to solve specific problems as well as furthering other scientific development. Mathematics has been crucial to the development of all the modern sciences such as physics, chemistry, and biology. Today we still use mathematics to solve a wide range of business problems, from calculating changes in restaurant placement to computing the trajectory of a space craft.

Modern branches of mathematical science, such as the fields of statistics and probability, are typically used to classify and predict different business scenarios and forecast future activity, like with many financial and engineering problems. This chapter focuses on a relatively new scientific method (at least when compared to the legacy of mathematics), often called Knowledge Discovery in Data (KDD). Within this discipline, a variety of techniques and algorithms are used for data exploration and prediction. Data mining can be considered a sub-discipline of KDD. Data mining can further be divided into two distinctive modeling approaches, namely supervised and unsupervised methods. Supervised methods are algorithms that are used to classify data and require a target variable to train the models. The unsupervised approach, however, is used to describe scenarios, particular situations, and patterns based on measures of similarity or dissimilarity.

Supervised models include a training stage in order to learn the behavior of a target variable. The target variable is the item of interest and typically a well-known attribute. Training considers past correlations between the target variable and the rest of the available data. The training process seeks to predict future occurrences of the target variable, in future events for which the outcome of the target is unknown. Thus a target variable is predicted, and is validated with a hold-out, naïve data set as part of the model-development process. Both neural networks and decision trees are usually assigned to these supervised, predictive models.

Unsupervised models aren't based on any prior target or occurrence and instead recognize patterns of behavior in data. With unsupervised models, there isn't any previous sort of known pattern in relation to the data to be analyzed, so there isn't any particular supervised training task. Clustering and segmentation models are good examples of this type of method and create groups of observations due to particular similarities or dissimilarities found in the data.

Both supervised and unsupervised methods are used to solve distinct business problems, and a combination of methods might improve the effectiveness and the accuracy of the overall analytical project.

INTRODUCTION TO ANALYTICAL MODELING

Statistical approaches are used to understand current behavior based on analysis of past events using historical data. Statistics also creates useful insight regarding what happened in the past, helping organizations better prepare for what could be expected in the future. Statistical, supervised methods like regression or forecasting can be used to foresee the forthcoming month of sales based upon the past 12 months of historical sales, for example. These are flexible methods that establish the likelihood of a future event, whether that event is churn associated with a specific customer, the possibility of bad debt, the potential for insolvency, the occurrence of fraud, sales in the next quarter, the possibility of being an acquisition or purchase, and so forth. Based on the prediction (like a churn event), corporate processes (such as retention strategies) can be used to affect the predicted rate, by changing one or more of the factors or conditions that are driving the prediction. Predictive models are very useful to organizations that want to proactively understand future scenarios so that they can encourage, change, or diminish the predicted event with better defined strategies, approaches, and tactics.

Other supervised data-mining methods, such as artificial neural networks, decision trees, forecasting, and association rules, are also used to examine the past to understand current behaviors, thereby helping prepare companies to address different business scenarios. These methods are specific to the business situation and, with fine tuning by adjusting parameters, coefficients, iterations, and so on, one can make the outcomes more accurate, and the model itself more reliable. This fine tuning is crucial to modeling simply because these models learn patterns based on the available data, and data is based on the scenario. When the business scenarios change, as they so often do, the data consequently changes and thus the model should be updated accordingly. For example, if the business problem is churn and an organization creates a model to identify potential defectors, then attempts to prevent customers from leaving by using relevant marketing offers, the expected (do nothing) churn rate should decrease if the offers are effective. By decreasing the churn rate, this company correspondingly changes the business scenario because the problem would no longer be the same churn rate. As such, with regularized updates, these methods can be considered more adaptable and even possibly dynamic to the business situation.

Unsupervised models are often used for customer behavior segmentation, typically applying clustering techniques to define some type of structure in customer characteristics. For instance, a customer's behavioral (unsupervised) segmentation might lead the company to adjust their products and services into specific bundles according to the identified needs and propensities resulting from the cluster segmentation. Specific product bundles may better fit the customer's aspirations and therefore could improve overall sales. Groups of customers with particular similarities might be handled by using similar approaches, with specific channels used for communications and particular offerings. In this way, companies are able to establish different types of business actions—whether they be campaigns, bundles, channels—according to the derived data-driven customer clusters. By narrowing the population to similar, segmented groups, business actions can be more focused and often more relevant to the shared characteristics of the cluster segment.

Unsupervised models, like clustering algorithms, group a set of observations into subsets based on similarities (or dissimilarities). Other models, such as association rules, are used to discover correlations among different factors—especially in those contained within large datasets. Such correlations are often sought to discover business rules, based upon events or transactions (defining the dependent variables), with regard to one or more attributes, which are defined as the independent variables. Association rules don't require a target variable to train the model, and as such they can be considered an unsupervised method. Association rules used for business modeling are often referred to as market basket analysis—focused on discovering the statistical correlation among different product purchases, like sales transactions from people purchasing wine who also buy cheese and bread. There is an old and popular example involving nappies and beer that popularized this method to retailers.[1]

---

[1] http://www.dssresources.com/newsletters/66.php includes some of the early thoughts on this, perhaps mythical, example.

As with associations, sequence association rules also examine business correlations between subsets of variables to estimate cause and consequence effects. Unlike association rules, however, sequenced associations include the dimension of time. For example, a sequence rule might examine transactions in which people purchased wine, only to later buy cheese and therefore bread. The timeframe inherently becomes a dependent association lag in the occurrence of the event sequence.

Link analysis, another unsupervised method, provides a clear connection between subjects. Often represented graphically, link analysis can highlight new insights associated with data-derived relationships. Useful to understanding potential business outcomes, link analysis can be used to examine the connections among consumers that have been targeted for cross-sell or up-sell campaigns by identifying the linkages between target groups. Analogously, social network analysis (an unsupervised investigative approach) can reveal the strength of particular connections among social structures within naturally networked relationships. Strong connections may be ascribed to influential members, who might lead other network members toward similar behaviors. This linked process of influence can be considered similar to that of a diffusion of behavior. Social network analysis can be highly useful to identify and investigate patterns of product/service adoption, cascading effects of churn, and the spread of fraud among rings of participants in collusion with each other, for example. These models aim to uncover the relationship, based on defined criteria between subjects or members who share common social ties.

Finally, there are optimization models, another unsupervised approach, which are used to improve a particular business process. Optimization models usually identify the possible paths, the peaks, and the troughs in connected flows of data and the potential alternatives. And while the objectives of optimization are to minimize (or maximize) an outcome based on defined constraints, they can address a range of business problems, identifying the shortest (or fastest) path within a supply chain to represent network flow patterns, with identified bottlenecks, and solve for ways to diminish them. Discovering alternative paths to redistribute network traffic for a telecommunications company, the shortest path needed to minimize travel costs, or the optimal route for speediest delivery all reflect problems scenarios for optimization. Once identified by the model, business processes can be changed to improve service quality, the stocking of goods, changing delivery routes, and so forth, in order to improve customer satisfaction. With increases in customer satisfaction companies tend to retain customers for longer periods of time, correspondingly increasing assigned revenue and thus the financial health of the organization. By improving financial health, companies can then compete in new markets, can afford better promotions, and/or are able to deliver higher-quality products and services.

Irrespective of the type of model used, whether it be supervised, unsupervised, investigative, or optimized (or a combination of one or more methods) the ultimate objective is to gain new, useful business knowledge. If correctly applied, this knowledge can encourage practical corporate action and yield effective business gains.

When all is said and done, all elements in a business are connected—so a change in one aspect of the cycle alters another, just as with the butterfly effect. If an organization invests resources (say, in the form of money, effort, capacity, or skill) to improve quality, customer perceptions should recognize services have improved. By delivering better services, companies might also be able to acquire more customers and correspondingly see increases in product-consumption patterns. With more products and services being consumed by a larger customer base, companies are able to increase their revenue and their profits. And given increased profits, companies can invest more resources into further improving quality. A perpetual cycle of improvement is supported by fact-based decisions which analytical models support at every stage of the process.

THE COMPETITIVE-INTELLIGENCE CYCLE

Storage capacity and processor speeds continue to decline in price, making new, high-speed computer processing systems, once only available to large corporations, accessible to small and medium-sized businesses. With increasing capacity afforded by these increasingly powerful systems, more applications and programs are developed and, as a result, more data is maintained. Fortunately for data miners, more data means more models. Answers to more complex questions can be developed. Transactional and operational systems seldom improve decision making. They are very important to operational management, focusing on how daily activity occurs, sometimes even on an hourly basis. They do not, however, tend to contribute substantially to the decision-making process or to analytical processes, with the exception of serving as a source of input data for analytical modeling. These increasingly large volumes of data often provide the main source of inputs that feed mathematical and statistical modeling efforts. These data typically require some type of additional processing to identify and select the relevant information for analytical model input.

Sometimes the absence of information reflects a lack of decision making in a corporate environment. On the other hand, an abundance of information can also lead to a lack of decisions, with increasingly complex IT environments leading to a type of corporate paralysis—limiting the ability to pick the right information to effectively use in decision-making processes.

In order to use transactional data from operational systems, data transformation routines typically change these inputs into information for use in analytics—with the goal of creating new knowledge that was not previously known. However, in order to improve the business based on this newly derived knowledge, it must be applied to a specific scenario; in other words, it needs to be used, in order to become intelligence. This process of changing data into intelligence can be described as a cycle of competitive intelligence. This process is described as a competitive-intelligence cycle because it lends itself to ongoing learning that continues to be improved upon when it is maintained, and as such leads to ongoing improvements, so business activity grows and flourishes in response to competitive marketplaces.

The majority of companies experience some sort of competition. In such competition, it is a race to have first-mover advantage, to introduce products first, to have customers using their services before they decide to go elsewhere, and/or to innovate and improve operations sooner than those competitors might offer similar capabilities. Say two engineers are assigned to fix a device. Assume that engineer A is unfamiliar with the task. He is seeing that device for the very first time, so in order to fix it he needs to work with the manual, reading it as he goes. He will succeed eventually, but it will take time. On the other hand, if engineer B has fixed the same (or similar) device in the past, he doesn't need the manual (perhaps he only refers to it for a few particular topics). Engineer B will fix the device much more quickly because of the familiarity with the topic and his knowledge from doing this before being maintained. In business, and particularly in competitive marketplaces, that competitive advantage improves organizations' capacity to not only do things accurately or well, but also do them faster than the competitors.

During each day we make many decisions, storing in our memories what worked well and what didn't. Over time it becomes easier to do similar tasks and make decisions because of this experience, and one becomes more effective in doing the same or similar tasks. In addition to this knowledge creation, if you also remember what was learned about the previous results, the outcomes, what to do, and what not to do, you identify ways to improve the tasks and make better decisions at the end. You can become aware of potential outcomes before you even run the task, understanding if conditions warrant a work around, the likelihood of success or failure, and so on. And this becomes a real advantage because you don't need to begin from scratch. You are using previous knowledge and past experience to succeed. Moreover, if you react more quickly you have more time to fix other problems, and possibly you can decide what problems you want to address first or at all, and which ones you want to give to your competitors. This can be thought of as a disease—the sooner you are diagnosed, the better the chances you have to be healed.

Analytics can provide a proper mechanism to help companies create this experience, particularly the business experience. Once the initial inputs are sourced (say, the broken device, the issue, and the documentation), and data are transformed into information about the task at hand. In organizations, these inputs are typically transactional data that is transformed into information that can possibly be analyzed. Distinct analyses are then applied to these inputs in order to create knowledge (the precursor to experience). It is at this second stage of the competitive-intelligence cycle that the analyses are applied. There are typically two distinct types of analysis, supervised and unsupervised. The basic difference between them is the existences of a premise for the first one and no proposition for the second. Both models are briefly described below, and will be covered in more detail later.

Typically, unsupervised methods that are often the first class of models that a company needs to develop. Given these models don't require a previously known pattern, history, or target (and thus aren't based on supervision related to other facts), they can be more difficult to develop and evaluate simply because there isn't the direction to assess them, comparative or otherwise. Even more difficult are the issues that can arise in transforming this unsupervised insight into business action. For example, pattern-recognition models such as clustering are commonly used as an initial step to group subsets of customers based on similarities. Customers with similar behavior in terms of product usage, payment method, time with the company, as well as shared demographic information are classified into similar groups.[2]

Supervised methods, which require a target variable in order to train the model, classify each observation in relation to their similarity to the target. For example, a bank may have historical information about bad debt and how some customers over time didn't pay their loans. Input data to the model would contain a set of historical information about customers who paid their loans and customers who didn't pay their loans. The variables pay or didn't pay could be used to create a class, defined as 0 when the customers pay their loans and 1 when they didn't. If the company wants to predict if customers will pay (or not) their loans in the future, the combined historical information about payment and the class variable could train the analytical model, predicting membership for customers for whom there isn't a target class defined by the historical data.

Often these types of models, supervised and unsupervised, are used in conjunction with one another. For instance, suppose a particular company needs to better understand a bad-debt scenario, with

---

[2] Collica, R. *Customer Segmentation and Clustering using SAS® Enterprise Miner™*, 2nd edition, Cary, North Carolina: SAS Institute Inc., 2011, provides detailed description of methods to create clusters for segmenting customer populations.

the goal of avoiding or at least decreasing the amount of insolvency. Initially creating an unsupervised model to cluster similar types of bad debt might identify different types of insolvency, in terms of the amount/volume or in terms of the timing of payments. Customers might be found to be in distinct groups, such as those who have smaller debts and pay with short delays, those with moderate debts who have short delays associated with their payments, or those with high debt who have longer delays. A clustering model can be used to identify these different debts as payment groups, each with their own unique characteristics. Given the behavior pattern is different for each of these three customer segments, it is reasonable to believe that the likelihood of bad debt may also differ for each group. Each supervised model might have some specific behavioral characteristics and different significant variables describing each particular segment's potential insolvency behavior. The overall accuracy of these three predictive models might indeed be higher than if one predictive model was developed for the entire population. This combination of both unsupervised and supervised models can predict, in addition to improved overall classification accuracy, some underlying business insight about the insolvency behavior between different customers. This knowledge can help specify more focused communications and campaigns aimed at avoiding the bad debt or improving the collection process. And while these different types of models can be deployed in conjunction with each other, and sometimes this is actually recommended, they are very often developed separately, regardless of whether they strive toward similar business goals.

Analytically derived knowledge, from supervised, unsupervised, or combined models, is only of benefit if applied to a business process, and it is this last stage in the competitive-intelligence cycle and is perhaps the most important. Companies are able to use enterprise software to control operational processes, addressing the first stage of the cycle. Information Technology (IT) departments often employ can use business intelligence systems that include data warehouses, independent data marts, query-based multidimensional applications, and on-demand interactive visual environments, all designed to help business managers with their daily decision making, as referenced in the second-cycle stage. There is a set of focused software solutions that deliver business analytics for production environments, allowing companies to create business knowledge to solve particular business problems. This third stage involves data mining, machine learning, statistics, and knowledge discovery from data and provides competitive insights for organizations. Unlike the previous stages, there isn't any formal science behind the usage of knowledge and how best to apply it to the business. This is very much an art, requiring subject-matter expertise. How to understand what to do based on a forecast from historical data or how to translate the likelihood to purchase or to encourage a purchase is indeed more an art than a science. Different people will create different business tactics and strategies based on the same data or analysis scores. And because of this it can be quite difficult. Sometimes, if not well executed, the whole process can fail. Even the best control systems operating the company, the best data warehouse providing input to analysis, and superior data analyses deriving the most accurate scores, are still not a guarantee for success.

As a result of this potential for applied-intelligence failure, a necessary fifth stage of the competitive-intelligence cycle is depicted in Figure 4.1. Derived from all previous stages, the intelligence associated with taking business actions needs to be maintained in order to ensure that learning continues for ongoing improvement. This is experience. All experiences should be remembered. Business approaches that have succeeded in the past should be remembered just as much as the business actions which failed. As in our individual lives, we are shaped by the actions we take, no matter whether the results are good or bad; so, too, are companies. Often, however, organizations don't centrally store experience like we do as individuals. Experience typically lives within the minds of employees, and in fragmented silos—but not in a well-structured environment designed to save and recover experiences, like our brains. Maintaining a record of experience requires focused effort by an organization, and as such,

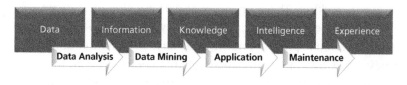

Figure 4.1 The Competitive-Intelligence Cycle

takes time. Not only are many companies ill prepared to maintain a record of experience, but many employees are not receptive to this final stage of the competitive-intelligence cycle. Many times people are afraid to share the intelligence and ideas they know. Fear of being criticized or not receiving credit can hold many back from realizing the benefit of maintained, shared experience. But rather than doing nothing when faced with a business problem, individuals typically draw upon their experience. Maintained within an organization, experience becomes a shared knowledge store, one that not only provides insights from collective wisdom but can be used as a simulation environment for testing alternatives.

Applied knowledge is a two-way street, a bidirectional vector, a round-trip route—it flows out and returns. The simple act of sharing knowledge persist the idea/notion/fact exchange for the listener, and also reinforces the concept for the speaker. It often teaches, and it learns and informs related scenarios and is a shared asset. Highly defined by the culture of the organization, experience that is maintained can become the most import asset to driving effective operations and innovation within an organization.

Data

Data can be characterized by the execution of a transactional system that controls and manages company business operations and processes. These systems collect and store data relevant to operations such as auditing and tracking/tracing events like fulfillment and provisioning, purchase transactions, sales transactions, and distribution and shipment events, among many others. Any information assigned to the daily operations is often in relation to transactional systems. The type of the data produced during this transaction processing is often called micro information, a set of attributes which describe a particular task or event that controls the operational process and permits event tracking. These operational data provide little or no relevance to business decision making as they contain too much detail of the operational process and little, if any, information about the business (and thus are not a focus of this book). As a result, data from operational systems is typically transformed and stored in a data warehouse or independent data store. During this transformation, the row data, comprising elements that control operational procedures is often aggregated into summaries that describe the business view of the activity, so that details about purchasing and fulfillment, for example, are summarized to customer-centric events.

One of the most important roles of a data warehouse is not to just aggregate operational data but rather to collect, transform, and store operational data from different systems, each of which controls different parts of the company's operations, making them available as a dimension of the business. Detailed information about the sales process, cost structures of different products, marketing campaign activity, and customer events all traced in operational systems are combined into a customer-centric view regarding customer experiences with the company across the entire business value chain, for example. The central perspective in the data warehouse can be the customer, as opposed to the operational system, which describes the operational activity they are designed to run.

When operational information is aggregated and oriented to a business perspective it becomes quite useful for analysis. Most often, data warehouses and stores are the foundation for strategic planning and tactical business actions. Very often, forecasting and portfolio optimization are based on information provided by these kinds of environments. And analytically derived estimates and likelihoods established in relation to customers (like churn probability, payment propensity, and fraud, among others), can be appended and recorded into these stores to support planning and tactical decisions. That being said, if something goes awry with operational system-transaction recording, then the remainder of the competitive-intelligence cycle shall fail too. The famous acronym GIGO (i.e., garbage in garbage out) starts with accurate data.

Information

During the information stage of the competitive-intelligence cycle, the operational data sources are identified, mapped into a data-collection strategy, and formatted in a storage environment needed by analysts and managers to aid them in their decisions. This includes the need to identify raw information fields from these systems, select the pertinent ones, translate this system data into business perspectives, join it to other, relevant data sources, and finally load the results into a database as a centralized store for multi-user inquiry. Commonly this process is referred to as ETL Extract, Transform, and Load (ETL).

Selection and extraction of operational data can occur from mainframe systems, Windows operating systems, Linux, and others, and most often is associated with a mix of different hardware and operating environments. Transforming essentially integrates these differently sourced fields into a single dimension and creates a record view that reflects the business perspective. And while loading these derived records into a table or centralized store of some sort may seem to be the easiest part of the entire process, it has its own complexities, with the need for definitions to address incremental updates, and distinct time periods refresh multiple destinations, among other considerations. As a reflection of this, one of the main characteristics in a analytical data environment is that of time. When a new cycle of business information is added, a decision about the past data needs to be made. Sometimes the previously retained data are rebuilt, incrementally updating history and appended to the current data as new content. Sometimes the historical data is discarded and a completely new stream of data is created. How new data is incorporated into existing stores becomes a business decision based on careful consideration of the importance of retaining consistency in the past and accurately reflecting the current information needs of the business.

As such, this ETL processing is part of a defined information-creation process, depicted as business intelligence layers in Figure 4.2. The ETL process typically includes a full dictionary component, which translates the operational elements into meaningful business field definitions. Additional tools are used to manage and govern development stores differently from production environments. And for this reason, as well as the complexity of the entire environment in relation to mapping definitions, extraction rules, transformation specifications, loading and managing the associated processing, and so on, this activity can be referred to as the integration layer. As with any database, information is stored for the sole purpose of retrieving it for some related activity. As the most important aspect of database design, how information needs to be retrieved defines how it needs to be stored.

Once the data has completed this integration processing, the results are maintained as data stores, shaping how the information is viewed and accessed by the organization. This aspect may consist of a single and centralized data warehouse, some extended data marts, independent data stores, and/or a combination of all of the above. Furthermore, a collection of small but highly accessed query-oriented multidimensional tables might be defined to address the most common questions. Sometimes referred to as data cubes, they describe a particular fact or topic from a set of pre-defined dimensions. For instance, a cube might be created to depict a set of indicators such as the sales volumes, revenue, taxes, and net profit across the dimensions of time, locations, category, product, and outlet. This cube may be computed overnight, creating a huge matrix of cells containing all possible combinations in relation to the defined dimensions. The conceptual model for this approach is called a star schema, because there are facts of interest that drive the business definition at the center, and multiple ways to see the facts from the different dimensions related to it. The computed results are maintained so decision making and downstream processes can access and utilize the results, often describing this aspect of the process as the persistency layer, as illustrated in Figure 4.2.

Once the data is stored it should be readily available for retrieving and, although it may be obvious, data is stored for the sole purpose of retrieving it; otherwise there would be no need to store anything at all. With the rise of big data, this retrieval may be delayed, and in fact, storage may simply occur without any consideration of retrieval needs simply because the potential value of the information is not well understood when it is gathered, nor will it be until business needs dictate. In such situations, commodity hardware is often utilized as the data attic—stuffing it with volumes of inputs that may be operational (say, from scanners), or from transactional or social media content. Once retrieval needs are identified, the attic of information needs to be dusted off and examined for usability—requiring assessment as part of the integration layer for use in any analysis and reporting activity.

Some of the traditional tools that allow users to retrieve information from data stores include pre-defined reports, dashboards, inputs to downstream systems (like modeling applications), relational queries, multidimensional queries, or some or all of these. Names such as Relational Online Analytical Processing (ROLAP), Multidimensional Online Analytical Processing (MOLAP), or Hybrid Online Analytical Processing (HOLAP) have been assigned to the presentation layer of a business-intelligence environment. More recently, attention has been paid to unstructured text data, which also requires some structure be applied in order for it to be usable for retrieval and reporting. Just as with transformation of operational data, text data is transformed with category and classification tags that provide dimensional structures (also known as facets) that enable retrieval. What data is included, what techniques need to be applied in the integration layer, and the vehicles for needed storage in order to be centered on end user retrieval needs define the purpose of text-based intelligence.

In assessing the retrieval needs of the organization, IT needs to address the different end user needs for the data. What kinds of reports or queries are needed? Will the users be making dynamic, ad hoc queries or do they need static reports about specific aspects of the business? How often does the data need to be refreshed? How many users will access the data simultaneously? All these questions (well, all the answers anyway) and a host of others define the type of the query and report layer(s)—the particular piece of the environment where the users actually touch the data. The aspect is depicted as the presentation layer of Figure 4.2 and represents the information stored in the persistence layer. This aspect of information delivery is fundamental because it is the way in which the end users see the business information. In fact, when business users refer to business intelligence technology in their companies, they are often referring to this presentation layer, the tools they are using to access the information required for their decision making. They really don't bother (and often don't understand) the other aspects of the business-intelligence ecosystem, how the integration process works, how the data is stored, and the overall architecture, nor should they. They simply want the information, and need to know how easy it is to get and what they can do with it is once they have it.

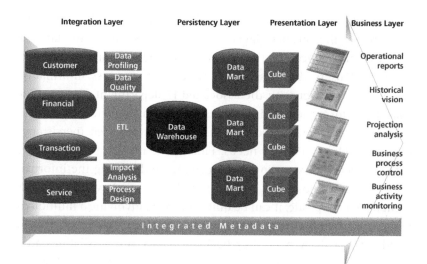

Figure 4.2   Business Intelligence Creates Information from Data

In order to deliver relevant business information to analysts and managers, as well as keep and maintain the information in a controlled and governed manner, all four layers need to be aspects of a single cohesive environment, as illustrated in Figure 4.2. The integration layer maps, collects, and loads all data into the repository stores, with information management requirements driving the mappings, aggregations, and transformations—and with corresponding governance policies and procedures ensuring consistency and integrity of the derived information. The persistency layer hosts all information delivered to the end users and thus is fundamental to the business perception on IT's ability to meet their needs. From a business perspective, the presentation layer is the business intelligence environment, forming evaluations of what is possible to understand from data. The final business layer is reflective of the end users, what they are going to do with the information, what they will use, and what they will ignore. And while this most important layer of the business intelligence cycle is easily understood, it is often not top of mind in IT system design—resulting in disillusionment and disappointment of end users and tarnishing the reputation of how information can improve decisions.

An alternate method, employed by many organizations, that helps retain the business layer requirements is simply to start the business intelligence cycle development at the end, and work backward. End users (business layer) state their business information needs and, together with the associated IT department, they outline plans to perform their analyses (presentation layer). Then, the proper data model can be defined to house the data required (persistency layer) to address end user needs. Finally, the mapping of the source data is executed, extracting, transforming, and loading the information into the repositories (integration layer). And while this may seem rather simplistic, it can be quite complex, involving a multidisciplinary team[3] and often stumbling when business users change their minds—particularly once they begin to realize the possibilities after interacting with data, and as such, this cycle will continue to develop, evolve, and grow—dynamic to the every changing needs of competitive organizations.

Knowledge

While many organizations are quite mature in their development of data and intelligence, many are just beginning to develop their knowledge. It is at this level, however, that insights associated with the impact of issues on activities are fully realized. Informed by data and text analysis, predicting into future scenarios can provide new knowledge that organizations can exploit. The focus of such analysis tends to be directed to specific business problems. Say, for example, a company is faced with increased numbers of customers leaving, that is, increased churn. Seeing this, they realize that they first need to understand why they are defecting, find appropriate ways to address or stem the tide, and quickly respond with targeted communications and offers. But how does the company do this? How can they improve the targeting beyond what they are already doing? What would be

---

[3] Such multidisciplinary teams often include business analysts who collect the requirements, software and database engineers who build/acquire the repositories and presentation applications, programmers who specify the data integration processes, and data administrators who manage the information map and environment.

the best promotion to offer? A predictive model can be developed, possibly on different customer segments, trained and deployed to classify customers with the higher likelihood to leave. This likelihood or churn score is then assigned to each individual customer, describing their specific propensity to churn. Based on this new knowledge associated with customers who haven't left but have greater propensities to leave, the company can create distinct promotions that reflect the needs of that individual and/or segment. Customers with higher churn scores might be contacted with an aggressive offer, customers with more moderate scores may have a less assertive offer, and those with low scores may not be given any offer at all—particularly if their calculated lifetime value is also low. Tiered offers to different customer types (in this case based on churn propensity) can dramatically improve customer response, more so than if the same offer went to every customer. Moreover, the marketing costs would also likely be lower, given that the communication would not be sent to everyone, just those who are desirable to be retained and who also have a reasonable likelihood of leaving.

The churn scenario is a focused analysis, and defined with straightforward business actions in mind. The historical information from the data warehouse (or data mart) is used to build a classification model by using past occurrences of churn to train a model to foresee future customer-churn events. These results define the suitability of a customer-retention campaign. Similar approaches may be deployed for sales events, product adoption, or even fraud and bad-debt prevention. Any business event with a reasonable history of occurrences, and which contains a flag that describes some target class such as churn or not churn, fraud or not fraud, pay or not pay, buy or not buy, can be used to develop a predictive model.

In terms of business processes, analytics and data mining can be deployed for each stage of a customer's lifecycle. Distinct models are built to identify the best acquisition candidates, targeting prospective customers and encouraging them to become consumers of the company's products/services. Cross-sell and up-sell models are used during the consuming phase to determine which candidates may buy more or higher-order products/services. At the end of the process, consumption stops. For many different reasons, consumer goods-related consumption will always end. What companies can do is slow the voluntary reasons for consumption ending, such as attrition and discontentment, by addressing issues like variety, price, quality, usability, innovation, and so on in their offerings.

No matter the industry, products, or services offered, there is a cost to each stage of the customer lifecycle. During acquisition, costs may be in relation to advertising, installation, fulfillment, provisioning, discount promotions, or initial support during setup and usage. For instance, when you acquire a broadband telecommunications service, there is a cost associated with the equipment and installation due to initial usage. Telecom companies invest in new customers with the belief that the ongoing, monthly broadband fees will not only help them recover this initial investment but will also generate a profit over the longer term. A flyer sent by a retailer to consumers has an associated cost. So, why send this out to all customers if you can send just to the most likely buyers? Better targeting of consumers improves the hit rate, that is, the number of consumers who will take the desired action, decreasing the cost of operation, and diminishes possible attrition by avoiding those consumers who don't fit the offering profile.

Analytics has a natural evolution within companies, as illustrated in Figure 4.3. No matter the size, companies usually start to develop query and reporting tools. During this phase of development, queries are affiliated with what has happened in the past and what changed with a particular business indicator (like sales). As questions begin to extend, going beyond deciphering what has happened or what current conditions are, companies start to explore how they can answer what will happen. Looking toward the future, data-mining tools are often used to foresee future business scenarios. Based on the historical data assigned to a business event of interest, predictive models can establish the future likelihood of these events. So while a key sales indicator may have decreased, this more-advanced stage of analysis can now be used to predict what will happen if that trend continues in the future.

Extending beyond the prediction of future events, companies may further their analytic prowess by modeling what would be the best option to solve a particular business problem. Optimization is used to simulate business scenarios, which can in turn utilize predicted

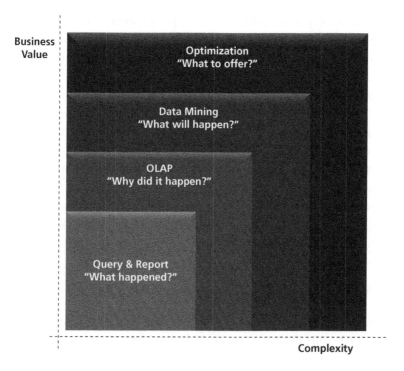

Figure 4.3 The Evolution of Analytics over Time

inputs, so that the best solution in a future scenario can be estimated. Scenario definition is the heart of optimization models, requiring explicit definitions that answer questions such as: What is the ultimate objective? What are the constraining factors? With the goal of maximizing sales, production, and distribution costs and limited marketing budgets constrain the activities that can actually be done to improve sales, and are inherent to optimization problem definition. That being said, optimization models can help organizations better understand their business scenarios, simulate marketplace and operational options, and help to identify the best (or at least a possibly better) approach or offering. From analysis of the underlying causes identified by decreasing sales indicators, including the establishment of predictive scores for high potential buyers, the optimal offering can be defined so that the realized response rate is the best possible (or at least good enough) to address the defined need.

While query and report tools are typically used by many commercial businesses operating in competitive environments, they address historical activity, providing a thermometer that can measure past and current conditions. OLAP, and its variants, helps organizations explore the possible rationale behind the existing and historic conditions. Moving from query tools to exploratory reporting systems there are increasing demands, in terms of both IT infrastructures that support such business intelligence creation as well as the analytic skill set of the end user. As companies continue to evolve their analytic environments, the technologies can become more specialized, leading to different skills sets needed by end users to generate the models while at the same time providing even greater business value by applying predictions and thus proactive direction to improve business processes.

Intelligence

To make use of knowledge, business action needs to be taken based upon the results derived from analytical models, as depicted in Figure 4.2. Consider a company that develops a particular predictive model to understand who is most likely to default in their payment. Without any analysis customers may have been ranked by the amount of outstanding funds to be collected, triggering collection when a threshold is crossed. Presume that part of the organization is tasked with calling customers when they cross that threshold; they'd then be contacting those with the largest debts first. However, based on a predictive model that classifies customers based on their likelihood to repay, calls instead would be made to those with the highest probability of repaying in the event of collection. And while funds may not be retrieved from all insolvent customers, the organization can anticipate the amount that will likely be recovered from the collection process, based on the bad-debt volume relative to payment collection probability. In fact, if those who are most likely to pay their debt are contacted first, overall recovery efforts would typically be more profitable, since the cost of capital is often more expensive than the cost of the collection process.

In this stage, knowledge application is defined, specifying how analysts and managers use the insights from the previous stages to improve decision making. Intelligence, in this context, refers to application of the knowledge for some particular purpose. You probably know that if you jump off a moving bus you might get hurt. With this kind of knowledge, knowing the result of jumping off a bus, that is, the action, defines specific fact. However, if you know you will get hurt and you still jump off, you are not being smart, you are not being intelligent. Intelligence can be considered, such as in this case, the *proper* usage of the information. Therefore, intelligence is defined as the use of knowledge to make better decisions, solve a problem, take effective business action, and so on.

Recognizing that data-mining and predictive models lead to new knowledge, we can map back this stage of the competitive-intelligence cycle to the customer lifecycle to understand at what stage of the acquisition, consumption, and churn phases a different model can provide useful knowledge. As depicted in Figure 3.1, the acquisition phase is largely a cost phase given that little if any revenue is generated from the marketing and sales efforts. Once a prospect becomes a customer, using products and services from the company, revenue is generated. Consumption does come to an end in the third stage, a consuming outage if you will, no matter the reasons.

Acquisition Models

In an effort to decrease losses from monies spent, companies can deploy predictive models to better target prospects that are most likely to become customers in the first place. This model might be based on historical information about customers that acquired similar products and services, training a model to foresee this prospect-to-customer-conversion event.

Losses can also relate to delayed or late events, such as bad debt. Suppose a company spends money and time offering and provisioning a product. If a subset of customers acquires the product and then become insolvent after two or three months, that company wouldn't recover its investment, thereby establishing a loss. Based on this history, another predictive model could be deployed to identify the probability of insolvency for each prospect before even targeting them for acquisition. Companies definitely don't want to sell to bad payers. By knowing possible bad payers in advance, that company could avoid future insolvency and corresponding losses.

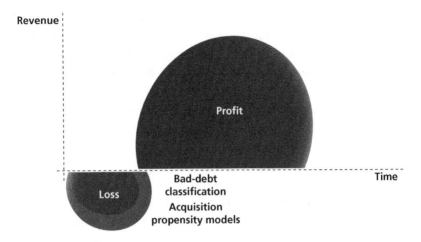

Figure 4.4   Predictive Models Supporting Customer Acquisition

Figure 4.4 illustrates how these predictive models can be used to reduce losses throughout the acquisition stage, either by using models to better target the prospects, increasing the response rate, or to anticipate possible bad debt, decreasing eventual insolvency. In addition to these models, many others can be developed, such as those who identify the highest revenue potential (encouraging them with more aggressive offers), or optimizing marketing and sales campaigns by timing them across communication channels with customized messages for each prospect, and even identifying what the most suitable products would be for a potential customer, targeting sales and marketing strategies.

Consumption Models

Basically, these models are aimed to increase the profitable use of products/services, leading to greater revenue, optimizing operational processes, reducing costs, detecting fraud, identifying risk, predicting bad debt, and in general, reducing losses. The popularized cross-sell and up-sell marketing models are commonly used at this stage, as illustrated in Figure 4.5. Very often initial segmentation models are used to better identify any unique customer groups. Clustering models are a common method used to better understand behavior,

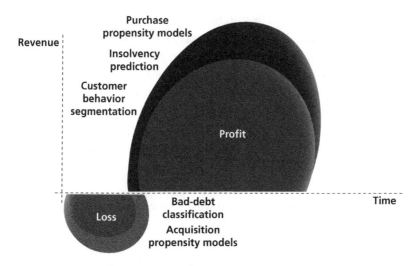

Figure 4.5 Supervised and Unsupervised Models Applied in the Consumption Phase

thereby decreasing the variability of the population with the goal of crafting more accurate models for each unique segment. In and of themselves, clusters can help direct which product and service packages are associated with the different, identified behavioral segments, but are harder to use because they produce descriptive results.

Continuing with the unsupervised methods, in addition to clustering and association rules (aka market basket analysis), customer transaction details that reflect a business event can be examined. In a supermarket, when you are paying for your purchases, every product is scanned by the cashier. This product-purchase data is stored in a repository. Over all customers, within a specific timeframe, the company collects a history of all product transactions. Association rules correlate all products within a single transaction, and across all transactions, identifying which products are purchased together—both by an individual and across their customer base. Based upon this derived frequency, two metrics are created, *support* and *confidence*. The *support* metric indicates how many times a particular combination of products is purchased together. For instance, wine, cheese, and bread may be purchased together in 20 percent of the transactions. The *confidence* measure indicates the number of times a subset of products is purchased if the presence of another product is part of the transaction.

For instance, wine might be purchased in 60 percent of the times both cheese and bread is also purchased. According to the values of *support* and *confidence*, the store might define specific promotions for sales. If the *confidence* is thought to be too high, wine with both cheese and bread, the supermarket might display them farther away from each other—compelling shoppers to wade through more square footage, hopefully buying additional items along the way. On the other hand, if the *confidence* is only moderate, the store might decide to set them closer to each other, persuading patrons to put them together, in the same basket.

Classification models are also used to predict the most likely customers to buy a product or acquire a specific service, another type of purchase propensity model, as shown in Figure 4.5. Similarly, classification models are also used to predict the most likely customers for upgrades to their products and services. These classification models can be deployed in conjunction with acquisition models to improve overall analytical effectiveness. Predictive models can foresee the propensity of a business event, like acquisition or adoption, and can be used in conjunction with prediction toward product disposition, to better target prospects with marketing and sales campaigns associated with more (predicted) appropriate goods and services while reducing the cost of operation and increasing acquisition response rates.

In fact, the right combination of supervised and unsupervised models can allow companies to identify complementary products and services for each customer, an overall and more effective offering. Augmenting with correlation analysis, which helps identify all customers who share a common product, and segmenting their behavioral pattern(s) in conjunction with rules defined to predict thresholds reflective of estimated patterns, can lead to even greater insight about how customers could behave even though they don't yet share a common product. This similarity analysis may, depending on the business scenario, result in a more profitable customer base than by classification methods alone. Similar to the acquisition-model methodology, bad debt predictions can also be deployed during the consumption phase. In this case, however, the intent is not to increase the sales but instead is aimed at preventing losses, with the goal of increasing overall profitability.

Termination Models

This final phase of the customer lifecycle is focused on actions that can be taken in order to extend the cycle as long as possible. Eventually, the lifecycle will come to end, for voluntary reasons or not. There are very few, if any, actions that can be deployed to avoid involuntary termination. Customers who move to a different locale, lose their job, die, or no longer require the service/product are difficult, if not impossible, to retain.

A lot of churn is based on voluntary reasons. When customers start to believe they are paying too much for a product, they experience disappointing customer service, buyer's remorse, or even if the service becomes obsolete, they will leave, soon or later. For these types of voluntary churn, a model can be deployed to help stem the tide.

Predictive models can be quite effective in establishing the likelihood for individual customers in relation to a particular business event. Using historical data about the event, translated into a target variable, the model is trained, correlating all other attributes about the event to the target. This target is a classification, such as 0 for paid and 1 for not paid; 0 for churn and 1 for non-churn; 0 for fraud and 1 for not fraud, and so forth. The target doesn't need to be binary (i.e., 0 or 1). It can also be a continuous numeric value, that is, an interval or ordinal target. Once the model is applied to the customer base, each observation is classified relative to the target, indicating the individual's probability of the event. For example, a value very close to 0 means that the customer is likely to churn, and a value close to 1 means that this customer is unlikely to leave (when 0 is defined for churn and 1 is non-churn). As depicted in Figure 4.6, estimating the probable way someone will behave, given the assumption that historic conditions will continue, can help target retention campaigns. The company can offer more specific offers to customers that are more desirable to keep, driving better marketing response and ultimately increasing revenue.

Models that focus on improving operations and contribute to profitability can be deployed throughout the customer lifecycle. Analytical methods like optimization, forecasting, and others can streamline efforts, minimize costs, and help project future scenarios.

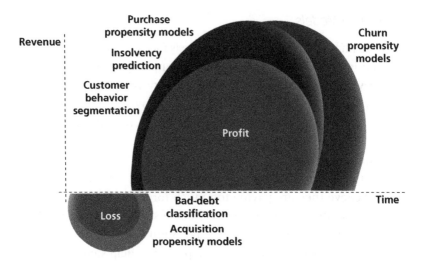

Figure 4.6 Predictive Models Can Help Extend the Customer Lifecycle before Termination

And while the focus has been on the customer lifecycle, given that it is fairly intuitive and common to most industries, data-mining models are not limited to the customer scope.

Experience

While we've examined each of the phases of the competitive-intelligence cycle, the only way to maintain the intellectual capital the organization has developed from all previous phases is to save the information used in the knowledge-creation process, the knowledge itself, the business actions, and the intelligence gleaned. Collecting, storing, and disseminating information assets, knowledge, and intelligence in such a way that it is accessible by the employees is crucial to learn from all previous actions and continuously improve strategies and tactics. All five stages outlined in the competitive-intelligence cycle, and in the sequence illustrated in Figure 4.1, constitute much of the corporate brand experience.

To succeed in the experience phase, a technological mechanism needs to be put into place that supports the collection, storage, and retrieval of the reports, conclusions, documents, and communications resulting from the competitive-intelligence cycle process. These unstructured data, when integrated or federated across the organization, become a reusable asset. This unified environment is not only tasked with collecting and storing the intelligence-related assets, but is also responsible for disseminating it. As such, search engines and content-management systems can be employed to help learn from previous endeavors and expedite decisions made in future processing. The knowledge-management discipline is focused on the methods used to elicit, extract, curate, and share organizational experience.

Enterprise search and retrieval systems, in many ways, direct the publishing and dissemination of the corporate experience, and as such these tools are considered to be a crucial piece of the IT infrastructure. These systems should be intuitive, user-friendly, and fast, and provide the desired, relevant informational assets when queried. Often, however, they fail to do so because these systems rely on predefined terms and keywords that are prescribed to the materials after they have been created by end users. And even when a defined list of terms (also known as a controlled vocabulary) is used, these dictionaries are used to *post facto* manually classify documents and can be unwieldy for document authors, who are typically not trained to classify content. Text analytics is another class of analytic methods that improves the relevance of retrieved materials, augmenting IT search and content-management systems. Text analytics methods can extend the metadata tagging done by these storage and retrieval systems to include additional metadata based on the content itself.

SUMMARY

This chapter presented how analytical models can be applied to solve common business problems, even with the changing dynamics of modern business scenarios. In addition to the models, some business actions were also described to provide a sense of how beneficial analytic-based results can be to companies, particularly large organizations that experience competitive marketplaces.

Analytical models create a competitive advantage for companies, enabling them to make proactive investment decisions and utilize tactics based on analytically derived facts. Improvements to operational performance and bottom-line metrics can represent millions of dollars, readily providing a return on investment from analytical platform investments.

As presented in this chapter, the task to transform data and information into usable knowledge represents the third step in the competitive cycle. Analytical models use these inputs to create specific knowledge about a business issue, such as how likely a customer is to quit, to purchase something, to not pay the bills, or to be fraudulent. This derived knowledge is put in place as an operational action, improving business decisions and task in both accuracy and in responsiveness.

One must be aware though that no matter how good an analytical model is, if it is not well deployed, in the appropriate time, with the right offering, it can be worthless. What's worse is that such failure could be ascribed to the model (knowledge) not being sufficient and not where the problem really lies—in the action (intelligence) from the model. In order to be successful, well-informed co-ordination needs to happen between the derivation of knowledge (the model) and that corresponding actions taken (intelligence). One of the most critical steps is to therefore understand the feasibility of a model to be implemented, working through the alternate scenarios even before the model is developed. In the formulation of the scenario to be examined, careful and thoughtful assessment as to how analytic results will be implemented is fundamental to success.

When intelligence is maintained, we end of up with experience, as described in this chapter, stimulating first-move advantage. However, the knowledge itself also needs to be maintained because it can be used in different actions, both in isolation for the issue for which it was defined, but also in combination with other endeavors. For example, suppose a company is experiencing bad-debt issues and the revenue-assurance department decides to develop and deploy a bad-debt predictive model to pinpoint specific customers for collection with the goal of reducing lost funds. As is often the case in large organizations, different departments can act independently. So a sales acquisition model is developed to increase sales for a new product. And given the focus to increase revenue, insolvency is not addressed. However, if these models (i.e., knowledge) are not combined, the company could create an even bigger bad-debt problem by selling too much to the wrong target. A better solution would be using the knowledge from the models, and combining them in order to increase profitable sales by focusing on prospects that are less likely to default on payments.

However, the analytical model itself is not a complete answer. The score provided by even a combined model doesn't fix the problem, avoid the churn, or improve the sales. The capacity of the company to take records scored with the model and translate them into real action is the driving factor for success. A poor business approach can destroy confidence in analytics, no matter how good and accurate the model is. Sound business approaches, on the other hand, can boost the profile of analytical models, creating a thriving organizational environment, learning from each and every action. A good analytical model requires a proper business action to show viable results. Very good business actions can be successful with even average analytical models. As a rule, the better the synergy between knowledge and intelligence, the better results companies will achieve.

Given neither the data phase of the competitive-intelligence cycle nor the experience phase are completely ascribed to the field of analytics, they are not addressed in detail in this text. With that said, the final chapter of this book does describe text analysis methods, and how they can improve aspects of the experience phase, in addition to their use in analytics. The intermediate steps, transforming data into knowledge and applying that knowledge to create intelligence, are, on the other hand, wholly assigned to the field of analytics.

The next chapter covers some examples and case studies about the competitive-intelligence lifecycle. Some problem-solving approaches are presented in order to show how to not just create the analytical model but also how to use the analytical outcomes in terms of practical actions.

CHAPTER 5

Knowledge Applications That Solve Business Problems

This chapter describes a series of real-world case studies revealing how knowledge is translated into intelligence. In corporate environments, this translation occurs by deploying the insight derived from analytical models—both supervised and unsupervised—in business actions. These actions can materialize in different ways, as marketing or sales campaigns, as product- and service-package definitions, as operational systems deployments, as alerts, or in any combination of some or all of these methods. The case studies discussed herein were developed and deployed in a production environment in a telecommunications company, and the actual results are cited. Even though these applications occurred in a particular industry, they are reflective of activities that are applicable to any competitive business such as retail stores, utilities, or financial institutions.

The important takeaway is to consider the potential gains, how to translate ideas into practical business action, and how the described outcomes resonate in your industry. These case studies were selected since they parallel issues that most competitive businesses are face.

CUSTOMER BEHAVIOR SEGMENTATION

One of the most important analytical models in marketing is customer behavior segmentation. Segmentation is the foundation to better understanding what individual consumption patterns are, how product acquisition differs, how customers pay, how they communicate, and when and why they leave.

Clustering models are most often used to create behavior segments—and are useful in refining customer data, dividing it into distinct subsets so that within each cluster more homogeneous characteristics exist than between cluster segments. Predictive models that classify any sort of business event (like fraud, acquisition, purchase, bad debt, churn, etc.) tend to be more accurate and powerful if they are developed upon each individual segment of customer data. As a result, several models are often developed to classify an event, rather than a single model for the entire customer population.

But even if you decide to not create distinct models for segmented behaviors, creating distinct cluster subsets provides an initial step for further analytical development. Because clustering delineates the differences among customers (averaging shared characteristics within each derived segment), companies are able to observe business weaknesses and strengths. Observed and strong customer features can be reinforced and protected, whereas weak or undesirable customer features can be adjusted and fixed. Knowing the distinct characteristics for different customer segments therefore gives companies the ability to define and create business plans. In knowing that some customers continually decrease their usage, the company may develop a churn prediction model. From identifying customer groups that lapse in their payments, bad-debt prediction models may be developed. In finding customers that don't change their usage behavior for extended periods of time, the company may develop cross-sell and up-sell prediction models. When these prediction models are built on a more homogeneous dataset—defined by a each cluster—the overall accuracy can be higher because the within-cluster characteristics more accurately reflect a target group whose signals aren't diffused with averages that are less relevant to their specific characteristics.

Most clustering techniques require that the number of desired segments be specified before the model is generated. There are basically two approaches to define this number, usually referred to as k. The first is based on a business definition defined by the operational capacity of the organization to create specific product bundles and/or campaigns, for example. If the organization can only manage five unique customer segments, then k can be defined to a maximum of five. The second approach is more statistical and is based on a technique that estimates the local optimal number of clusters within the database, using metrics such as R-square and Cubic Clustering Criterion (i.e., CCC). These techniques are also good examples of heurist processes. Both of these measures estimate a possible local optimal number of clusters based on the distance variance between observations. Intuitively, a good number of clusters minimizes the average distance between the cluster members and lowers the average distance between the members of adjacent clusters. Dependent on the type of data, these estimates can even be more heuristic. And regardless of the method used to define the number of clusters, distinct segments result from the clustering model. Each cluster holds some particular characteristics about the customer observations, and based on this derived knowledge business actions can be informed.

Figure 5.1 illustrates a project defined with SAS® Enterprise Miner™ depicting the development of cluster models.

In Figure 5.1, while six different clustering models are developed, the model labeled Cluster 2 is identified as the best one, and is used to score the population. In this model, seven different customer segments are found, each with its own blend of characteristics. We label the resultant segments based on highlighted features that characterize each group, as depicted in Figure 5.2.

The cluster Control Star (16 percent of the entire customer population) describes heavy users, generating large bills but with some delays in their payments from time to time. Customers within this cluster should be monitored in order to avoid eventual bad debts. The Star segment is quite similar, but with no payment delays at all. These customers just need to be spoiled. The Opportunity cluster refers to customers who have average usage and bills, but based on their known socio-demographic information along with their payment history, they are good candidates to spend more with the company. As such, they are good candidates for up-selling and cross-selling campaigns. The Cash Flow group is composed of average customers with

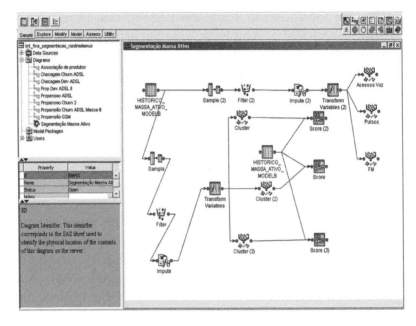

Figure 5.1 Clustering Raw Data with SAS® Enterprise Miner™

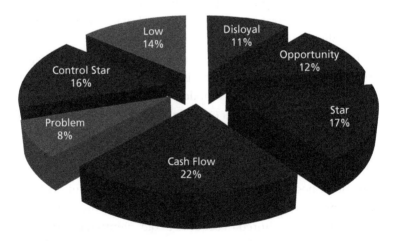

Figure 5.2 Customer Segments and Associated Business Naming Convention, Based on Highlighted Characteristics

normal usage, basically no payment delays, and the standard products and services. They are not as profitable as the Star cluster group, but given the large proportion of the customer population in this segment

(22 percent), their moderate purchasing behavior is helping the cash flow of the company. The Low cluster tends to have less than average usage behavior and lower socio-economic means. And while they might be candidates for a sales marketing campaign, it needs to be sensitive to the budgetary constraints characterizing this segment. So while they are solid customers, they aren't as profitable as other segments. Two cluster groups have naturally formed that contain less desirable customers. The aptly named Problem cluster is mainly characterized by insolvent customers who should be closely monitored to avoid significant revenue leakage. And finally, the Disloyal segment is represented by customers who substantially use competitive offerings. For instance, in some telecommunications markets, customers choose their carrier for long distance calls separate from the telephone provider. In other words, customers may have a contract with carrier A and make national and international calls using carrier B. This segment describes customers that are using more than one provider for their needs. As such the company needs to understand the competitive products/services being used and work to get closer to these customers, offering them appropriate packages and promotions, perhaps discounts in long-distance calls.

For each cluster defined by the model there is a set of marketing possibilities. The company may create particular bundles and campaigns for each one of the clusters identified. They can develop predictive models for specific clusters, establishing the best within-cluster customers for targeted up-sell and cross-sell campaigns. Given customer behavior can be quite dynamic, the clustering model should be periodically updated. In fact, if campaigns and modeling efforts are effective, then you'd expect behavior to change to the more desired behavior elicited by the marketing activity. Updates are done to identify changes in the customer behavior, properly re-classifying them, and flagging any new characteristics. An analysis that illustrates migration between the clusters should also be performed every time the clustering algorithm is run, since it can explain how the customer base is changing in reaction to business actions and the market. Such monitoring is important to evaluate the degree to which business actions are effective or if the company might need to change operational and tactical actions.

COLLECTION MODELS

Two distinct types of models are often deployed to aid in the collection process. Both are predictive, but they are utilized at different stages of the collection event. The first is in relation to payment delay, assessing how long it will take until a payment is made, and while it may seem trivial, identifying such candidates early can avoid substantial losses. The second is associated with the predicted likelihood a customer will pay once they are in the collection process. While this second case doesn't recover more money when compared to no model being deployed, it can help anticipate cash flow by targeting the most likely insolvents to pay.

Insolvency Segmentation

If the insolvent historical behavior is unknown, a typical first step is to build a clustering model to identify the most significant characteristics of customers who do not pay or who delay their payments.

In this particular case, a self-organizing map (Kohonen model) was developed to examine usage and payment behavior. The cluster analysis identified five distinct groups, labeled G1 to G5 in Figure 5.3, representing distinct insolvent profiles. The relationship between the proportion of the customer population, the percentage of total billing, and the amount of insolvency highlights some interesting findings. In Figure 5.3 we note that while the G5 group represents only 13.7 percent of the population, it is affiliated with 34.7 percent of total billings and is responsible for one quarter (i.e., almost 26.0 percent) of the total insolvency.

Examining each group individually allows business analysts to assess customer group behaviors and insights specific to each unique segment. Correlation analysis of this data can describe the average payment capacity associated with each cluster based on the billing and insolvency values relative to time delay of payment. Another important analysis would be the relation between insolvency to the average payment delay for each cluster. Most carriers operate with a tight cash flow and, as a consequence, reasonable periods of delayed payment for a substantial proportion of customers could severely deplete cash flow, putting overall profit at risk. If the company needed to borrow

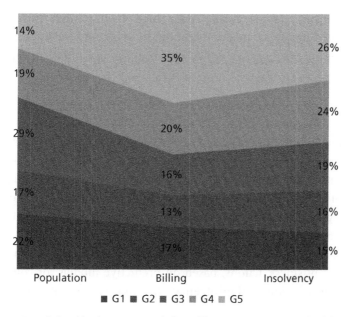

14%

35%

26%

19%

24%

29%

20%

17%

13%

19%

16%

16%

22%

17%

15%

Population   Billing   Insolvency

■ G1 ■ G2 ■ G3 ■ G4 ▩ G5

Figure 5.3 Relationships between Population, Billing, and Insolvency Derived from Clustering

market funds as a result, the financial damage could be even higher given interest rates and the cost of the capital.

Insolvent characteristics, such as the average billing value, amount of bad debt, product and service usage, and so on are all used to describe and label the clusters. For instance, as identified in Figure 5.3, G1 presents average usage and commitment of payment; G2 average usage and lower commitment of payment; G3 low usage and good commitment of payment; G4 high usage and low commitment of payment; and G5 presents very high usage and relatively low commitment of payment. Based on these core characteristics, the clusters can be labeled as:

■ Cluster G1—*Moderate*, with medium billing, medium insolvency, high delay, medium amount of debts, and medium usage.

■ Cluster G2—*Bad*, with medium billing, higher insolvency, medium delay, medium amount of debts, and medium usage.

■ Cluster G3—*Good*, with low billing, moderate insolvency, medium delay, medium amount of debts, and low usage.

- Cluster G4—*Very Bad*, with high billing, high insolvency, medium delay, medium amount of debts, and medium usage.

- ClusterG5—*Harmer*, with high billing, very high insolvency, high delay, high amount of debts, and very high usage.

Given the observed insolvency behavior, the company can create distinct collection policies and rules, each addressing different types of insolvents. Some collection actions might be more aggressive in an effort to avoid huge losses while others may be more moderate and focused on continuing to track insolvents. Other actions might be envisioned as soft as they could focus less on collection, but more on avoiding attrition by targeting customers who will pay their bills with only short delays.

Clustering to understand insolvency behavior can also inform proactive business actions, based on predictive models for collection notification, action, and insolvency prevention as described below.

Collection Notice Recovery

In a company, collection actions take place in an appropriate time-frame, according to the period of the payment delay and given any specific governing regulations or policies. In some industries, when customers are insolvent for 15 days they receive a collection notice informing them of the possibility of having their services reduced if payment isn't received. After 30 days of no payment, they may have their services partially interrupted—say, becoming unable to make outgoing telephone calls. After 60 days, they have their services totally cut off and are not able to make or receive calls. And after 90 days, their profile (including their name and associated identification) could be forwarded to a third-party company to proceed with collection processing. In this type of scenario, the company usually earns a percentage of the recovered revenue. After 120 days of no payment, the insolvent may be sent to judicial collection. In such cases, besides a percentage of recovered revenue given to the collection company, a portion would also be used to pay attorney fees. And finally, after 180 days, the insolvent customer would be considered a loss and wouldn't be a future prospect for the company, having the bad debt recorded with credit rating agencies.

Each action associated with this collection process represents some type of operational cost. For instance, and as part of the goals of this case study, the printing cost of letters sent after 15 days of arrears might be $0.05. The average posting cost for each letter is, say $0.35. And while a total of $0.40 may seem quite trivial, when it is accumulated across the number of letters required for managing a portfolio, the final investment can be substantial. Consequently, it is advantageous to identify customers who, although late in their payments, are more likely to voluntarily pay, saving collection costs, and focusing collection efforts on those that it is harder to recover late payments from.

In order to estimate possible incremental gains from deploying analytical models for current collection actions, a predictive model can be developed. It would focus on customer records for a specific collection-related timeframe—say, those individuals with at least a three-day delay in their bill payment. The goal is to predict those customers that will indeed pay their bill independent of any collection action—denoted as good customers for this particular example.

Considering results with 95 percent or more predictive accuracy, in this case the model identified 340,490 customers that would pay their bill irrespective of a collection notice within 29 days of the bill being due. For these customers, issuing collection notices are not likely to change behavior and it is quite likely that many of those customers will voluntarily pay before any collection notice is issued. As such, not spending money on collection notices for this group would significantly reduce collection-notice costs. For estimating purposes, and taking into account that average printing and posting costs are assumed to be around $0.40 per collection notice, a monthly investment of approximately $383,983 would be needed for the 957,458 collection letters to be issued. On the other hand, and taking into consideration the misclassification error rate the predictive model, about 15 percent of these customers would still need to receive the collection letter to encourage and hopefully accomplish payment. Thus, a total of 51,075 could be notified (based on the model's misclassification rate), receiving a collection letter after 30 days in arrears according to organizational collection policies, thereby minimizing collection costs.

Figure 5.4 illustrates an example model for collection notice-related recovery using SAS® Enterprise Miner™, a data mining tool used to for clustering and predictive data mining. The approach first clustered insolvents into groups with similar characteristics, delineating the population into not paying and those with delays in payments. For each insolvent cluster, a unique predictive model was developed to establish the likelihood of payment once the customers became insolvent.

In Figure 5.4, the top 15 percent of predictive scores for each of the cluster groups is examined relative to the recovery costs—depicting the total saving associated with voluntary repayment. Given this is a monthly analysis, the ongoing application of such methods can not only save substantial costs but will also improve the company's reputation and relationship with insolvent customers. Moreover, the insolvent customer segmentation can help inform communication refinements for collection letters as they provide insight to distinctive behaviors in relationship to the likelihood of payment estimates.

Anticipating Revenue from Collection Actions

Commonly, the process of sending collection actions to insolvents is based on the amount of debt. The collection department prioritizes insolvent customer communications based on the outstanding

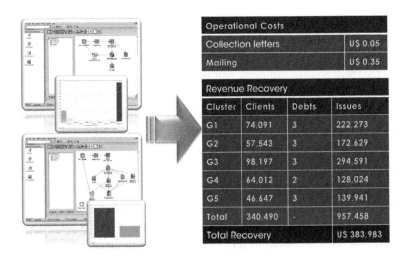

Operational Costs			
Collection letters			U$ 0.05
Mailing			U$ 0.35

Revenue Recovery			
Cluster	Clients	Debts	Issues
G1	74,091	3	222,273
G2	57,543	3	172,629
G3	98,197	3	294,591
G4	64,012	2	128,024
G5	46,647	3	139,941
Total	340,490	-	957,458
Total Recovery			U$ 383,983

Figure 5.4 Avoided Collection Expenditure Determined from Analytical Model Application Estimating Voluntary Insolvency Payment

balance, with those having the highest outstanding amount having the highest priority. A single customer may have multiple insolvent accounts—say, if they have separate statements for their landline, mobile, and broadband accounts that are all unpaid, then there will be three distinct bad-debt accounts associated with the same subscriber. Other insolvents, given bundles and packages, may only have one account associated with multiple products/services. Without analytical models, customers who owe the highest amounts would be contacted first. And while ranked bad debt might be an intuitive approach for the collection department (aiming to recover the greatest amount of money first), there is no correlation between the amount of debt and the probability to pay, at least no straightforward statistical correlation.

On the other hand, a predictive model can estimate the likelihood to repay given past payment events and characteristics—such as the period of delay, the customer profile, their products and services, the usage behavior, and certainly the amount of debt. If the customer had historically been insolvent and paid the open bill afterward, the target class would be 0, while if the bill remained unpaid, then 1. The supervised model is then trained based on the target class, correlating its value to all the other variables. Depending on the method used, these correlations might be translated as a set of rules and thresholds or as a numeric probability ranking. In either case, this predictive model defines a likelihood of payment once a customer becomes insolvent. This is possible given that the definition of the target variable, and corresponding training, are based on customers that had historically been insolvent before paying. Therefore, the average behavior assigned to the payment probability after insolvency is better recognized. It's not a predictive model indicating the overall propensity to pay. Such a model might actually be developed, but in that particular case study, the event of bad debt requires a former payment delay.

Given the likelihood of payment estimates, all insolvents can be ranked by their likelihood to pay rather than simply the amount of debt. With this approach, the company can expect to first collect from customers who are most likely to pay and can also anticipate the amount of funds to recover. Considering the tight cash flow in many industries, this could represent a substantial amount of money.

If the company contacted all customers regardless of ranking, they'd not recover any more funds than simply ranking by amount. The key benefit of the applying the analytical model in this scenario is to recover funds faster by only contacting customers who are most likely to pay their debts.

More accurate estimation of bad debt repayment using analytics can be very valuable to cash flow projections, particularly when the cost of capital charged by financial institutions is considered relative to the interest rates charged (if any) to customers with outstanding debt. By doing so, organizations are better informed to make financial decisions, such as choosing to not take money at the capital market rate, realizing a relevant financial gain at the end of the collection process. Figure 5.5 represents an example of how customers can be better prioritized for bad-debt collection, with insolvents ranked by amount of debt compared to their rankings based on the likelihood to repay. The estimated gain by using a predictive model could reach a half-million dollars each month, especially in countries where the inflation rate is relatively high.

From Figure 5.5, customer ID 23456895343 has a debt of $456.43 and due to this they are ranking with the highest outstanding amount

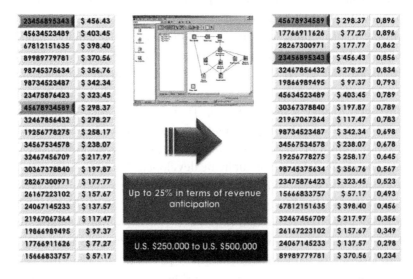

Figure 5.5 Amount of Recovery Ranked by Amount on the Left, and by the Predictive Collection Model on the Right

and would be contacted first if insolvent amount prioritized communication strategy. Analogously, ID 45678934589 is the eighth in that same ranking. However, after ranking with the predictive model, the first customer with the highest outstanding amount has a likelihood of 85.6 percent to pay, while the formerly eighth-ranked customer has an 89.6 percent likelihood. As such, ID 45678934589 would be first one in the collection list and customer 23456895343 would be the fourth to be contacted.

The range of likelihood scores for payment can also be used to further direct the collection process. For instance, customers who have very low propensity to pay might be sent out to third-party collection companies, who typically charge a percentage of bad debt recovered. The organization can minimize collection costs, weighing the expected gains and collection activity investments by focusing on the most likely payers, thereby decreasing the overall pool of insolvents addressed by higher-cost strategies. That being said, usually the older the bad debt is the lower the chance to recover it, and the higher the amount the less likely it will be fully recovered. Including these two general principals along with the predicted high propensity to not pay, such insolvents are good candidates for the judicial collection process, abiding by the term delays associated with such a process.

In the end, collection probability score(s) can be used in a variety of distinct business actions, helping to anticipate the money to be recovered, directing collection strategies, and even improving the operational process associated with contacting the insolvents.

INSOLVENCY PREVENTION

There are basically two types of bad debt, the involuntary event and the voluntary one. The first is naturally assigned to unforeseen causes, such as job loss, unknown whereabouts, or simply an unforeseeable circumstance impeding payment. These customers generally don't have deliberate intention not to pay their bills. The second type of event is intuitively understood as a fraud. The customer, or better yet, the fraudster, deliberately uses services and products with the intention not to pay their bills, no matter the time past due. They actually subscribe to services being aware they won't pay for them.

The following examples consider voluntary bad debt specific to a telecommunications company who was interested in minimizing losses.

Bad-Debt Classification

A bad-debt collection model was built considering all insolvent subscribers, taking into account their historical events of nonpayment. A classification model that predicts payment events requires a target variable in order to train the model for future assignments of payment likelihood. The model-training process basically looks at the historical events of payment, trying to correlate the defined target class (pay or not pay) to the rest of the variables in the training dataset. The difference in the type of model—regression, decision tree, or artificial neural networks, among others—is essentially related to how correlations are calculated by the dependent and independent variables. Which best characterizes the event of payment upon the variables available in the training dataset? Which better describes the customers who do not pay their bills according to the variables within the training dataset?

Some models are more intuitive than others in explaining historical payment behavior. Decision trees, for instance, result in a set of rules based on correlation thresholds, which tend to be clearly intuitive to business analysts. They can then take these rules and readily translate them into business logic and therefore into practical application. Regression models are somewhat intuitive, giving a sort of formula that explains the historical event behavior. However, the more complex the regression model becomes, the more difficult it is to translate the formula into business intelligence. Artificial neural networks, on the other hand, are generally difficult to interpret and are commonly referred to as *black box models* since they are harder to explain. However, this type of model very often provides good accuracy and tends to be quite robust when implemented in production environments.

For model-training purposes, customers are classified as good (G) or bad (B) according to their history of payments. The average distribution between good and bad customers over the course of a year for this particular telecommunications company was 72 percent good customers and 28 percent bad. This distribution illustrates that there is essentially a huge amount of money stuck in nonpayment rather than serving as cash flow for the company. The objective of the model is to predict bad customers based on their profile, before any payment delay occurs. This allows the company to decide the best preventive action to take—based on each customer segment. Figure 5.6 depicts the methodology used to segment and predict bad customer behavior.

Prediction based on a segmented database allows the set of classification models to deal with more homogeneous data sets, given clients in each segment supposedly share similar characteristics. Feed forward neural network models were used to predict bad customers within each segment. The parameters of each subclassifier were optimized to each respective subset of data and the corresponding accuracies are listed in Table 5.1. The sensitivity ratios listed by group (i.e., segment) in the table describe the percentage of correctly classified good and bad relative to the total records in each segment.

Table 5.1 Sensitivity Scores Associated with Bagged Neural Networks

Group	Sensitivity (percent)	
	Good	Bad
G1	84.96	96.45
G2	82.89	96.89
G3	85.78	92.14
G4	83.87	89.04
G5	81.59	88.36
G6	80.92	88.57
G7	82.09	89.92
G8	86.44	97.08
G9	88.69	91.32
G10	87.23	93.98
Average	84.45	92.38

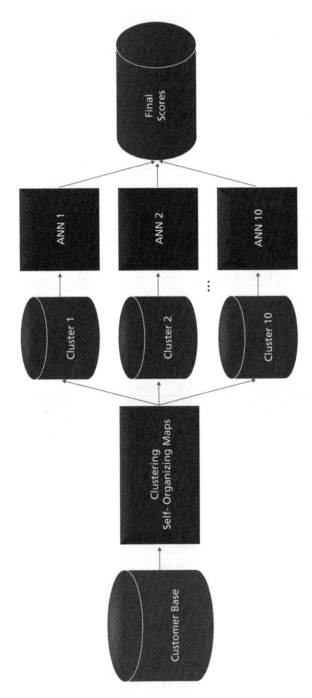

Figure 5.6 Data Analysis and Mining Method Used to Create Predictive Customer Segments Based on a Bagging of Artificial Neural Networks

The bagging aspect refers to the development of a classifier model based on averaging 10 different classifiers, each of which corresponds to a segment prediction. This procedure enabled more accurate predictions in the final results. For comparative purposes, a simple neural network model was also developed using the same parameter specifications but based on the entire database, that is, without any customer segmentation (i.e., bagging). This model reached a sensitivity ratio of 83.95 percent for class good, and 81.25 percent for class bad. And while the bagging approach only slightly increased the sensitivity ratio of the good class by 0.5 percent, the sensitivity ratio for the bad class was improved by more than 11 percent.

Since collection procedures are focused on the bad class of customers in general, the gains seen in the classification ratio of good payers was of little relevance to the business. However, the gain in the bad payers was extremely important given that this was the target group of the business scenario, improving business actions more precisely, and decreasing the risk of errors assigned to collection tasks. The results of both unsupervised and supervised classification models allow for a better business action plan to be defined, aimed at decreasing the losses assigned to bad debt. The next section describes one such action.

Avoiding Taxes

One of the important issues in data mining that is not often discussed is the feedback action taken from the knowledge discovery in databases. Besides the steps of the model formulation (the identification of the business objectives and the functional requirements), data analysis (extraction, transformation, and manipulation of the original data), and knowledge development (i.e., model building), is the fundamental step of knowledge application, that is, the associated with practical business action. Intelligence creation and the corresponding business actions are designed and executed based on the knowledge gleaned from data mining, and this crucial step is responsible for returning the investment made by the company in business analytics environments.

Many business departments might benefit from analytically based actions. Marketing departments can establish better channels and relationships with customers and prospects, creating bundles of products and services specific to the derived intelligence of client needs. Financial departments can develop different policies for cash flow and budget due to predicted payment behavior. Collection departments can define revenue-assurance actions, including different collection plans and credit-analysis procedures based on likelihood of insolvency. Each of these business plans should also take into account the specific characteristics the market, industry, and customer profile. For instance, in our telecommunications case study, there are a host of market regulations. When carriers issue their bills, they have to collect most of the taxes in advance of the service provided. Whether the subscribers pay or not, almost all of the taxes are collected in advance, with average amounts varying between 25 and 30 percent of the total billing.

A bad-debt predictive model can be very effective in foreseeing the payment event based on the assigned likelihood of whether or not a customer is going to pay their bill(s). Bear in mind that the model described was developed considering both voluntary and involuntary insolvency. High likelihoods might be associated with voluntary insolvency, possibly representing those customers who use the telecommunication services being fully aware that they are not going to pay for them. Also keep in mind that taxes are still collected for these outstanding bills.

Suppose then that the carrier decides to put a very unusual procedure into place. If the carrier knows ahead of time that a particular customer has a very high likelihood of no intention to pay their bill, they can consider this as a potential fraud event. This carrier also knows that they need to collect the taxes associated with this bill in advance, when it is issued, no matter if the customer pays it or not. So why issue a bill and collect the taxes if the company is quite sure that this particular bill won't be paid? While this may seem a strange scenario, let's take a look at the numbers.

The bad-debt classification model assigns each customer in the database a particular likelihood to pay. The average accuracy, based on a sensitivity confusion matrix is 92.38 percent for bad debt and 84.45 percent for good, that is, receiving the payment as stated in Table 5.1. If we isolate just the customers with statistical confidence of greater than or equal to 95 percent from the bad-debt class we count more than 480,000 customers. These are the highest risk segment for the company, behaving like fraudsters. They may very well be subscribing and using the telecommunications' services anticipating a nonpayment event. The average outstanding bill amount assigned to this fraud-like group is around of $47.50. Thus, possible insolvency losses may reach $22.8 million. Associated with this potential loss the carrier is responsible for collecting approximately $5.7 million in taxes. And recall, this $5.7 million in taxes should be collected in advance, no matter if the customers pay their bills or not!

Considering the misclassification rate for this particular model, that is, the number of incorrectly estimated customers is around 36,000, there is approximately a $1.7 million estimated billing loss in question. However, if the company had issued the bills for these customers, it would have collected more than $420,000 in taxes. The net loss equates to around $1.3 million. Summarizing these figures, the predictive model would still produce significant financial savings. Including the classification rate, the model would help the company to avoid $5.3 million in taxes. This classification rate also means that the company would fail to charge the good segment $1.3 million (i.e., $1.7 million in bills minus $427,000 in taxes). The overall savings balance in terms of savings is still substantial, about $4 million a month.

By following the competitive intelligence cycle outlined in Chapter 4, the company might recover the investment made in this analysis (in particular, the investment in data mining), in just one model application. This, for some, is almost too good to be true—especially when we consider that many information systems never reach expected return on investment (ROI), or simply continue to be nothing more than a financial drain on the organization.

And finally, the organization can be assured that those good customers who were left behind because their bills were not issued (due to the misclassification rate), can be eventually addressed. If company decides to cut services due to nonpayment (otherwise this would be a fraudster's paradise) and chooses not to issue bills, these good customers might eventually complain. Very rarely do fraudsters call to customer care claiming their rights. The company may decide to appeal to the potential outrage, admitting to a terrible mistake, apologize, and provide some bonus or compensation—continuing to work to improve that relationship.

You may now be wondering what happens when the fraudsters realize that the company will try to appease customers when they have their services cut off. If they also complain about the outage, and earn, say a month of free telecommunications services, they will not pay the next bill issued, and the company will eventually recognize this particular customer is a fraudster (perhaps without an analytical model). If all fraudsters started taking advantage of this, the data will reflect this behavior, and may raise the necessity of creating a different prediction, one that estimates fraud from customers who have complained after a services outage. The data will always change and as such, models not only need to be adjusted and fine-tuned, but new scenarios considered in response to emerging patterns. Model adjustment may not always be significant, but other times it is, and not only is this dependent on market and behavioral changes, but also on the technique used, how adaptable the model is in the production process, and so on. Regardless of the ongoing maintenance, there is typically always a benefit to creating analytical models in companies, no matter the size, industry, or even the goals.

FRAUD-PROPENSITY MODELS

The last case study described in this chapter is specific to fraud detection. There are a number of good fraud-management systems currently available, some of which are particular to very specific types of fraud, while others are more encompassing of alternate fraud scenarios. These fraud-management systems are very often embedded into operational systems, tracking and monitoring usage transaction by transaction, trying to detect fraud in near real time.

Fraud is a business. Fraudsters are focused on making money by crafting ways to use services and buy products without paying for them. Fraudsters will also often sell their services to others. For example, in both utilities and telecommunications, fraudsters create extensions to the physical lines transmitting power or communications. These transmission lines are outside of the known system or the plant so that the service takes an alternate route to the end (fraudulent) consumer. Fraudsters will then sell this service for a fixed monthly rate.

The most common approach to detect fraud is to look at consumer behavior and note changes in patterns over time. Each customer will have known average behavior based on historical data. This average behavior can be established as a set of easily interpreted rules and/or thresholds, or in a more complex way, by using data-mining models (like artificial neural networks or support vector machines). As their transactions continue, the customer's consumption patterns can be matched to their past behavior. If something relevant has changed, an alert can be issued, indicating some type of suspicious activity for that individual, directing the need for further investigation.

Fraud also evolves over time and fraudsters tend to be up to date with fraud-detection techniques in order to successfully continue their fraudulent ways. Sometimes fraudsters actually develop new ways to commit fraud, which are rarely considered in the deployed fraud-management systems. Although vendors actively track new types of fraud by refreshing applications, there is often a delay before such updates are formalized into the operational systems they support. For this reason, it is a good business practice to have the data-mining group also supporting the fraud department. When fraud analysts perceive a potential new type of fraud (ones that are escaping current detection methods), the data-mining group can perform the appropriate analyses to understand the new type of fraud and ideally develop predictive models to anticipate this new event.

Fraud is fought using built-in transactional intelligence to monitor activity on an ongoing basis and exploratory fraud modeling. Both are relevant and both are commonly needed. The following case study examines exploratory fraud modeling—identifying fraud that the transactional system hasn't been prepared to address.

New Fraud Detection

In this scenario, a telecommunications company is expanding beyond landline and broadband services to also launch a mobile operation. The marketing department is keen to acquire as many mobile subscribers as possible and creates a new campaign aiming to attract customers from mobile competitors. In this particular scenario, there were three mobile companies operating similar services, making the company the fourth incumbent in the marketplace.

As the last operator to start in this mobile market, any marketing and sales campaign needed to be quite aggressive. The entry-level campaign was aggressive indeed, offering a bonus to subscribers to make calls even when they were incoming to the subscribers. Any call received from a competitor network generated interconnection rates. Given the majority of the subscribers belonged to the competition, the likelihood of incoming calls to the new network from other operators was very high. But even with a few subscribers, the new company could make some money from the incoming interconnection rates (i.e., the fee paid by one operator to another operator to carry on its calls).

The acquisition campaign was devised to give the same number of minutes to a subscriber to make calls as the amount they accumulated based on received calls. For instance, if subscriber A received 100 minutes of calls (regardless of which operator they were from), they would be granted credits to make 100 minutes of calls for free. However, one small detail was overlooked. If customer A decided to make their calls to a competitors' mobile network, the company would have to pay the associated interconnection rates. Furthermore, the chance that this customer was going to make calls to competitive networks was significantly high.

The market was completely shaken by this aggressive promotion, including the fraudster market. Fraudsters immediately started requesting landlines from the company. They didn't intend to pay for these landlines at the end of the month, or at the end of two months—when service would be to be cut off due to insolvency. They acquired landlines to make uninterrupted calls to prepaid mobile phones they subscribed to. By doing so, they created a perfect tool to generate credits from prepaid mobiles allowing them to make free calls on the new mobile carrier network. Due to the huge amount of credit minutes they received, they were practically guaranteed free mobile service for a long period of time.

Fraud, like any other business, seeks publicity and advertisement to sell the illicit service. These organizations started announcing free calls on prepaid mobiles in the black market. For a fixed price, customers could purchase a prepaid phone with almost unlimited minutes to talk. Great business for the fraudsters, not so great for the operator.

From a detection point of view, the fraud-management system wasn't designed to examine the numbers called. Fraud was usually examined in terms of the caller number, not what number was dialed. But in this particular case, if the fraudster linearly distributed the calling from the landlines they took on (which most likely wouldn't be paid for), making calls to the prepaid mobiles acquired in some sort of regularized pattern (say, several landlines making calls to several mobiles—creating a normally distributed matrix), the fraud-transaction systems wouldn't identify this as a fraud event. It would simply be recognized as a set of landline numbers making regular calls to a set of mobile numbers, appearing quite normal—in fact, the associated data was normally distributed. This particular type of fraud would never be identified by looking just at the called numbers.

However, when the called number was examined, a different pattern emerged. The called mobile numbers would never make calls, only receive them. And right after activation, they received an excessive number of calls from a consistent set of landlines and never other mobile devices. Fraudsters know that it is fairly easy to acquire a landline—carriers are often compelled to provide landline service to consumers. With trivial documentation, such as ID and proof of address, one tends to get a landline. And while you may think that ID and proof of address are pretty substantial, for fraudsters, fake/stolen IDs and false proof of addresses are a part of the toolkit, combining information to subscribe to a number of landlines. Typically, they were found to have at least 30, and upward of 45 landlines in just 60 days—each making excessive numbers of calls to prepaid devices—and filling them to the brim with credits for free calls.

While a fraudster's profession can seem quite ingenious, analysis of the data can help find them. And while the fraud-management system didn't look at called numbers and, therefore, couldn't have identified this pattern, data mining was deployed to not only discover the characteristics associated with this pattern but find it on an ongoing basis.

Classifying Fraudulent Usage Behavior

The supervised model used to detect this type of new fraud needed to look at the past behavior (i.e., the historical data) and correlate that with the new landline/mobile usage behavior. The target variable needed to be defined in order to train the classification model.

The definition of this target began with insolvent landlines. The insolvency or collections department selected all landline numbers that didn't pay their bills. Within this group, a particular subset of landline numbers were selected that had the particularly unusual behavior of always, and only, calling just mobile numbers, and never receiving calls. This subset of landline numbers were forwarded to the fraud analysts. These analysts could determine if all called numbers were in fact to mobiles that not only never made calls but only received them—from the same set of landlines. The target variable defined as 1 (potential fraud event) when these subset conditions applied and 0 otherwise. The original group of insolvent landlines created over the same time period constituted the historical population and along with the target, the predictive model was developed and trained.

There were several approaches that could have been used to develop a supervised model, each using different techniques. As mentioned previously, some of these methods are easier to interpret than others. Business rules and thresholds tend to be more straightforward for general management (like decision trees). Some are more complicated and harder to translate into business rules, but they provide minimal understanding about the correlation between the target variable and the rest of the model attributes (like regression models). Others still are virtual black boxes (like artificial neural networks), providing no practical end-user understanding about what possible business rules could be.

Given this scenario required the fraud event to be well described so that not only could business actions be designed and deployed, but if need be also defended—decision trees were chosen for the data-mining model as illustrated in Figure 5.7. The decision tree branches are pruned and split according to the value ranges of the other attributes (i.e., variables) as they correlate to the target. The rules resulting from the decision tree, detailing the correlation between the target variable and the other attributes describing the fraud event, could readily be implemented in the operational environment in production—to detect fraud during transaction processing.

When a customer makes or receives a call, a unique transaction is created. This transaction comes from the network systems that includes collectors, tabs, switches, and so on and is captured by the

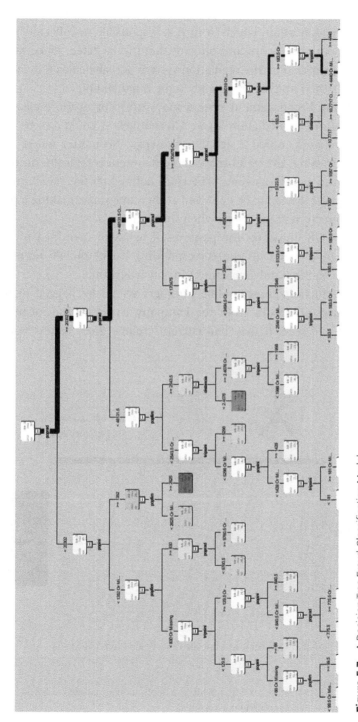

Figure 5.7 A Decision Tree Fraud-Classification Model

125

mediation application, which in turn is responsible to collect all calls from the entire network and prepare them to be rated. Once rated, the calls formatted by the mediation system are labeled as Call Detail Records (CDRs) and are then ready to be rated and billed.[1]

The fraud-management system may run prior to the mediation layer or after the mediation layer. Alternatively it could also be in a parallel network, called a signaling network. No matter where it is in the processing, the fraud-management system is typically running against near-real-time events. The rules defined by the classification model therefore need to be deployed at the same stage, making it possible to detect the fraud event when it is taking place.

Figure 5.8 illustrates the patterns of behavior identified by the fraud-event model with the corresponding list of mobile numbers being sent to the fraud department for investigation.

In production, these mobile numbers would be flagged to not receive any call credits from the company based on the incoming calls they received. If they had current credits, those credits would

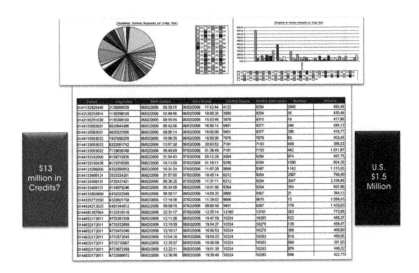

Figure 5.8 List of Prepaid Numbers Identified by a Fraud-Predictive Model

---

[1] The rating may instead occur in the mediation application as opposed to outside of it. For this example, either scenario is acceptable.

be erased and the landlines used to generate the credits could be also blocked or cut off.

After some time running and tuning the predictive model, fine tuning it for more accurate predictions, part of the process was automated. It could never be completely automatic, as typical with most fraud analysis, the goal is to prioritize the cases for further investigation. Companies try hard to avoid upsetting their good customers, and misclassification rates, among other things, deem it prudent to engage specialists and investigators who are appropriately versed and trained before taking action. For some very specific scenarios however, policy permitted immediate disconnection of both the mobile units and the landlines.

SUMMARY

This chapter covered some real-world business problems and possible solutions using analytics.

It began with a study to segment behavior of a customer population. This sort of segmentation might also be used in different business approaches, to better define offerings, bundles of products and services, and also channels of communications to be used with clients. Behavioral segmentation can also be used as a precursor for other analytical models, splitting the general population into more homogeneous datasets, according to particular characteristics.

After examining population segmentation, a more specific clustering model was presented, this one focusing on just insolvent customers. In telecommunications, particularly in emerging economies, insolvency can lead to large problems for the provider. In the scenario, companies can realize that there are good insolvents and bad insolvents. The segmentation method presented can help identify which customers fall into which bucket.

In addition to the clustering model, a set of classification models to predict the bad debt was developed. These classification models were developed from the segments, improving the overall hit rate of predictions, given the input data was more homogeneous per segment.

Collection actions can also be improved with predictive models, providing a crystal ball of estimation that helps foresee the most likely customers to pay their bills. This model does not recover money by itself, but it anticipates revenue by ranking customers based on their probabilities, identifying the low bill probability customers for communication strategies.

Fraud or voluntary insolvency is not only expensive to telecommunications companies but in any industry, especially when taxes are collected before the bills are even issued. Models that identify customers who have higher propensities to behave like fraudsters (or bad payers) can be developed to avoid tax issues.

Finally, a traditional model to detect fraud in prepaid mobile phones was used to describe how analytical models effectively improve business performance. Most fraud-management systems detect fraud in telecommunications by the caller number. However, in some particular marketplaces fraud should be focused on the numbers called. Understanding the market and the potential fraud schemes helps recognize alternate approaches that can be used to expose illicit activity.

These issues are not unique to telecommunications. Similar problems are common to all industries that offer products and services. And in addition to the transaction systems currently operating, batch data-mining processes can almost always be of help—enabling better understanding of strengths and weaknesses, and threats to the organization.

In fact, this highlights one of the greatest benefits of analytics—there are a host of possibilities to develop very specific models that can highlight areas of interest and expose business problem patterns. In Chapter 6, we describe a unique method that is gaining acceptance for practical application of pattern identification.

CHAPTER 6

The Graph Analysis Approach

The previous chapters presented techniques such as artificial neural networks, decision trees, association rules, and clustering used to better understand the present and foresee the possible future. Such techniques, in addition to statistical approaches like regressions, can be described as traditional analytics, often used to solve business problems like customer segmentation, sales and churn prediction, financial forecasting, and fraud and bad-debt detection, among others.

However, other techniques are starting to be utilized that in many ways extend current analytical portfolios. These methods are designed to recognize patterns of behavior and are based on graph analysis, social network analysis, or even complex network analysis. Used to improve business understanding and optimize operational procedures, these newer methods hold great promise to contribute analytic prowess, leading to significant returns for companies in a variety of industries.

This chapter describes graph analysis, its fundamental components, method, objectives, and foundation. Specific, real-life examples of graph analysis application are detailed in the next chapter.

INTRODUCTION TO GRAPH ANALYSIS

Graph analysis is similar to social network analysis (SNA methods), albeit the former considers all relationships among individuals, permitting flexibility in how both an individual is defined as well as what constitutes a relationship. In this approach an individual could refer to any element, be it a person, a thing (like a mobile phone or bank account), or a role (such as a policy holder of a claim). And relationships can extend to those that are between people (friendship, workmates, classmates, relatives, etc.), between things (a phone call between mobile phones or transactions between two bank accounts), or between distinct roles (between a driver and a policy holder of a claim). With such a wide range of definitions to the parameter settings of graph analysis, this method is adaptable to a wide range of business scenario investigations.

Behaviors within networks are crucial to understanding connections and their implications inside communities and groups of relationships. One of the most relevant areas in graph analysis is to first identify where the influence comes from within a network, no matter the type and regardless of the type of relationship event. Influencers are network members that may diffuse a message (to buy, to churn, to be fraudulent, etc.) inside the community. Influencers lead other individuals to follow them in similar activity and event behaviors.

Formal analysis of networks involves the definition of a set of nodes that represent network individuals/members, and a set of links that correspond to the connections between the members, thereby relating individuals to each other. Different types of links can be defined depending on the business scenario in question, but regardless of type established they represent the relationship between two members. In the financial or banking industry, nodes may consist of customers or accounts, and links could consist of transactions or claims. In telecommunications, nodes might be mobile phones or cells, with the links depicting calls or traffic. One of the first steps, and also a very important task in network analysis, is to define the different roles of nodes and links within the network. This initial definition governs how close the solution is to the problem shape being examined. The process to identify appropriate nodes and links in a particular network is not always a straightforward task. A reasonable effort should be spent identifying roles for nodes and links within the network because these definitions determine whether or not the graph analysis will succeed. And once again, this definition reflects a heuristic process in analytics development. Given that different types of nodes and links may be assumed to generate distinct types of networks, alternate solutions can be used to properly address the same problem. Defining the roles of the nodes and links, as well as the network itself, becomes a trial and error process.

Furthermore, with graph analysis, an individual is considered to be a member of a group. However, instead of a traditional descriptive analysis of individual attributes wherein individuals are grouped together when they have similar characteristics, in graph analysis they are grouped together when they have relationships between them, regardless of if they hold particular similarity for some individual attributes. The links between members of the network essentially define the group attributes and these groups are commonly known as communities.

One of the most common network structures to be identified is a communities of individuals, formed when they interact with each other. There are some distinct algorithms to detect communities, and most of them are recursive, when groups of individuals are breaking down along the process. Community detection is best achieved when it is iteratively identified, which essentially means, another heuristic process. To begin this process, the entire network is split into two or more smaller sub-subnetworks. Each one of these sub-networks is again divided into two or more smaller subnetworks, and the process continues until some criterion is satisfied. This criterion may be the number of minimum nodes within the community or the strength of the links within the community in relation to the external links, the links that connect one community to another, or both criteria together. There is a mathematical measure to identify if the division of the network into smaller groups (communities) is good or not. This metric is called *modularity*. Modularity is measured as the fraction of the links that fall within the communities minus the expected fraction if these links were distributed randomly. However, this modularity merit (or measure) may be initially set at distinct values and therefore the division of the network into distinct communities would also vary based on this measure. The closer the modularity is to one, the better the communities' divisions, theoretically.

When working with a large network such as telecommunications for instance, it is common to get a huge number of communities. Usually the distribution of members and communities follows a power law, where few communities have a great number of members and a huge number of communities have a low number of nodes. Hence, a business definition might also drive the community detection process. As with most analytical model development, business definitions can drive the defintion process from end to end, fitting and adjusting the entire process to the companies' particularities. And one of these business definitions is the expected average amount of members within communities. As data miners, we may set a list of different resolutions and therefore end up with a distinct list of community distributions. We might find 6, 7, or 10 different configurations for community detection. The expected average number of members within the communities may also help us in choosing the best distribution. For instance, if we look at the call detail records (including SMS and MMS, for instance), we can compute the average number of distinct connections all subscribers have. This average number can drive our selection of what the best distribution of communities is, or where the best resolution should be set in the community-detection process. For instance, when the average number of distinct connections for all subscribers is around 30, perhaps it doesn't make too much sense to find a distribution of communities where the average number of members is 10 or 100. The graph analysis, therefore, also needs to consider business strategies, marketing assumptions, commercial perspectives, sales goals, and any other factors that may affect the inter-relationship dynamics.

When creating a network and selecting nodes and links, weights can be assigned to distinguish their importance within the network. The node's weight is used to indicate that emphasis is to be placed on the associated node, for example, due to its average revenue, billing activity, or account importance. Analogously, the link's weight is used to indicate that one particular relationship is more important than another one, perhaps that a voice call has more value than a short message, or a deposit is more important than a withdrawal, or a claim is more important than a quote. Weight values are based on business decisions and are totally heuristic. There is no predefined rule to create weights, so the business needs solid guidance given that there are several ways to establish weights. And while both the relationships and the participating members in the relationship can be emphasized with weights, sometimes it isn't until the analysis outcomes are examined that it is apparent that the assigned weights are correct or not. Moreover, the weight-definition process could be completely different given the same set of nodes and links, and even the same network, but defined for a different purpose, being even more heuristic. Once again, there is no rule to better perform this than to examine all conditions, requirements, and constraints, and heuristically define the values.

Graphs Structures, Network Metrics, and Analyses Approaches

The type and structure of a graph changes the output metrics and measures, which in turn influences the distinct approach used to explore the network. For example, network links may be widely distributed based on node locations. It could be sparse or dense concentration, containing lots of shortcuts or none at all. Networks can also be slightly segmented or, alternatively, well connected. Regardless of the type of graph, all data associated with the network is critical to correlation assessments. Such information should include data about the types, attributes, relevance, and weights of both the nodes and the links. The way nodes and links are weighted can also alter everything in the graph analysis—including the outcomes.

Very often, network analysis is aimed at recognizing patterns of behavior and, in particular, the relationship patterns. The network relationship patterns are completely assigned to the relations between the nodes, and so proper node definition becomes mandatory. We may define nodes and links in a particular way and build a network. From this network we may then compute all network metrics which in turn, would be constant based upon the graph, built upon those nodes and links. However, the way the metrics are combined and thus the way they are analyzed might change according to the business objectives. This, in turn, can completely change the network analysis. Consider churn analysis. Some metrics may be more significant than others, whereas for product adoption a different set of network metrics may be more relevant than others—both associated with the same resultant network. As such, a distinct subset of nodes might be raised as influencers, some of them in encouraging churn, while others are influencers of product adoption. A critical factor in graph analysis is therefore the definition of problem to be solved and how that subject is understood as a network. So, although the node and link definitions are both very important, the definition of the main objective (i.e., the target analysis), is a critical factor for success.

In telecommunications networks, links may be described by frequency, duration, call type, call rate, and call period, among other factors. Nodes may be described by average revenue of a subscriber. In this case, nodes (i.e., subscribers) that hold several links (calls, text and multimedia messages, etc.) are very important and correspondingly those nodes also become important. So while links describe frequency, amount, relevance, and other attributes, nodes are described by their value within the network. However, the node importance is influenced by the links, and correspondingly the importance of the links is influenced by the nodes. What makes the subscriber nodes important is essentially the links associated with those important nodes—the nodes and links are codependent.

Different values for node and link attributes also change network metrics. As mentioned, it is possible to include some individual attributes for nodes and links, such as subscriber segment, average revenue, product and bundles held (for nodes), and call price, call duration, call period (for links) in the graph analysis. Distinct values for these attributes, or even their usage, changes the weights for nodes and links and thereby the network metrics that are computed. And by changing the network metrics, we definitely alter the network analysis result.

Graph analysis is focused on explaining some particular problem or event. What affects node weights, what differentiates influencers in a social network? Considering churn events, we may find that some network metrics better describe/distinguish churn influencers, relative to other customers, than other metrics. These influencing customers could have *degree-in*, or *closeness*, or *authority* that is higher than other customers. On the other hand, when looking at product-adoption events, we may find a different subset of network metrics might better describe influencers in comparison to the rest of the customers. These product adoption influencers may have *degree-out*, *betweenness*, or *hub* characteristics that are higher relative to other customers.

In practical terms and due to the business needs, depicting network metrics for both nodes and links is one of the best ways to understand the network characteristics as well as their impact associated with a particular business event. And while there are many network metrics that can be used to describe a resultant graph, luckily some will make more intuitive sense than others for examining appropriateness to a particular business scenario. The following section describes some of the most important network measures used in graph analysis.

Network Metrics

Each network measure has an appropriate interpretation relative to the business goals. These metrics are used to describe the main characteristics of the overall network and individual node and link behaviors, and each highlight some useful knowledge of the graph analysis. For example, the *degree* centrality describes how connected a particular node is to other nodes, while *influence* also takes into account the adjacent links. The *closeness* centrality measure is an indication of how fast a message can flow throughout the network while *betweenness* centrality indicates how much control a particular node has over the information flowing throughout the network. The *hub* centrality, on the other hand, indicates how many nodes a particular node refers to, while the *authority* centrality describes how many nodes it is referred by other nodes. The centrality *page rank* shows how likely some nodes are to being influenced by other nodes. Key metric associations are described below.

Most of the network metrics described as following were excerpted from the paper *Community Detection to Identify Fraud Events in Telecommunications Networks*, presented at SAS Global Forum 2012.

Degree

Degree centrality represents the number of connections a particular node has to other nodes. In a directed graph, wherein the direction of the node is relevant, there is a differentiation between *in-degree*, the number of links a particular node receives, and the *out-degree*, the number of links a particular node sends. These directional elements are particularly important in telecommunications and other industries that have an inherent succession in network behavior. The sum of both in-degree and out-degree nodes determines the degree-centrality measure.

This particular network metric is quite useful for understanding how popular or connected a particular node is to others. For instance, in the telecommunications industry a high degree of centrality for a particular node means a subscriber is well connected, probably making and receiving both calls and texts to and from many other subscribers. The degree centrality is typically one of the first possible network measures that describes a formula for customer influence. Usually this influence factor is described by a set of network metrics formalized in an expression and most often degree centrality is one metric in this influence formula.

Closeness

The *closeness* measure indicates the mean of the geodesic distances (i.e., the shortest path in the network) between a particular node and all other nodes connected with it. In other words, this closeness describes the average distances between one node and all other connected nodes. It can be used to understand how long a message will take to spread throughout the network from a particular node, n, essentially describing the speed of a message within social structures.

The closeness centrality is very often used to indicate what constitutes a central node, that is, a particular point within the network that is close to other points—measured by short paths to reach other vertices from its position. In some business applications, such as in telecommunications, it is a good measure to describe subscribers who are closely knit to others and therefore are more likely to influence them during an event in which the strength of relationship is important, like churn or portability.

Betweenness

Betweenness represents how many shortest paths a particular node is involved in, or related to. Nodes that occur on many short paths relative to other nodes have higher betweenness than those that do not. Betweenness can help clarify how central a node is in relation to the entire network and all connections that exist. It also represents how far a message could reach within a network from any particular node, n. It is a measure that describes the extent or span of a message within social structures.

The centrality betweenness becomes a good measure to indicate who might be a better candidate to diffuse a particular message throughout the network. A node with high betweenness (inversely computed) describes a point within the graph where most of the shortest paths pass through. If a node like this (one with high betweenness) can control the information flow, it can also diffuse a message the company wants to advertise, such as a product launch or adoption campaign.

Influence 1

The centrality measure *influence 1* is the first-order centrality for a particular node. It describes how many other nodes are directly connected to it. This measure is popularly understood as how many friends a particular node has. It indicates how many nodes can be expected to be directly influenced by a particular node. The influence 1 for a particular node, n, considers the weight of nodes and links adjacent to n.

Sometimes the number of connections doesn't matter as much as the importance of the connections. The centrality influence 1 takes into account the relevance of the links (from the weights) and the importance of the node itself (its specific weight). For example, how many customers a particular subscriber is connected to in a mobile telephone environment is less important than the strength of the connection links and the value of the subscribers themselves.

This centrality is often used to understand the impact of a business event that requires strong relationships between the members, such as churn.

Influence 2

Influence 2 represents the second order centrality for a particular node, reflecting how many nodes that a particular node is connected to are, in turn, connected to other nodes. This measure can be best understood as how many friends my friends have. It describes how many nodes can possibly be influenced by a particular node. The influence 2 for a node, n, considers the weights of nodes and links adjacent to n, as well as the weight of the links for the nodes adjacent to the nodes adjacent to n.

The centrality influence 2 extends the concept of centrality to the second order by adding the importance of the links that influence 1 connected nodes have. While a subscriber may not directly have important friends, his friends may have important friends—and thus a second level degree of influence is useful to evaluate possible impacts. In terms of business applications, a node with a high value of influence 2 may indicate that the individual may be a good candidate to spread a particular message. In telecommunications this may be a subscriber who has an average number of connections (with average relevance) to other customers, who have a substantial amount of connections (and valuable ones). In this case the average subscribers might be good potential starter candidates for a product-adoption campaign. If a mobile operator identifies two customers, the first well connected to few important people and the second one connected to few less important people, but in the second case the people she is connected to are well connected to a substantial number of important customers, then the second customer may be in fact a better prospect to initiate the campaign, instead of the first one. That first customer would have an influence 1 centrality higher than the second one, and the second customer would have an influence 2 centrality higher than the first one. On the other hand, for a different business scenario, say for churn, the mobile company would more likely select the first customer to spread the message for retention, but not for diffusion.

Eigenvector

An *eigenvector* measures the importance of a particular node inside the network. Relative scores for all nodes are computed based on their connections, considering both the frequency and strength of the relationship. The eigenvector is assigned to a recursive algorithm that calculates the importance of a particular node considering the importance of all nodes and all connections within the network.

The centrality eigenvector is similar to the influence 1, but for undirected links, wherein the direction of the connections doesn't matter. Applications using this centrality would therefore be similar to the ones using influence 1, but in a different network graph, one that involves undirected links rather than directed links.

Hub

The *hub* measure represents the number of important nodes a particular node, n, points to. This measure describes how a node refers to other, important nodes. The higher the number of important nodes it refers to, the more important the node is.

The centrality hub considers just the important nodes in the subgraph it belongs to. If this particular node points to several important nodes, no matter its own importance, it constitutes a hub.

For example, in an airline traffic network, a node would be the airport and the links could refer to the flights. If most of the international flights for United Airlines stop in Houston, this airport would be a hub when depicted in the graph network. From Rio de Janeiro, Brazil, to most of the U.S. destinations, if you were to take a United Airlines flight, you'd have to stop in Houston first and then continue the rest the journey. Houston is a hub given it connects many other important airports.

Authority

Authority represents the number of important nodes that point to a particular node, n. Similar to the hub, this measure describes how this node is referenced (versus what nodes it refers to as with the hub). The more important nodes that refer to it, the more important it is.

If many important nodes in the network refer to a particular node, this node should therefore be even more important. The concept of centrality authority is quite applicable, for instance, in authorship networks. Authors may often refer to other authors in their papers. A particular author, referenced many times by other important authors, is definitely an authority in a particular subject. This concept is straightforward and may be applied in distinct types of networks, such as telecommunications, insurance, and banking.

Page Rank

The *page rank* measure describes the percentage of possible time that other nodes within the network might spend with a particular node, *n*. Originally an algorithm from Google used to rank web sites according to performed searches. In networks other than the Internet, this measure may infer how a node might be relevant to the network based upon the contact frequency (such as visited web sites) by other nodes.

Networks representing corporate relationships can use this network measure as a way to predict contacts among employees, vendors, consultants, providers, and so forth. The page rank of a particular node, considering its historical relationships, might also indicate the probability of it being contacted by the other nodes in the network or in its own subnetwork.

Clustering Coefficient

The centrality *clustering coefficient* computes the number of links between the nodes within its neighborhood, divided by the possible links that could exist among them. It is a metric about how connected a neighborhood of nodes is to each other.

If I am connected to 10 people and these 10 people are connected to another 10 people, the centrality clustering coefficient would measure how connected my neighborhood is by computing the number of connections between all my connected neighbors.

Many different types of networks rely on clustering coefficient to identify good diffusion nodes. If a company needs to target a segment of customers for a specific message (like a product advertisement), customers with high values for the clustering coefficient would be good candidates because they are members of well-connected neighborhoods, encouraging the advertising message to reach further.

Types of Subgraphs

In addition to network metrics, there are some additional computations that can be made for graphs. Some of them are quite useful indeed, particularly for large graphs, like those associated with telecommunications networks. Large networks are typically sparse, in which most of the members are connected to only a few other members. In calculating the associated network metrics, we can envision a matrix. Suppose we belong to a community of 30 people. We usually talk to only some members of the community, not to all members. This restricted type of communication is common to all members in this community. In order to understand all relationships among these 30 members, we'd have to create a matrix with 900 cells. And given most of the members don't talk to all other members, many cells in this matrix would be blank, resulting in a sparse matrix. More realistically, the mobile carrier could have one million subscribers. The connections, as well as the other subscriber's relations, would be flagged in a matrix with one trillion cells! This makes the calculation matrix even more sparse.

One reasonable workaround to the issues of sparse matrices is to consider just groups of members, defined as those who are well connected to only each other. In this way, the entire network can be divided into *subnetworks*, or *subgraphs*. All network metric computations are then based on these subgraphs instead of the entire network, making the analysis less computationally intensive and more manageable for typically available time and resources. For example, if we calculate the centrality clustering coefficient for groups of nodes, such as communities, the algorithm will consider far fewer neighbors than if this measure is calculated for the entire network. If we compute this measure for the entire network, the number of my neighbors would be huge. If we belong to a community with 30 other subscribers, for instance, the clustering coefficient would be calculated considering all 29 neighbors, instead of the 10 million subscribers the carrier may have. In other words, it simply doesn't make sense to consider the entire network for some of the network metrics. When computing some network metrics it does make sense to assign neighbor roles to just those people I'm connected to and then perform the graph analysis and the network measures calculation.

Furthermore, there are different clustering procedures that can be used to generate subnetworks depending on the type of the group required. Analysis goals may be to describe more or less connected network segments that may include or exclude some members and consider all links or only a portion of links, for example. The following outlines alternate methods used to cluster subgraphs from entire networks.

Connected Components

When a group of nodes exist wherein each node can reach any other node and can be linked with more than one node in its path, this group of nodes are considered *connected components*. These connected components can best be understood as a very close group of nodes, separate from the rest of the network but composed of nodes that are reachable by any other node within the subgraph.

Bi-connected Components

Another important concept to network analysis is *bi-connected components*. These exist when there is a connected component composed of a particular node that, if removed from the subgraph, would split the connected components into two distinct groups. This original connected component's associated originating node is called an *articulation point*.

Core

The *core* decomposition is an alternative approach to detect communities within networks. This method gives a coarse approximation of cohesive structures composed in the network.

Clique

A *clique* of a graph is an induced subgraph that is also a complete graph. Every node in a clique is connected to every other node in that clique.

Cycle

The path generated by a sequence of nodes in a graph is considered a *cycle* when each of the nodes has a corresponding link to the next node in the sequence. A cycle is then formed when the start node and the end node are the same.

Shortest Path

A *shortest path* in a graph is the path between two distinct nodes that link the source node to the *skin* node—that is, the one that ends the particular path—with the lowest total link weight. If there is no weight assigned to the links, the shortest path becomes the lowest number of steps (the sequence of nodes) in the graph from the source node to the skin node.

SUMMARY

In spite of the more popular use cases about network analysis, particularly in social network analysis, the computational approach is founded in mathematical science. As a mathematical science, graph theory explains the relationships within a network. As evident in the terminology, many concepts and most of the measures that relate to network analysis come from graph theory. Based upon graph theory, the mathematical formulas can be applied to computing resources and therefore the method can be used to solve big data business problems.

Graphs and networks may be viewed as mathematical structures used to model pairs of relationships between distinct objects. The graph analysis considers a set of nodes and a set of links that connect pairs of nodes. The explanation of networks in social science is basically the same of that of graphs in mathematics; however, in the latter case there is the benefit of mathematical formalism. Upon these mathematical formulas it is possible to deploy different algorithms, employing then social network analysis to solve practical business problems.

The increasing power of computing is also a great benefit in applying social network analysis in real business problems. Social sciences usually involve small networks, comprising a manageable amount of nodes and links. On the other hand, in industries such as telecommunications, banks, and credit-card, for instance, the social network analysis might be huge, with a massive amount of nodes and links to be processed. Even in a moderately sized telecommunications company with 10 million customers, a typical network can be as large as 10 million nodes with a billion links! Efficient algorithms, based on properly formal methods, become mandatory to successfully address business issues for such industries.

A graph may be undirected or directed. Undirected links indicate that there is no distinction between the two vertices associated with each other. In other words, there is no direction in relation to the link that connects two nodes. Node A relates to node B in the same way as node B relates to node A. This concept can be illustrated by considering a friendship. A is a friend of B and thus B is also a friend of A. There is no differentiation between the links that connect the nodes, such as A being more of a friend to B than B is to A—albeit some may be accused of this in real life. Directed links, on the other hand, indicate that there is a direction in relation to the connection between two distinct nodes. In this case, node A may relate to node B in a different way than node B relates to node A, just as with parent-child relationships.

In telecommunications, traditional graphs are always directed: node A calls node B or node B calls node A. Analogously, if A calls B 100 times and B calls back to A just 10 times, this differentiation should be clear in the network definition, as those two links are (at least from a volume perspective) quite different and thus would hold distinct importance within the network. The way to clarify this is to establish a directional element to the links. There are two possible approaches to represent this scenario. The first one is to create 100 arrows from A to B and an additional 10 arrows from B to A.

The second approach is to create one single arrow from A to B, and another single arrow from B to A. In the latter case, the arrow from A to B should be 10 times thicker than the one from B to A. The arrow becomes a visual representation of the relationship. Mathematically, the link AB would be 10 times more valued (i.e., weighted) than the BA link. When computing the network metrics, the values that have been assigned to the links (AB and BA) would be considered.

Graph theory's concepts are commonly used to find communities in large networks. Algorithms assigned to detect the community make this method a feasible alternative to business problems in big companies, and quite often those with big data volumes. By dividing large networks into small groups of members such as connected components, cliques, cores, and communities, it is possible to apply network analysis to several distinct types of problems while reducing the computational and analysis effort. It is easier to make multiple computations for a set of network measures for small subgraphs than to compute the same set of network measures for the entire network. Furthermore, subgraphs can be essential to properly compute network metrics for some scenarios. At other times, it may be infeasible to compute network metrics for large graphs, particularly in relation to distances or matrix calculations.

The types of problems that can be solved with graph analysis continue to increase. Different industries are addressing questions regarding customers or users, operational procedures, internal processes, and cost distribution, for example by using graph or network analysis to better understand the relationships between components in an interdependent system.

And finally, the use of graph analysis has been spurred on by the hot topic of human mobility. Mobility behavior analysis has been capturing the attention of more researchers and practitioners over the years, becoming a key issue in many areas and industries, including both private and public organizations. Understanding human (user, subscriber, customer, or consumer) mobility, organizations are better equipped to understand the paths, average trajectories, and workload distributions to improve traffic planning efficiency, communications network effectiveness, public transportation requirements, and even extending to evacuation and emergency procedures, among other applications. Companies also look to better understand consumer paths for employing individual campaigns, exposing web content, and evaluating the impact of social media based upon graph analysis. There is likely an entire suite of business and public applications that have yet to be realized, given the lagged adoption of graph analysis relative to other analytical methods.

The next chapter describes network analysis case studies and the possible business outcomes. And while most of the case studies described are based in the telecommunications industry, they are relevant to virtually any industry that examines churn, product adoption, fraud, and mobility.

CHAPTER 7

Graph Analysis
Case Studies

n the previous chapter we looked at an analytical new approach to performing behavior analysis. The most common approach to understanding individuals' behavior, whether customers, subscribers, account or policy holders, tax payers, and so on, is to cluster the observations into groups based on similarity. It is quite common to do so in banking, telecom, retail, and insurance industries. Network analysis—or graph analysis—is an old discipline that allows us to deploy new analytical approaches, particularly when trying to understand group behavior. Based on graph analysis we can now look at the customers, subscribers, and account and policy holders not just in terms of who they are and which particular attributes describe them but also, and maybe most important, we can look at them in terms of how they behave when interacting with other individuals. It is a relationship approach to describing individual behavior.

Telecommunications has a definite, straight forward association between nodes and links and subscribers and calls (and texts). The way people use telecommunications services describes them better (for this particular purpose) than the individual attributes they may have, such as payment and usage history, products and services acquired, age, economic class, salary, gender, marital status, professional category, and so on. For mobile operators, it is more important to understand how their subscribers use and relate to each other than to know all those individual attributes. You may be a physician, just like my brother. My brother is passionate about text messages. He actually doesn't like to call that much, but he texts his friends, patients, and colleagues with very high frequency. But maybe you don't like these brand-new technological devices, or this new-fashioned way to get in touch. Perhaps, believe it or not, you are like us. We would rather chat in person than call or text. Anyway, you and my brother are both physicians, and perhaps have a similar salary, same gender, both married with kids, and so on. You both have very similar individual attributes, but totally different relationship attributes. Okay, let's take usage. Suppose you also use talking or texting an average of 300 minutes monthly, again exactly like my brother. But you always call home, and talk or text to your child. My brother uses the same amount of minutes to talk and text to lots of different people. The usage history, aggregated, might even be the same. But the relationship behavior is definitely quite different. And this is about network analysis. This is something telecommunications companies are interested in.

In this chapter, we explore three real-world examples of how to apply graph analysis to better understand relationships between people or entities. The first one describes a process to recognize subscriber behavior in telecommunications. The goal is for the company to exploit a viral effect that can exist within networks for a benefit, like decreasing churn or increasing sales. The second case study is related to the insurance industry. Social network analysis is used to identify claims and possible exaggeration of claims. And finally, the third case study relates to identifying fraud in mobile telecommunications operations.

Graph analysis is a flexible methodology, and as you'll see, network definitions related to customer behavior can be used to identify targets to increase sales and to avoid churn. Validity assessments can be used to detect suspicious activity, such as exaggerated claims and overpayments. And fraud is something all industries seek to minimize. While each of these case studies is described in terms of specific business scenarios, the principles associated with these graph-analysis applications are similar to other market sectors.

CASE STUDY: IDENTIFYING INFLUENCERS IN TELECOMMUNICATIONS

The telecommunications industry has evolved into a highly competitive market, demanding that companies invest in effective customer relationship-management programs. Graph analysis can be used to better understand key customer influencers in social networks and communities. This knowledge becomes useful to companies that want to continuously improve customer relationships or who want to better understand how business events percolate throughout a social network. By understanding the viral effect that influencers can have, companies can impact the entire process of marketing and sales, identifying targets for key messages and campaigns such as those for retention and adoption.

Background in Churn and Sales

Churn and portability is a day-to-day reality for the telecommunications sector. Customers come and go, switching operators based on the latest disappointments and deals. The cost of churn is high. The old adage still holds; it is far more expensive to acquire a new customer than to retain an existing one. With the pervasiveness of socially based relationships that are now common, dissatisfied customers also have a big virtual soap box to air their grievances. It's just typically better (and more economical) to keep them happy.

Analytics has proven its value to identify at-risk customers, that is, those that have high likelihood to churn. In developed markets, most major service providers have adopted churn-propensity models that have succeeded in helping to reduce churn for post-paid subscribers from about 3 percent a few years ago, to about 1 to 1.5 percent today. While we might not be able to attribute all of this decrease to analytic intelligence, we do know that the models have helped deliver dramatic improvements.

Organizations can improve their results by using graph analysis output as additional variables in existing predictive models. But developing this new set of attributes is not trivial. The additional insights are based on the relationships that customers have within the network of telecommunications subscribers. As illustrated in this case study, by using attributes based on graph analysis predictive model lift improved by about 30 percent. This translates to being able to better predict business events 30 percent more accurately by including the new knowledge gleaned from social network metrics.

If a mobile operator acknowledges that consumer purchase behavior and loyalty are increasingly influenced by friends and acquaintances—say, from social networking sites—they can try to better understand all social relationships within the network and use that information to target the customers who count the most. These influence effects take place in both churn and product acquisition. If community leaders are identified—the ones that influence others to follow them—they can try to stop them from influencing their followers to defect or encourage them to follow and adopt products they have.

Customer-link analysis considers relationships based on network theory. Nodes in this case are the individual actors (or entities) within the network, and links (or ties) are the relationships between them. In its simplest form, this social network is a diagram of all the relevant ties between the nodes being studied. The network diagram can be used to identify connections and commonalities that would otherwise not be apparent and provide deeper insight to a host of business questions.

The power of customer link analysis stems from the unique view it takes of the customer, the account, or the entity. Rather than focusing solely on the attributes of each node, customer link analysis considers the relationships and ties across nodes. This perspective makes customer link analysis particularly well-suited for business problems in which connections are key, such as identifying spheres of influence and where connections can be clearly identified.

Customer link analysis, however, goes much deeper than showing the ties between nodes. Depending on the sophistication of the analytical tools used, customer link analysis can differentiate between weak and strong links, close and remote relations, influential relationships and casual ones, and more.

In this case study, we examine how network analysis augments traditional analytical methods to include the effect of influence on customers.

Internal Networks

All communities are defined by the relationships among members. Any sort of community is established and maintained based on relationships. With the plethora of technologies and communication devices available today, the possible types of relationships continue to increase. Because of these different ways to communicate, people are more apt to participate in virtual communities, relating to each other directly and more and more frequently. The shape of the network and the different types of relationships can indicate potential influencers within communities. Using this information can be a great advantage for mobile operators.

Identifying and highlighting influencers puts customer value in a new perspective, one that is no longer simply based on individual attributes to one that is now also based on their relationships. Telecommunications connects people, and the network is simply a route, a path if you will, to connect people to each other. This can be either an active or a passive connection. Calling your child, texting your mother, or tweeting to your friends is actively connecting to someone else. Reading a blog, following a hashtag, or reading a forum is a passive connection.

Some events in the network may be understood as a chain of events in which the occurrence of one event can trigger the occurrence of many other events. Relationships among the subscribers can be considered a chain of events and this type of pattern can be leveraged to trigger a process of diffusion throughout the network. Triggering business events that can cascade in a community might be one of the most effective approaches to establish new customer relationships. Understanding customer connections and identifying influential subscribers inside social networks might even be the best way to prevent churn events as well as improve product adoption in the entire network.

Customer Influence

A customer influence network can disclose correlations between a particular business event (such as churn or product adoption) and customer influence. This can be recognized within communities by examining the (oftentimes) massive impacts that happen after an event has been triggered by an influential subscriber. Influence constitutes the extent to which others will follow the initial influencer when associated with the same type and timing of a business event. It is observed as a cascade process, and so the influential customer is assigned as the initiator of the event. In targeting one, companies may hit many.

The influencer is identified by looking for what happened to customers during a given time period—did the customer decide to leave or remain—and then comparing that to what happened in the following time period, and the one after that. Suppose a customer decides to leave at time 1, and in time 2 a related customer also left. In time 3 we can identify if there is a pattern, and if there is, we can consider the first subscriber as a leader, the person who can convince others to follow them, and the other customer as a follower.

The effect of influence isn't limited to single customer relationships; we can compare all churners and nonchurners, or all early and late buyers, to each other—and then average the customer base—in order to isolate the attributes of customers in various categories. Analysts can then apply this knowledge to the entire customer base as new variables to understand the effect of influence on the likelihood to churn (or adopt products). This influence takes place essentially among connected customers as well as customers with similar attributes and relationship patterns. All of this intelligence can then improve the effectiveness of retention and diffusion programs.

To do this, we start by aggregating the call data for three months prior to the time period in question in order to build the social network, detect communities, and understand the relationships within them. After the three-month period, at a designated point in time—time 0—all customers who decide to defect (or acquire a product) are flagged. Moving forward in the timeframe, we analyze what happened with related customers. Did they also decide to churn (or to buy similar products) after those initial customers left (or bought something)?

In this study, a social network was built and the network metrics calculated for call-detail records from September through November. The subscribers that left the company or decided to buy a product were flagged in December. Post time 0, analyses regarding the influence effect throughout the network was based on the following January through March timeframe (with January defined as time 1, February as time 2, and March as time 3). This post-time 0 analysis observed what happened to customers related to the ones who already decided to leave or buy. Business questions included: What happened within these communities? Did churners have an effect on others? Did their purchasing have an impact on other buyers? Did customers related to influencers also leave or buy a product?

In the data-gathering process, more information than simply who was calling whom was utilized. Data analysis activity included weighting the nodes and links in the network based on the subscriber profile and call-detail records. Links were weighted by the type of call (prepaid or postpaid, incoming or outgoing, voice or text message, etc.), the time period (weekday or weekend, early morning, work time, leisure, or night) as well as call frequency and duration. Nodes were weighted using the average revenue per subscriber. Given the business questions in this analysis, the node weights could also have included distinct profiles for each subscriber, such as products and bundles in service, tenure, market segment, and others.

Customer Influence and Business Event Correlation

The first correlation analysis was based on the question of product adoption. This viral effect analysis examined a relatively new product, 3G broadband data access service. A new product was selected for this analysis because it was believed that the influence effect on message diffusion might be more apparent than with an older product. Given that an older product would have been in the market for some time (and assessments and conclusions may have already been made in the network), it could have dampened the degree of potential influence. The viral effect of new products was thought to have fewer preconceived notions and, therefore, was selected as a better candidate to evaluate the impact of influential subscribers.

At time 0 approximately 3,000 customers had acquired the new 3G bundle. From these 3,000 customers, 136 subscribers were randomly selected who were found to often be related to 1,420 other subscribers. After three months, that is, from time 1 through to time 3, 95 of these 1,420 subscribers (6.7 percent) had acquired the same 3G bundle.

Similarly, we took another set of 136 3G subscribers from the pool of 3,000, but this time the 136 selected were the most influential subscribers. How did we know that these were the most influential ones? We knew this because of the following events in our timeframe (i.e., in times 1, 2, and 3) these 136 people related to others that had also purchased a similar 3G bundle. As in any traditional predictive model, these customers were flagged as belonging to a particular class of buyers. In fact, these 136 top influencers were connected to 3,585 other customers, 550 of which decided to purchase similar 3G bundle between time 1 and time 3, more than doubling the relative acquisition rate (15.3 percent).

Simply from the number of calls, we knew these top influencers talked to more individuals, but they also interacted with more people, both in absolute and in relative numbers. A regular (or random) customer talked, on average, to 10 other customers, which represented less than 1 person (i.e., 0.7) purchasing the bundle after time 0. At best, these regular customers might affect up to 6.7 percent of related subscribers. On the other hand, each top influential customer talked, on average, to 26 others, of which four subscribers were seen to purchase a similar bundle. Thus, the influential subscribers might affect up to 15.3 percent of the customers they usually connected to. This influencer rate is 132 percent better than the random event.

If we plot these random customers, as well as the ones they relate to that also adopted the product, and made a side-by-side comparison to all the influential customers and their connected purchasers, we would see subgraphs such as those depicted in Figure 7.1.

From Figure 7.1 it is apparent that the influential customer network is much more densely populated. If we amplify this subset and extend it to the entire database, selecting customers with similar behavior, we might end up with a significantly reduced list of subscribers to better target 3G bundle promotions to.

These influential customers have characteristics that may be described better in terms of network metrics than by individual attributes. They had 40 percent higher value (node weight) in terms

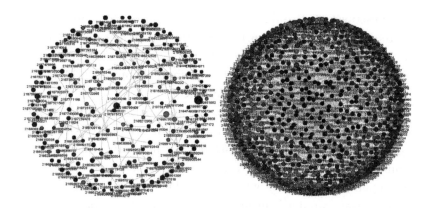

Figure 7.1   Product Diffusion Networks of Random (left) and Influential Customers (right)

of revenue than regular customers. They also made and received 200 percent more calls (links in and out), had 200 percent more distinct connections (i.e., degree), 200 percent more important connections (influence 1) than average customers, 500 percent more connections to people who were connected to important customers (influence 2), 400 percent more important subscribers they are pointed to (hub), 150 percent more important subscribers pointing to them (authority), 40 percent greater likelihood to be contacted (page rank), and so on. As in a traditional predictive model, or even in a clustering approach, these metrics are a set of variables that describe a pattern. In this case, it uses social metrics to describe the pattern of influence.

All network metrics can be inputs to traditional predictive models, thereby including additional relevant information about behavior. As is often the case with new insights, additions of knowledge that improve understanding tend to increase the accuracy of the predictive models.

Analogous to the product-adoption approach, at the designated time, time 0, more than 6,000 customers had defected. This group of subscribers had related to more than 100,000 other customers, having a relationship ratio of 1:17. From this churn pool, 53 percent were dedicated customers, that is, those who belonged to the same mobile operator. The remaining 47 percent were subscribers to competitive networks. Beyond time 0, and considering the network associated with the same three months (January through March), there were

677 subscribers that could be ascribed to an associated churn event. In other words, from those 6,101 subscribers who defected in time 0, 677 of them were connected to other customers who also left between time 1 and time 3. In time 1, 419 subscribers left, another 228 left in time 2 and an additional 212 left in time 3.

Another fact came to light during this analysis. Dedicated subscribers (i.e., those who were from the company that was conducting this study) had on average 47 percent of churners defecting to competitor A, another 22 percent to competitor B, and 31 percent to competitor C. However, when the viral nature of churn within the network was examined during time 0 to time 3, the percentage of defectors to competitor C increased from 31 percent to 55 percent. Company C was well known to offer substantial incentives for calls and texts that remained within their own network, often allowing this at no charge to subscribers. When an influencer leaves, they will often take other subscribers from their community with them, so they all benefit from these discounts. By comparing all churners, the top influencers and the regular churners, it was possible to identify that each regular churner had in average 17 related contacts, 9 of whom belonged to the same operator, and just 0.14 of them were affected in the same event (churn). This constitutes a viral effectiveness of just 1.6 percent. On the other hand, each top influential churner related to an average of another 33 customers, of which 16 belonged to the same mobile operator, affecting 1.28 of them. This translated to enhancing the viral churn effect by about 8 percent, five times more than average churners.

As with the product-adoption analysis, there are a set of network metrics that describe the characteristics of the influential churners that differ from average subscribers. They had 155 percent higher value, 83 percent more connections, 120 percent more peers, 156 percent more traffic, 89 percent more relevant customers they pointed to, 107 percent more relevant customers pointing to them. And most of them were also postpaid subscribers, connecting largely to other postpaid numbers. Furthermore, in the majority of the cases the demonstrated churn was seen as a portability event, when they left, they simply ported their number and service to a competitor. To port out of a network, customers typically have to be quite upset with their carrier.

And being really upset, these subscribers had to have used the provider's products and services well. It is because of this that a well-defined profile exists for these influencing churners. They are vested in the carrier, and as much as they use the product/service they are unhappy. If it was good, high usage would be associated with a very happy customer.

Influencers are only leaders because there are followers. An additional viral churn-effect analysis was done to examine this follower behavior. In this case, we also considered the regressive direction inherent in the timeframe. Starting backward, from time 3 when the followers defected, investigating back through time to the beginning of the study period, when the leader triggered the cascade of events. At time 3, 5,091 subscribers had churned. From this group, 1,058 used to have relationships with subscribers who had previously left in either time 2, time 1, or time 0. For instance, 821 subscribers of the 1,058, used to have known relationships to subscribers who'd defected in time 2. Another 226 had relationships that ended because they left the network in both time 2 and time 1, and a total of 11 of the time 3 subscribers used to relate to other subscribers who churned in time 2, time 1, or time 0.

These followers also had a specific network metric pattern, just as the leaders did. In comparison to the average churners, they had 18 percent higher value, and they were 292 percent more often postpaid than the average. They also had 25 percent more incoming calls, 20 percent higher traffic, 10 percent more distinct connections, 41 percent more central, and 31 percent higher information flow. Recall from the last chapter that these last two measures are ascribed to understand closeness and betweenness centralities.

Unlike the product-adoption analysis, the churn study included a community analysis. There are different algorithms used to detect communities, but the methods generally include similar concepts. These algorithms attempt to split the network into smaller subnetworks, trying to keep the relevant connections among the members. The criterion to cut a particular link between two nodes, separating them into different communities, may vary.

In this study, 666,281 communities were detected, comprising 16,163,728 members (technically nodes/ties, or in terms of the business, subscribers, from the operator or not). During the timeframe analyzed (time 0 to time 3), 52,998 communities had some churn event, affecting a total of 1,460,311 members. The total portability rate in that period was about one percent. However, if we consider just the communities that experienced at least one port out during the timeframe, the port out amount is the same, but the number of members lost from those communities was smaller. Based on these figures, the portability rate increases to up to 9 percent. However, if we look at the communities with historical portability in the same period, we found that the average rate of port outs increased substantially over the time. This can also be interpreted as the likelihood to port out increases in communities that experienced previous events of portability. For example, in time 3, there were 10,414 communities with portability, comprising 285,290 members, with 4,871 port outs. The average rate of portability increased to more than 10 percent in time 3 (considering the overall 9 percent of port outs in communities with portability). In examining communities with portability in time 3 and time 2, we found the port-out rate has increased to 24 percent (344 communities with port outs in both time 3 and time 2, comprising 10,480 members with 417 port outs). If we also look at communities with port outs in all periods—time 3, time 2, and time 1—the port out rate increases to 49 percent (16 communities with port outs in those three time periods, comprising 524 members with 38 port outs). This means that as long as subscribers are porting out, the likelihood to take others with them increases dramatically. In fact, the likelihood to port out in communities with previous port outs is up to five times higher than in communities with no previous port out events. The fact that some subscribers decided to port out to a competitor increases the chances of the remaining subscribers porting out afterward.

In this study, graph analysis produced a set of important customer behavior variables, that is, the network metrics, which described the general shape of the network and the types of relationships within it. These network measures were very important in explaining the exhibited behavior, and therefore were included as variables in the traditional predictive churn models. When this was done, the model lift increases varied from case to case, but on average the models that also included network metrics improved churn probability accuracy by more than 30 percent.

The measured accuracy used was based on a confusion matrix (and this is really an appropriate name for that type of matrix), which indicated the positive-positive, positive-negative, negative-negative, and negative-positive relationships among the scored records. There was a substantial lift for the false positives and false negatives, the cases when the model incorrectly predicted if a subscriber would defect or not. If the model predicted that a particular subscriber would churn and they didn't (false positive), the company would waste money in retention campaign investments. If the model predicted that the subscriber wouldn't churn but they do (false negative), the company wastes even more money, because by doing nothing to retain this subscriber they've now lost the longer-term subscriber revenue.

Possible Business Applications and Final Figures in Churn and Sales

Mobile telecommunications is a very dynamic market. Operators are constantly offering new deals, attracting subscribers from one company to another and back again. Due to this, analytical approaches become critical to proactively examining the customer portfolio to optimize investments, improve operational processes, and secure successful business performance.

When the market changes, the data reflecting the market also changes. Any analysis, including graph analysis, therefore needs to be monitored and assessed to minimize model staleness and, when necessary, tweak (and even at times redo) the analysis to represent the new business reality. A benefit of graph analysis is its adaptability to changes that occur in the underlying data, such as when companies launch new products and services, subscribers change their consumption behaviors, and so forth. Fortunately, all these types of changes, and in particular, the relations across behaviors tend to continue to be present in the data—even when individual behaviors change. Graph analysis is somewhat more immune than other analytical methods given the often stable relationship patterns that remain in the face of changing conditions.

In this study we observed how important relationships are in the telecommunications network, how people relate to each other, how communities are shaped, and how leaders and followers are identified.

This approach can be used to not only track customer activity, but also the market itself. We found that some subscribers behave like leaders and diffuse messages for new products and services, making them excellent targets for marketing and sales campaigns. Leaders in product adoption were up to three times more effective in spreading adoption news than the average buyer. This cascade effect also included a second wave of influence, a trickle effect, when the subscribers that had been influenced by the leaders also illustrated characteristic changes in their relationships. This secondary influence improved product adoption rates by up to 50 percent more when compared to the average customer.

For churn, 11 percent of the churners were found to behave like leaders, influencing up to 8 percent of their relationships to follow them in the same event. When customers ported out their service to a competitor, up to 21 percent that did so were related to leaders. Portability leaders were in fact up to five times more effective in taking related subscribers with them than the regular port-out subscribers. Comparatively, leaders for churn were up to three times more effective in taking others with them than regular churners. This illustrates that churn really is a viral event, and in special cases—like that of portability—the effects can be even more devastating. The viral effect of leaders was seen to be up to five times greater than that of regular churners. And to make it worse, very often, these were good customers with high level of usage. The viral effect was also seen to affect communities. The occurrences of portability within communities increased up to four times than that of other customers to port their service out in the subsequent months.

And finally, the accuracy of the traditional churn predictive models was increased by almost 30 percent when social network metrics were included. The attributes associated with the relationships exhibited in the network were useful to improve probability estimates of churn within the network.

There are basically two main approaches to using the outcomes from the network analysis and community detection for business application, both considering the identification of the leaders and followers. The first is to seek out the leaders within the communities, estimate their churn probability, and thereby identify the key subscribers to be contacted for retention efforts. There were roughly 36,000 postpaid subscribers identified as community leaders, and from this study about 1,500 had a reasonable propensity to leave. The second approach was to monitor the followers. Given the insight that once churn within communities increased, the likelihood of defection for subscribers who remained in the community also increased, key retention targets became those subscribers who belonged to the churner's communities. With around 80,000 postpaid subscribers meeting this criterion, there were approximately 12,000 subscribers identified who had a high propensity to leave.

In a rough exercise to explore the possible best business actions based on the network analysis outcomes, a comparison between the effectiveness of contact actions measured in terms of the rate of contacted subscribers and the number of possible customers retained was done. This was recognized to have been a completely theoretical exercise because it assumed that once the target subscribers were contacted they'd simply stay and that the retention offering wouldn't be refused. Even with this assumption, it did provide a guide as to the number of contacts that would need to be made.

Given the number of subscribers and the exhibited churn rate, it was determined that in order to retain all possible customers, the carrier would contact all subscribers once the possible churn targets were identified. The average retention rate was understood to be 1 in 53, that is, to retain one subscriber the company needed to contact up to 53 customers. Using a traditional predictive model with an average success rate (i.e., predictive accuracy) of around 80 percent to 85 percent, the operator only needed to contact 48 potential defectors to retain 1. Based on the calculated model lift, and selecting only the top 30 percent, the rate further decreased to 32 contacts to retain one subscriber. And by isolating on the top 10 percent, the rate improves to only 26 contacts. Without inclusion of community factors, but adding network metrics, the contact rate was 1 in 24 (i.e., out of 36,000 leaders there were 1,500 potential churners). However, when communities were included, and assuming that each leader took along at least one other subscriber, by retaining one leader the company would retain two subscribers. This, in turn, further decreased the contact rate to 1 in 12. And finally, by including the follower metrics in the model, with 80,000 subscribers needed to retain 12,000, the contact rate becomes 7 to retain 1. Nice? Analytics can do a really good job helping direct how investments can be most economically made, particular when we are talking about big volumes of data—whether that be customers, subscribers, calls, texts, transactions, or more.

CASE STUDY: CLAIM VALIDITY DETECTION IN MOTOR INSURANCE

When unusual behavior occurs in the insurance industry, it can represent different things, like heavy users due to specific claimant life events or suspicious transactions. From the company's point of view, neither business scenario is good. Although in most industries like retail, entertainment, communications, and banking, heavy users are something to celebrate, in insurance, heavy users mean higher costs. When these heavy users are claiming for factual damage, it is simply the cost of business and insurers have to pay. But what if some of these heavy users are actually exaggerating their claims? And what if some of the different actors within these claims are somehow tightly connected and colluding with one another?

Background in Insurance and Claims

A network analysis that considers all the different roles involved in claims can be used to gain relevant business knowledge of average customer behavior, therefore making it possible to distinguish unexpected patterns. Regardless of the reasons for high usage of insurance services, it can lead to substantial increases in operational costs, either by the claims payout and expense processing or possible fraud events. Correlations raised by network analysis can be used to evaluate the roles assigned to the actors and their relationships, so that insurance organizations can deploy more effective programs to better understand and monitor claim transactions.

Network Definition

This case study is based on data specific to a car insurance company. The raw data inputs are transactional details about the claims. The goal of this network analysis is to highlight unusual behavior in relation to the participants assigned to a claim, such as policy holders, suppliers, repairers, specialists, witnesses, and so on. The idea is that unexpected relationships among participants can be identified, including those associated with suspicious groups. This approach reveals possible suspicious connections within distinct social structures, thereby describing which claimants may be exaggerating their transactions.

The network definition in this study was established from claims records in which the participants, and the different roles they play, were first selected and then their relationships to other participants were established. This is typically the first step in any network definition, to create links and nodes, evaluating the actors and their roles.

All participants in one particular claim are connected to each other, describing all possible links. For instance, claim 1234, illustrated in Figure 7.2, has one policyholder (A), one claimant (B), one supplier (C), and one approved recommended repairer (D). All links between these four players creates a combination of three by two parties, creating a social structure containing four nodes and six links, namely nodes A, B, C, and D resulting in links A-B, A-C, A-D, B-C, B-D, and C-D.

In this case study, 22,815 claims were considered in order to produce the social network. All claim records were aggregated to examine distinct claims with multiple occurring participants. Furthermore, these participants were selected based on a match code of their names and addresses, avoiding any obvious duplicates. From this, 41,885 distinct participants (nodes) were identified and involved in 74,503 relationships (links).

By connecting all participants to each other, a huge number of linkages were found. For instance, in the network illustrated in Figure 7.3,

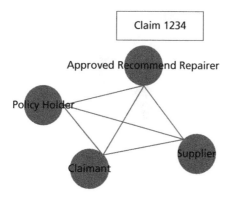

Figure 7.2 Network Links among Four Participants within a Claim

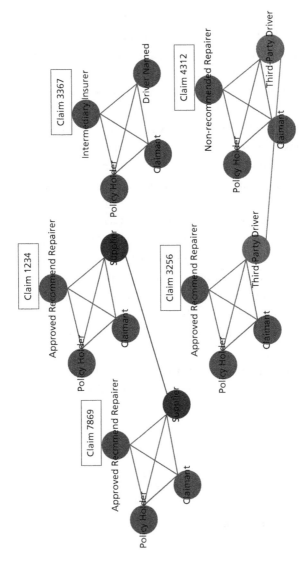

Figure 7.3 Social Structure Considering Participants within Distinct Claims

two participants appeared simultaneously in two subnetworks. Claims 1234 and 7869 interacted with the same supplier, and claims 3256 and 4312 had the same named third-party driver in both claims. This fact means that in some way, all participants associated with claims 1234 and 7869 were connected. The same thing happened in claims 3256 and 4312, where all participants were also connected.

In order to analyze the entire network structure and all correlations between the nodes, the network analysis considered all types of roles within the claims, but performed distinct analyses according to each claim type. The network measures were computed based on the entire network, considering all nodes and links, regardless of the participants' roles. Then, all metrics assigned to the individual nodes were evaluated. The same approach was performed for organizational nodes. Distinct analyses could then take place according to the participant's role, such as policyholder, third-party driver, repairer, and so on. These detailed analyses tended to readily highlight the unusual behavior in relation to each type of claim participant. A particular repairer, for example, could be an outlier according to his network metrics when only the category repairers were considered, but not when all types of participants (including the category approved recommended repairer) were included in the analysis. Figure 7.4 presents the network of nodes with bold labels, while the organizational nodes are illustrated with faded labels. In this way, the network was viewed in terms of analysis rather than in terms of the construction method.

The analytical methodology deployed in this case combined graph analysis to build and compute the network metrics, and subsequently, exploratory analysis to identify unusual behaviors, including those based on outliers associated with either nodes or links. The outliers were identified using different methods, including univariate, principal component, and clustering analyses. These analyses were performed with the network measures, a times including the entire network, while others were based on sub-network categories.

As with any traditional exploratory analysis, outlier occurrence (and therefore the unusual behavior) can then be used to define a set of rules and thresholds describing suspicious events. However, in this analysis, the unusual behavior and outliers were defined by

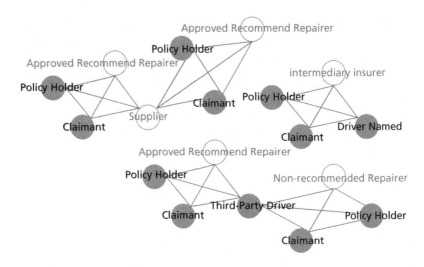

Figure 7.4 Distinct Social Network Analysis Illustrated by Different Roles of Participants

relationships instead of the individual attributes. The relationships among actors considering all claims defined a suspicious observation.

A high number of similar addresses (or participants) involved in different claims can trigger an alert, and therefore, highlight the participants and their associated claims. Different analytical methods can be used to create distinct sets of rules based on thresholds derived from the network measures. A combined approach to indicate suspicious events should consider all sets of rules.

The network is used to expose suspicious participants, or participants with unusual or outlier relationships, considering the network connections associated with the claim transaction. Traditionally, if several claims have average values for their attributes, such as total amount, number of participants, number of roles, addresses, and so forth, none of these claims would be identified as suspicious and wouldn't issue alerts. However, if a particular participant, such as a supplier or a claimant, is involved in all those claims, their relationship level could be considered too high relative to the average of the network, and an alert would be issued, flagging it for further investigation. In this latter case, all individual claim values can still be considered in regard to the transaction norm. However, the strength of the connections among actors in different claims was much higher than the normal, expected values within this type of network structure.

This graph-based analytical approach, however, doesn't eliminate traditional methods. The investigative subject matter expertise encapsulated in business rules is always quite effective and should be used in conjunction with analytically derived knowledge. The gains achieved from this analysis were specific to identifying the possibility of unexpected behavior because of network relationships. Each analytical method is more or less suitable to find a particular type of suspicious event, and thus a combination of distinct approaches, in combination with subject matter expertise, makes it possible to track a wide range of different types of risk within one system. Typically, when it comes to fraud detection, any action that might increase effectiveness and performance is more than welcome.

Participant Networks

Network participant metrics describe how participants relate to each other, in what frequency, and their importance to the network. From the analysis some suspicious relationships can be found and hence some potentially fraudulent actors can be identified. Due to this, investigation should not only be for the claim itself but also should be done for the participants—and any other claims they are involved with. The measures discussed in this section are used to describe the structure of the claims and the participant network.

From 41,885 nodes within the social structure analyzed, 30,428 were individuals, and 4,423 were organizations. Additional analysis based on the distinct participant role (both individual and organizational) was conducted to highlight unusual activity stemming from groups of participants, either in terms of nodes or links. Analysis of the nodes constituted description about the participants and how they related to each other through the claims, while the links portrayed their reach across the network.

Different types of group analysis were also performed within this study, including community, cluster, connected components, and biconnected components investigation.

Group Analysis

In addition to the analysis of participants and claims, other analyses were performed considering different types of groups. These groups were clusters of participants found among the claims associated with a particular claim category. They were detected by using sub-graphs within the entire network. The approach was used to find clusters of outliers within the network, in addition to participant outliers. A special group of actors behaving differently from the rest of the network can readily be exposed when examining groups of behavior that may be undetected when only individual behavior is considered.

For example, in this particular study there were 6,263 connected components. It is quite important to note that during the data-cleansing routines some entities were removed from the network. There were some participants within the claims who occurred frequently, such as government agencies and some insurers. By including these participants the entire network would be completely connected, given that these participants appeared in almost every claim.

Furthermore, this network had 15,734 bi-connected components and 2,307 articulation points. Analogous to the connected components, the articulation points were highlighted for further investigation. And from those 2,307 articulation points, 984 of them were individual participants, which was even more suspicious.

And finally, 13,279 communities were detected in the network, considering all nodes, regardless if they were classified as an individual or organization.

Identifying Outliers

The next phase considered the overall measures relative to individual ones. By doing this, the most relevant aspects of social structures within the network were identified. In order to do this, the entire network was considered in relation to the computation of individual measures. These measures were then assigned to each node and link within the network.

The second step was to compare the individual measures (for both nodes and links) against the average metrics of the entire network, and in relation to some particular categories, such as individual, organization, policy holder, repairer, and so on. Unusual or unexpected behaviors in relation to nodes and links were also found with these comparisons via an outlier analysis of the network measures. The outlier analysis took into account the average measures for the entire network, and therefore compared these measures with those assigned to the individual nodes and links.

Distinct approaches that highlighted the occurrence of outliers were put in place. Based on univariate, principal component, and clustering analyses, a set of different conjunction rules was established. A link analysis was also performed in order to identify outlier links and therefore highlight the nodes involved in those linkages.

A comparison of the social structures within the network was done in order to highlight the outlier occurrences of connected components, bi-connected components, and communities, thereby identifying the nodes associated with these groups. Specific to the bi-connected components, the articulation points were deeply analyzed because they were very relevant to the connections that associated two or more tight groups. When an individual node played a role in an articulation point it was deemed suspicious, and hence susceptible to further tracking.

Rules and Thresholds Using Univariate Analysis

The univariate analysis evaluated the network measures and defined a set of observation ranges based on predefined percentiles. All observations that satisfied the established rules assigned to the outlier percentile were highlighted for further investigation.

In this case study, when the degree was greater than nine, the eigenvector was greater than 6.30E-03 based on network measures. The closeness was greater than 1.46E-01, the betweenness was greater than 1.12E-04, the influence 1 was greater than 2.32E-04, and the influence 2 was s greater than 1.44E-01. Based on these thresholds, a node was considered an outlier and was flagged for investigator scrutiny.

According to the univariate analysis, there were 331 nodes that satisfied the network metric thresholds and were defined as outliers. The average behavior of these 331 nodes was associated with 21 different individuals when traced back to the transaction database detail.

Rules and Thresholds Using Principal Component Analysis

The principal component analysis evaluated the network measures by reducing the dimensionality of the variables. All measures were reduced to a single attribute that represented the original characteristics of the nodes. Similarly, the outlier observations were identified according to the high values relative to this derived attribute.

When the degree was greater than 13, the eigenvector was greater than 3.65E-03, the closeness was greater than 1.42E-01, the betweenness was greater than 9.10E-05, the influence 1 was greater than 3.22E-04, and the influence 2 was greater than 8.48E-02. And when these conditions were met, the node was considered an outlier observation and was flagged.

According to the principal component analysis, there were 305 nodes that were outliers. The average behavior of these 305 nodes satisfied the individual network thresholds, which lead to the identification of 23 individual participants who were identified as involved in the suspicious activity.

Rules and Thresholds Using Clustering Analysis

Clustering analysis evaluates the network metrics that create distinct groups of nodes based on their characteristic similarities. These similarities could be based on measures such as degree, eigenvector, closeness, betweenness, and influence. The outlier observations are not identified based on buckets or percentiles but instead according to unusual clusters that are derived. The vast majority of the clusters identified within the network usually contain several nodes. Based on this, when a cluster includes only a few members they are identified as being uncommon, and thus outlier groups of nodes. As a consequence, all nodes within these uncommon clusters would were also considered to be outliers.

The average network measures for outlier clusters established thresholds that highlighted which nodes within the network were also outliers. According to the derived cluster thresholds, when the degree was higher than 36, the eigenvector greater than 1.04E-02, the closeness greater than 1.45E-01, the betweenness greater than 6.50E-04, the influence 1 greater than 9.35E-04, and influence 2 greater than 1.49E-01, then both the cluster and the nodes within it were pre-scribed outlier status and were flagged for further investigation.

Based on the cluster analysis in this study, three clusters were found to be outliers, composed of 18, 2, and 3 nodes, respectively. And in turn, these 3 outlier clusters were composed of 23 nodes (also outlier) nodes. The average behavior exhibited by these 23 nodes sat-isfied thresholds which translated to identifying just two unique net-work participants from the transaction's database.

Rules and Thresholds Using Link Analysis

The previously described rules and thresholds were based on the anal-ysis of outliers that examined measures of individual nodes. Although the clustering analysis considers groups of nodes, the individual node measures are computed to establish the thresholds themselves. However, in social network analysis it is also possible to analyze the behavior of the links that join the nodes. Such link analysis can iden-tify the occurrence of outlier links, which means beyond average rela-tionships, thereby highlighting the potential outlier nodes associated with the corresponding outlier links.

Similar to the clustering analysis wherein outlier node groups as well as the individual nodes within them are considered uncommon, outlier links and the nodes associated with them are also ascribed out-lier status. For link features, the geodesic distance (i.e., the shortest paths assigned to them), was examined. The link betweenness in this case represents how many shortest paths a particular link partakes in. Analogously to nodes measures, links that take part in many shortest paths have higher link betweenness than those that do not.

In this study, the average network measures for outlier links were calculated to establish the thresholds defining which nodes within the network to be considered outliers according to their uncommon links. Based on the link thresholds, when the degree was greater than 9, eigenvector greater than 4.30E-03, closeness greater than 1.41E-01, betweenness more than 2.32E-04, influence 1 higher than 2.26E-04, and influence 2 greater than 9.37E-02, then the node was defined as an outlier and should be flagged for further investigation.

According to this link analysis, 300 links were identified as being outlier connections, comprising 199 nodes. The average behavior of these 199 nodes met the criteria of the thresholds, which, when applied to the production environment, raised 18 individual participants from the transaction database that should be subject to further scrutiny.

Rules and Thresholds Using Bi-Connected Components

The social structure in this case study contained 15,734 bi-connected components. Interconnecting these bi-connected components were 2,307 articulation points, of which 984 were associated with participants classified as individuals. The articulation point recall was an individual who binds two connected components. Claims in insurance typically should not have too many individual participants involved in them (i.e., connecting them). Companies may appear several times in a claim, such as suppliers, repairers, or the insurers themselves; however, individuals who appear several times, connecting different claims can raise eyebrows, and should be investigated further.

There are two different ways to use articulation points. The first is to simply highlight them. The second is to calculate their average behavior, similar to other methods described, and identify all nodes that match or exceed the derived threshold criterion. In the latter case, the average network measures for the articulation points established the thresholds used to highlight outlier nodes. Based on this, when the degree was greater than 20, the eigenvector greater than 5.05E-03, closeness greater than 1.43E-01, betweenness greater than 4.27E-04, influence 1 greater than 5.00E-04, and influence 2 greater than 1.03E-01, then the node was considered an outlier and was flagged.

According to this bi-connected component analysis, 99 articulation points were identified as outlier observations and the average behavior of these 99 nodes met the derived threshold criteria, which when assessed, identified 15 individual participants who were suspicious.

Connected Component Analysis

Connected components depict strong relationships between nodes. All nodes can reach each other, no matter what the path is. A connected component analysis was performed over the entire network.

Different from the analysis methods already described (wherein evaluations considered just participants classified as individuals), the connected components method of identifying outliers takes into account all nodes, both individual and organizational. In this analysis, additional information was considered, including the numbers of both the individual and organization nodes as well as the total number of claims that were associated with the connected component nodes.

A principal component analysis was performed over the network and, in addition to node measures, business metrics were also used to assess the connected components. Node metrics including the number of nodes within the connected components, the average values for degree, eigenvector, closeness, betweenness, and influences 1 and 2 were examined. Business information including total ledger, amount claimed, number of vehicles involved, number of participants, and others were also included.

The average network measures for the nodes comprising outlier-connected components therefore established the thresholds necessary to identify the overall outlier nodes. Based on the calculations, when degree was greater than 7, the eigenvector greater than 6.97E-17, the closeness greater than 8.33E-02, the betweenness equal 0.00E-00, influence 1 greater than 1.89E-04, and influence 2 greater than 1.50E-03, then the node was considered an outlier and should be flagged for further investigation.

According to this connected component analysis, 3 connected components were identified as outliers, comprising 30 nodes. The average behavior of these 30 nodes highlighted 555 individual participants flagged as involved in suspicious activity.

Due to this high number of participants, this approach was not considered as an appropriate technique to be used in the production systems. Business rules prevailed. Highlighting such a large number of participants was thought to be inappropriate and this particular set of rules and thresholds was discarded.

Community Analysis

Similar to the connected components evaluation, the most relevant characteristic of communities is the type of relationship between the community nodes. As previously described, additional information in terms of number of nodes, individuals, and organizations, and the total amount of the claims associated with the community nodes were taken into consideration to accomplish this analysis.

Once again, a principal component analysis was performed over the network and (what has become) the traditional graph analysis metrics were calculated—the average node degree values, eigenvector, closeness, betweenness, and influences 1 and 2. Business measures for the communities were also considered, including total ledger, amount claimed, number of vehicles involved, number of participants, and others.

The averages network's measures for the nodes comprising the outlier communities established the thresholds to highlight the overall community outlier nodes. The calculated results identified threshold for degree greater than 13, eigenvector greater than 3.20E-03, closeness greater than 1.42E-01, betweenness greater than 7.10E-05, influence 1 greater than 3.26E-04, and influence 2 greater than 8.02E-02 as the thresholds used to flag nodes for further investigation.

According to this community analysis, 13 communities were identified as outliers, comprising a total of 68 nodes. The average behavior of these 68 nodes met the threshold criteria when applied to the production data, identified 24 individual participants for further investigation.

Final Figures in Claims

The process of identifying outlier observations based on all of the different types of analyses described resulted in distinct sets of rules. The core notion in this approach is not to separate these calculations into different analysis, but instead to include all of the derived rules into a single framework and then evaluate all claims with all of the rules. Table 7.1 lists the different techniques performed and the number of resultant individual participants associated with satisfying the suspicious threshold criteria.

As stated before, the number of suspects raised by the connected components analysis was too high, and for this it was discarded. Outliers' participants were identified by different techniques, such as univariate analysis, principal components, clustering, link analysis,

Table 7.1 The Number of Unique Suspicious Participants Discovered Using Various Graph Analysis Measurement Techniques

Technique	Individual participants
Univariate Analysis	21
Principal Component Analysis	23
Clustering Analysis	2
Link Analysis	18
Bi-Connected Component Analysis	15
Connected Components Analysis	555
Community Analysis	24

articulation points, and within communities. Each technique raised a range of 2 to 24 participants. If we summarize these total amounts we would reach 103 participants. However, if we remove duplicate individuals, considering the entire number of outlier participants across all techniques, we found about 33 unique individuals. These participants were involved in 706 claims.

Visualizing for More Insight

Individual claim attributes contain useful information regarding the transaction event. However, these attributes might poorly explain correlations for particular events such as fraud or claim exaggeration, whereas the relationships between claims can reveal unusual recent and frequent behavior that can be associated with suspicious claim activity. Social network analysis has the potential to reveal different participant roles, as well as groups of participants that may be colluding; often, visual depiction of relationships can quickly highlight graph analysis derived patterns.

Figure 7.5 depicts a particular medical specialist who was quite frequently found to be associated with claims above an acceptable value amount. He connects to a high number of distinct policyholders. The resultant star network shows a central node (the specialist) having a high number of connections to different nodes (presumably

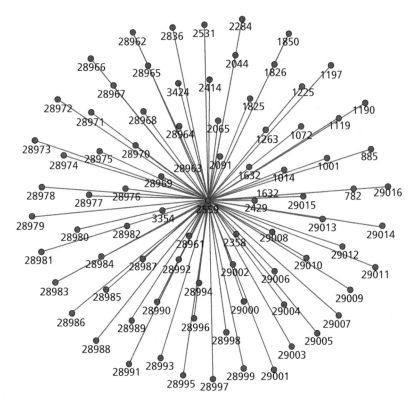

Figure 7.5 Star Network Presenting a High Central Node with Lots of Distinct Connections

patients). Further analyses uncovered widely distributed geographic addresses for these different connected nodes. This was considered uncommon in this particular motor insurance study, and thus this specialist was identified for further investigation.

Another graphical method that can be used to highlight unusual behavior stems from visually examining groups depicting connected components, bi-connected components, and communities. Some groups are found to be rare, or outliers, because their network measures are outside the norm of the average for the entire social structure. Other groups might be recognized as uncommon due to business attributes such as the amount of claim, the number of distinct roles, cars involved, different addresses, and so on. These business attributes affiliated with group measures should also be compared to the average figures for the entire social structure.

Figure 7.6 shows a set of connected components and bi-connected components that were found to be unusual because of their social network measures or their business attributes.

Final Figures in Insurance Exaggeration

Distinct approaches can be combined to highlight heavy claim users in the motor insurance environment. High volumes of payment claims, fraudsters, and even exaggerators can all jeopardize corporate profits and cash flow. All companies need to maintain operational cost control, especially those in competitive marketplaces such as insurance. Profit is a reflection of contained costs, which is, at least in part, best achieved by rigorous monitoring of claim transactions.

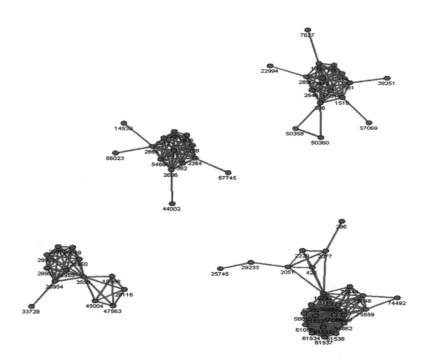

Figure 7.6 Uncommon Groups of Participants Highlighted by Visualizing Community Network Metrics

High claim payments, although not specific to fraud, can still significantly impact profit leakage. Claim exaggeration is typically a substantial problem in most insurance companies, sometimes instigated by customers, other times by suppliers. Hence, it is not simply fraudsters who are responsible for losses, but exaggerators can also lead to substantial financial damage to insurers. All these types of participants need to be closely monitored to help identify and ultimately avoid possible unexpected payments.

As in many industries, the vehicle insurance market is quite dynamic. As we now know, when the market changes the underlying data related to it also changes. An analytical model based on social networks analysis needs to be monitored and intermittently assessed to ensure adaption of the network and the underlying metrics to new business realities, new scenarios, new regulations, and other changing conditions. Even though motor insurance is dynamic, social network analysis holds great promise as a very adaptable method that fits comfortably to different data types and changes.

CASE STUDY: FRAUD IDENTIFICATION IN MOBILE OPERATIONS

This last graph analysis case study presents a unique approach to finding fraudulent behavior in telecommunications. For this method, a set of outlier analyses was performed in conjunction with processes to detect communities. The overall analysis of the entire network and a subsequent investigation over the sub-networks was very effective in finding new ways to detect suspected cases of fraud. Instead of examining transactions or the overall network to find usage outliers, this approach considered groups of subscribers, trying to highlight unusual usage behavior within the particular group. The most common approach to detect fraud in telecommunications is based on transactions analysis or the calls originating from subscribers. Typically, these calls are compared with a set of rules (with derived thresholds), and when the corresponding criteria are satisfied, an alert is issued to flag the transaction for further investigation. If the system is set with lower thresholds, a higher number of alerts might be raised and time would more likely be spent on investigating a number of false positives. On the other hand, if the thresholds are set too high, fewer alerts might be issued, and thus a good number of possible events of fraud could be missed.

Background in Telecommunications Fraud

This is an inherent problem with thresholds. The approach used in this study was based on network analysis and community detection to define groups of subscribers in order to apply distinct sets of rules for each sub-graph found. So while rules are still developed (based on derived thresholds), it is done on a smaller (community-based) network. Just as with segmentation methods, dividing the entire network into a large set of smaller sub-networks, the average behavior within each one segment is a more specific reflection of behavior than that between segments. A heavy user in a business community could be flagged as suspicious by the traditional approach, once usage surpasses the thresholds. However, when examined within a high usage community, they may well be within the average for that sub-group, and thus not be deemed an outlier.

Not only can individuals within communities be highlighted using this method, but particular groups of individuals can also be readily identified. Totally different shapes of communities with completely unexpected behaviors can also be detected by using this sort of graph analysis. Groups with very low numbers of members and with very high usage should be considered quite suspicious, for instance. A community where just one member makes all the calls and the rest of them just receive calls is also odd. Simply based on transaction analysis, such behavior would be missed because the relationships aren't considered.

This case study presents how social network analysis and community detection for calls and text messages within a communications network can be used to understand different aspects of customer behavior. As we've seen, the analysis of relationships can point out aspects of customers and their possible viral effect throughout the network or sub-networks. Do viral effects take place in events of fraud as they do in churn or product adoption? Do fraudsters influence others to conduct illicit activity?

Just as network analysis creates knowledge about customer relationships and the patterns of these relationships in social structures, fraud in telecommunications is often exhibited in patterns of relationships. There are some fraudsters who focus on interconnection rates, others who avoid last miles (i.e., the last piece of traffic, usually delivered by another carrier for a charge), some who conduct fraud between operators, and others who use different schemes. Essentially, fraud in communications is done to provide a cheap way to make calls, and thus to connect people. In this study, the focus is on communities within the telecommunications network, so all individual social metrics are compared to the communities they are members of.

Most fraud analyses take into consideration usage and demographic characteristics that describe individual subscriber behavior. Social network fraud analysis evaluates the relationships between customers, regardless of their individual information. Customers are assessed for fraud based on their connections rather than their individual attributes, distinguishing their importance within social structures.

Social Networks and Fraud

Network analysis can disclose correlations among potentially suspicious subscribers, describing their consumption patterns. Monitoring and analyzing social structures over time, particularly those that are interconnected, allows companies to recognize the emergence of suspicious events within communities, enabling a more proactive approach to addressing the resultant revenue leakage.

To detect the viral effect of fraud within communities, the goal was to describe what happened in the rest of the community after one community member commits fraud. Do these other community members also commit fraud after the initial fraud event? If so, this would be representative of a viral influence that fraudsters have within communities. What happens when one subscriber finds out about a possible fraud? Does she reveal this fraud to her connected members? Are communities notified of building momentum for fraud in advance of the event?

Based on call detail records, the network was established, connecting the initiating caller to the call receiver as links. Both nodes (mobile phones) and links (calls, text messages, and multimedia messages) were weighted to distinguish their relative importance and further differentiate the call types. Multimedia messages were weighted higher than phone calls, which in turn were weighted higher than text messages. Important nodes were found to contribute more in some particular networks, as did important links. The node weighting was based on the customer's average billing, while the link weights were based on the call value, frequency, and duration. All calls were aggregated by type, based on frequency and total duration.

Once the network was built, community detection was performed to find existing groups of customers that had closer relationships to each other than to other members of the network. An exploratory analysis was then done to highlight unusual or unexpected behavior for groups of subscribers within the communities. Unexpected behavior was recognized by outlier observation. Analogous to any traditional exploratory analysis, the presence of outliers indicates unexpected behavior, which arises from a particular set of rules and thresholds defining that highlighted suspicious event. The main difference here is that, according to the social network analysis, the occurrence of outliers is based on the relationships and not the individual attributes. Particular values assigned to groups of nodes might also indicate unusual behavior, as well as the sum of individual values for all nodes within a community.

Community Detection

One of the most important outcomes from a network analysis is the measure related to consumers and how they relate to each other, at what frequency, and how relevant their connections are. A suspicious node might be recognized by the node metrics themselves, by the link measures, or even by the community measures. Nodes with very high values for some measures might be suspicious, as could the nodes defined by the links with high metric values. And finally, nodes that belong to communities that have high values might also be suspicious.

In this study, communities were initially detected and then, for each node, the community-related metrics were computed. Different approaches were considered to detect communities. For instance, some basic rules were defined, the heuristic part of the job.

A trial-and-error process was used to detect the best number of communities to describe the network and the best average number of members within each community. There were also some mathematical measures used to help describe how well the network was divided into sub-networks. Additionally, business rules were followed to split the entire network, making the community-detection process quite heuristic.

Two different types of algorithms were also used to help identify communities. Different from connected components identification—which are isolated from the rest of the network—a community can hold some nodes which also has connections outside the community, described as branches or arms. In this way, communities connect to other communities, which can often occur through more than one node. Communities inside networks can be described as clusters from a population. In big networks such as in telecommunications, it is quite common to find large communities that follow a power law distribution. In other words, there are often a few communities that each containing a large number of nodes, but the majority of communities contains only a few nodes. To address this problem, we worked with different resolution values, created by examining different community distributions.

The resolution defined how the network was divided into communities, and constitutes a reference measure used by the algorithm to decide whether or not to merge communities based upon inter-community links. In practice, larger resolution values produce more communities with a smaller number of members in each. In order to produce big communities, the algorithm needed to consider more links between the nodes, even those connections that were only weakly binding nodes. In this way, we were able to define bigger communities with higher numbers of members who had weaker links connecting them. The smaller communities defined had fewer members, but held together with stronger links joining the nodes.

The modularity metric was also used to identify the potential best resolution for community detection. The larger the modularity value, the better distribution of members within the community. However, deciding the number of communities and desired average number of members in each was done with business definitions. Fraud analysis often requires strong links, as does churn. On the other hand, purchasing and product adoption may be better reflected by communities with higher member counts to enhance the desired viral effect. Business knowledge can direct nuances associated with different analysis objectives.

As a heuristic process, there is no single formula to identify the best distribution of communities or the optimal resolution number to divide the network into communities. This trial-and-error process needs to consider the size of the network, the business problem to be solved, and the analytical questions being asked of the data.

Finding the Outliers within Communities

Once communities were defined, we set out to identify outliers, based on community membership relative to the average measures for each community. There were several networks, community-based metrics that were calculated. Outliers were sought based on degree, influence, closeness, betweenness, hub, authority, and page rank. Each of these measures was calculated for every community, and then the values of individual community members were assessed relative to the community average. This helped describe outliers inside the network, not so much in relation to individual calls and texts but in respect to the groups of consumers and their usage behavior.

Individual calls were known to have expected values for some attributes like call origin, destination, durations, type, time, day, and so forth. However, it was found that the relationship among calling subscribers also revealed unusual frequency, recency, and density measures, based on network behavior Social network analysis was therefore used to reveal unexpected behavior for node attributes when they were defined for a group.

As with any business, fraud events have a beginning. This initiation was clearly identified when a fraudster created the proper environment to diffuse illegal usage of the telecommunications network. As long as this environment was available to use for illicit purposes, the fraud events were seen to span throughout the network, diffusing across social structures. Very often, these events were found to be highly concentrated among the smaller community groups that would likely have been aware of the fraud, and hence presented a different type of behavior than did the non-fraudulent community groups.

The outlier analysis method for individuals within the network wasn't believed to adequately identify suspicious behavior in this scenario. Instead, this study examined outliers associated with groups of consumers so that investigation was directed toward a suspicious cluster, and the individual participants within these flagged communities. So while the procedures used were only slightly different from that of the previous case studies, completely different results were achieved.

Rules and Thresholds for Community Outliers

After computing the social metrics for all communities, outlier analysis was conducted to expose unusual behavior. A univariate analysis was also done to classify all measures into percentiles in order to separate the higher value occurrences. For instance, by taking the 1 percent or 5 percent percentiles we highlighted a selected number of nodes, associated with a limited number of communities. Examples of these are illustrated in Figures 7.8 through 7.10. These nodes held average values for all the calculated social network measures, degree-in and degree-out, closeness, betweenness, influence 1, influence 2, hub, authority, and page rank. We also considered the number of members within communities and the density of some specific network metrics assigned to each group. By applying the metric thresholds for the entire network, a number of nodes surfaced, highlighting those members for investigators to validate for the occurrence of fraud.

Defining and applying rules for community outlier detection subsequently required a sequence of steps, starting with defining network communities, computing the social network metrics for each community, identifying the outlier percentile (1 percent for instance), establishing the average values for the outliers' network measures, and then applying these thresholds to the entire network. This outlier percentile, which defined which nodes were considered to be suspicious, was not only determined based on the distribution values for the network metrics, but also reflected the operational capacity to handle further investigation by the fraud analysts.

Fraudster Visualization

The following figures illustrate some communities that exhibited suspicious behavior based on the exploratory analysis of network measures. The red node located in the middle of the social structure shown in Figure 7.7 is a subscriber who made calls to almost 7,000 distinct phone numbers, which, in and of itself, was quite suspicious. This potential fraudster had absolutely huge degree-out value when compared to the rest of the sub-network he or she belonged to, pinpointing this particular node as a well-qualified candidate for further investigation.

The red node in the middle of Figure 7.8 received calls from more than 1,000 distinct phones, which was deemed suspicious. In this particular case, the social measure degree-in was used to highlight this outlier observation.

In Figure 7.9, the red node in the social structure represents a subscriber who made more than 16,000 calls to the member node beside it (yellow). The thin arrow illustrates how strong this connection is in comparison to the other links. A combination of the link strength and the social measure hub was used to highlight this particular outlier.

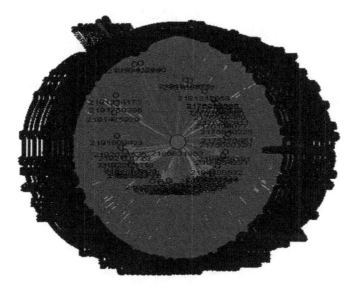

Figure 7.7 Outlier n (big node in the center of the network) Graphed According to the Social Measure Degree-Out

Figure 7.8 Outlier (big node in the center of the network) Graphed According to the Social Measure Degree-In

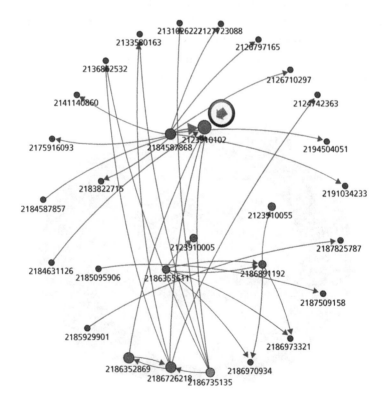

Figure 7.9 Outlier (big node highlighted in the figure) and the Link Strength, Graphed Based on the Social Measure Hub

And finally, Figure 7.10 illustrates a subscriber who received more than 20,000 calls from just 26 distinct phone numbers. This is depicted by the red node with thin arrows connecting to other nodes. These arrows represent the strength of the links between the suspicious node and their correlated connections. A combination of the link strength and the social measure authority was used to highlight this particular outlier.

Final Figures in Fraud

As with most of the procedures assigned to fraud management, this graph analysis approach is able to identify suspicious activity and

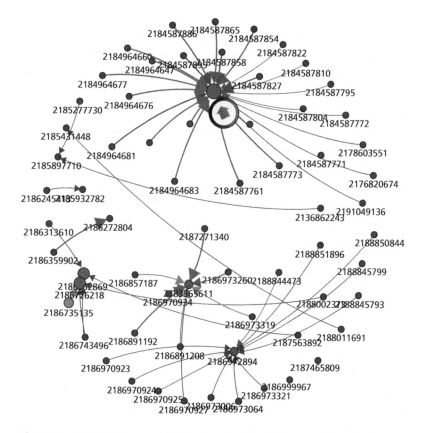

Figure 7.10 Outlier (big node highlighted in the figure), Link Strength Graphed Based on the Social Measure Authority

potential fraud. This study presents a compelling argument for fraud detection to also consider relationships as part of the detection process.

Outlier analysis using the social network measures describes possible behavior for groups of consumers who may be committing fraud. Average community and network behavior can be translated into a set of rules and thresholds in relation to the network metrics. This set of rules and thresholds can then be deployed in transactional systems to issue alerts associated with possible fraud events. Alerts are not conclusions about fraudulent activity. They indicate the likelihood of a particular event, subject to further investigation by qualified experts.

SUMMARY

Social network analysis can be applied to solve different business problems, as illustrated by the case studies described. The first step in graph analysis is to properly identify the network by recognizing which entities play the role of nodes and which events connect the nodes, defining the links. Roles assigned to even the most complex networks are simply nodes and links. The definitions, however, determine model outcomes. A wrong definition will result in bad network construction, lead to improper network measure calculations, and incorrect business conclusions.

Deeply examining the problem and all the different business aspects involved is the best way to appropriately judge the entities and events that define the pattern of nodes and links. Building the proper network is not only the first step in such analyses, it is the most important one.

We examined how social network analysis can be used to examine marketing and sales issues in telecommunications by highlighting possible influencers in two different business scenarios, churn and product adoption. An influencer has a particular meaning when it comes to network analysis. Labeling someone an influencer happens when they encourage a specific, demonstrated behavior. If you bought an iPhone and influenced your friend to buy an iPhone too, you could be called an influencer. Yet there is a difference between the general influencer who has an impact on those close to their surrounding network, and an influence effect (the viral one) that some nodes have. It is this viral effect that marketers seek when they want to exert influence over other nodes in the network.

Social network analysis can be used to simply calculate network metrics for all nodes, and rank them by their corresponding metrics (which may be a combination of degree, influence, closeness, betweeness, etc.). This ranking can essentially be described as the power of the nodes in the network. Naturally, if a node has high degree it is very connected. A high influence also describes well-connected nodes. High closeness describes a wider spread of information throughout the network, high betweeness describes controlling information flow within the network, and so on. A node can have high power (strength) within its network, but such strength is not the same as being an influencer—at least not before it has influenced another node to do something.

All the network concepts described in this chapter are important when nodes and links are not particularly intuitive, such as in telecommunications. The insurance example highlighted how node and link roles, the approach to detect sub-graphs, the way to compute network metrics, and how to interpret the results is key to analyzing the correct problem.

Social network analysis can be applied to any number of industries and scenarios such as retail, taxation, money laundering, political and corporate lobbying, education and research, biology, chemistry, and much more. Although network analysis can provide deep knowledge about relationships, it isn't an analytical panacea. In the majority of cases, graph analysis methods are better deployed in conjunction with other analytical methods.

CHAPTER 8

Text Analytics

T ext analytics is the use of software to analyze the written word. The focus of this type of analysis is to understand the intent, characteristics, and meaning of the author. Although based in well-established disciplines of linguistics and computational linguistics, statistics, machine learning, and information retrieval (others would also say philosophy, psychology, and other social sciences), this type of analysis applied to traditional business scenarios is relatively recent—making it by definition, heuristic.

Text analytics is distinct from content analytics in that text analytics considers electronic words, sentences, phrases, snippets, fragments, and documents and does not include the inherent analysis of video or audio recordings. Text can of course be extracted from either type of recording and transcribed to electronic text, manually or by using recognition software. And while there are unique attributes distinct to both video and audio such as time spent standing in a bank teller line captured on video, or the length of a pause by a phone caller, this chapter focuses solely on electronic text.

Seldom is textual data independent of structured data. Structured data such as date, time, author, source, title, and so on, is often captured automatically by the operating system or word processing software being used by the text author. This type of automated, structured data capture is common to all computing systems—so the remaining body of these documents (i.e., the free format electronic text), is associated with the context of this structured data. Unstructured data, on the other hand, has no frame of reference or associated system data (or even predefined context), other than what is intended by the author. It can be argued (and many do) that because of this there really isn't anything that is unstructured, and that all text is really semi-structured data. Regardless, even within the confines of semi-structured data such as the body of the document, like the commentary written in the other category of a survey, a pre-defined structure is absent.

Data from social media is similarly a combination of both structured and unstructured information. The internet protocol (IP) address, the author's chosen internet handle, the location of content on the page, the title of the post, and so on are defined in a standardized nomenclature, with universally accepted formats (such as the HTML markup). Locating the unstructured text elements relies on these structured fields to distinguish where the free format text starts and ends, if one or more authors comment, and how quickly the content is being updated, augmented, or changed, for example.

Purism aside, the ultimate goal of text analytics is to provide structure to unstructured text. As with the competitive-intelligence cycle described in Chapter 4 (and perhaps depending on your perspective), text analytics can be ascribed to all aspects of the cycle—including information creation, knowledge generation, and intelligence. In fact, text analytics can also help persist intelligence so that it is recognizable as experience.

Structuring unstructured text is used to decipher what the author intended to convey. What is the person commenting about? Are they happy or unhappy, angry or sad? Is this research relevant to what I'm investigating? Does this report describe a potentially hazardous situation? The applications of text analytics extends to virtually every field and every industry simply because content is everywhere. Text lives within organizations, in the form of verbatim comments, emails, document archives, field notes, product descriptions, claims summaries, service call detail, contact center snippets, operational system notations, and so on. By all accounts, text data is exploding outside organizations, within forums, reviews, blogs, posts, and tweets. Who has time to read it all? Text analytics software is believed by many to hold the original promise of computing—to do the work for us, reading and evaluating documents, freeing up humans (and other machines) to assess the derived insights and results, thus improving decisions.

A number of methods are part of the text analytics toolkit. There are methods that consider entire collections of documents—that seek to discover patterns, with or without target variables—including supervised, semi-supervised, and unsupervised approaches. There are other methods that emerged from an entirely different school of thought, focusing on evaluation of each document in isolation, albeit processing them very, very quickly. The latter are largely supervised methods, requiring some form of training corpus to successfully derive the models and then processing them in batches, (near) real-time, and event streams.

Conversations among text analytics practitioners often conclude in soft chuckles. This is an emerging discipline, about words, their meaning, and use—and yet we are limited by these same words to describe, communicate, and advance the topic. So what constitutes a topic, what is a concept, why that is different from a fact, often leads to definitional confusion for newcomers to this type of analysis. In fact, it is this very subtlety of language that is at the heart of what makes this an intriguing and evolving area of analysis.

TEXT ANALYTICS IN THE COMPETITIVE-INTELLIGENCE CYCLE

With text data everywhere, it is perhaps not surprising that text analytics can be associated with every stage of the competitive-intelligence cycle. Transactional systems control and manage company business and daily operations, creating data that describes tasks or events—tracking the activity and enabling downstream processes—the micro-information, as previously described. Text data is also captured in these systems, as part of daily operations. For example, call center agents make notes during their customer conversations. Field technicians and agents write descriptions that explain issues and document reports. Transaction and on-line applications capture narratives from staff justifying actions and requests. The list goes on.

In addition to such operational sources, electronic documents are also created in every organization, often for the purpose of communicating thoughts, research, or need. Collected from email servers, intranet wikis and platforms, web pages describing the organization to external audiences, document management systems, research archives, and so on, internal authors continue to update sources as part of daily operations. To these sources add the general population of web commentary written by Internet users, perhaps it's no wonder then that text is recognized as being one of the leading contributors to big data.

In his book *Too Big to Ignore*,[1] Phil Simon examines the reality of big data and practically describes how it not only impacts business but how business can act differently because of it. With content coming from so many sources and authors, it should be no surprise that data cleansing and normalization are required before text data is useful to analysis. As with structured data analysis, analysis of this seemingly ubiquitous data type is required before it can be consumed by other stages of the competitive-intelligence cycle.

Information Revisited

Crawler applications are used to locate and retrieve content from their sources, whether they are internal file systems or web pages. Depending on the settings, a new file can be created that stores the retrieved content, or a referencing link can point to the desired material. In either case, the content is marked for use with mapping definition as part of data integration layer processing. With text data, translation of operational elements into meaningful business field definitions, however, involves text-based processing.

Electronic text is available in many different formats, and for this reason, document conversion is often the first step of integration processing. From text, markup (like HTML/XML), and word-processing formats (like ASCII, and Microsoft document formats); spreadsheets and presentation formats (like Adobe and OpenOffice); and database formats (like Access, dBASE, etc.), documents are rationalized to meet the common format needs of the analysis software. Some of these

---

[1] P. Simon, *Too Big to Ignore: The Business Case for Big Data*, Hoboken, New Jersey: John Wiley and Sons, 2013.

Figure 8.1 Utilities within Crawler Technology Can Define the Structured Text Elements without Native Language Understanding[2]

formats contain predefined elements that relate to different aspects of the document—like the title, author, or body of text—that are described in the machine language of the formatting application. For example, if you right click on any web page and select the "view source" option, you're presented with a language that describes the format and the text associated with the page itself. And it is from these markups that the document parser identifies web page contents. The parser then carves this up into structural information components like headings, links, or other elements, isolating text (and structured) content.

Crawler technology typically includes the necessary routines to convert and parse documents. Many can also incrementally add updates to previously copied pages to minimize document duplication. And not only are documents in different formats, they can also be in different languages, and as such crawlers (or other text-import mechanisms) often also include language-identification routines. However, in order to capture the content, document parsers can be blind to the native language, and simply denote the language of the text for other processing routines. As illustrated in Figure 8.1, crawler

---

[2] Full article referencing multilingual considerations for information extraction: "Lost in Translation," Part One: May/June & Part Two: September/October, 2013, *Analytics Magazine*, http://analytic-magazine.org.

definitions are specific to the structure of the page, and are not sensitive to the text language (in this case Arabic).

Just as with structured data, text data can be maintained in a data store that shapes how the information is viewed and accessed by the organization. But unlike structured data, a new text repository is not required—at least not for content that already exists in storage devices. So while web content may be new additions (and thus stored as part of analysis efforts), existing operational stores and document- and content-management systems often contain copies of the desired documents. In the latter case, reference linkages to existing repositories ease the IT burden by accessing the content without replicating it. However, unlike structured data, text needs to be analyzed to create structure before it is in a form usable by traditional tools that allow users to retrieve the information in pre-defined reports and systems that expose the results.

Knowledge Revisited

Aspects of text analysis focus on what could be considered text data cleansing. Routines such as finding and correcting misspellings, associating acronyms with their full descriptions, detecting synonyms, and so on could also be considered part of the data-analysis phase. But before this can happen, even more rudimentary analysis of sentences are needed to recognize words and their associated use in a document. To do this, sentences are parsed (grammatical analysis), broken into their individual elements (like punctuation marks, white space, words, expressions), parts of speech are identified (words are tagged based on their use in a sentence, identifying if they are nouns, adjective, verb, adverb etc.), and different word bases are recognized, also known as word stems (like pluralization, tense, etc.). For example, *play* would be a word stem for both *plays* and *played*. More advanced text analytics software automates much of this initial processing.

Less pedestrian analysis can be associated with insight discovery. Understanding what a document is about, what is expressed in the words, and what are the key elements in the message are identified using statistical models and linguistic analysis. The level of sophistication of technologies to successfully define these aspects can widely vary, with more advanced packages providing the modeler with exacting control to define these key elements (defined below).

Category

Derived from Greek, *katēgoria*, meaning a declaration or assertion about something, a category has more commonly come to describe a characteristic expressed in a document. Category membership for a term or phrase can be indicated as a binary value, belonging to a category or not. Different methods can be used to classify a term as part of a category.

Concept

A concept is an abstract idea of a class of objects, a generalization that has a mentally inferred meaning. A robin, dove, blue jay, and finch can all be identified with the concept of bird. Concepts enable higher-level thinking through their simplification.

Entity

Often described as a person or place, an entity is a type of term that denotes something that physically exists, and is in that way a named concept (or a realized instance of a concept).

Fact

Facts can be considered a type of entity, one that represents a relationship between other entities. For example, a purchasing fact could be defined by the customer, the date, and the item acquired.

Taxonomy

Taxonomy is a collection of phrases, linguistic rules, and logic that describes how to accurately categorize a document or extract relevant concepts. Often expressed as a hierarchy, taxonomies define parent and child relationships wherein a child category automatically implies parent membership. Child categories can also have more than one parent. For example, a transportation vehicle could be a car, boat, train, plane, and so on. A car could also belong to both a transportation vehicle parent and a manufactured steel goods parent category.

Ontology

Ontologies may be reflective of analytic philosophy, with the remnants of Parmenides of Elea's poem *On Nature*[3] first describing ontologies as alternate views of reality. Ontologies describe relationships between concepts and entities, including the conditions under which these relationships are true (i.e., describe a meaning of interest). Ontology models describe the formal structures between terms and their use.

While aspects of text analysis can seem almost mechanical, since they teach computers to understand language, models of language can indeed be quite sophisticated in determining the intent of the author. Two broad categories of methods describe alternate modeling techniques to identify categories, concepts, facts, entities, and so on. The first is associated with linguistic methods that retrieve elements of text using Boolean logic and linguistic operators. The second uses statistical machine learning to discover patterns and is typically referred to as text mining. Both of these methods have merit, and in fact, a hybrid approach to creating structure from text is often used to provide the best of both approaches.

LINGUISTIC MODELS

Linguistic modeling approaches can be considered supervised methods, with defined taxonomies denoting the relationships between categories and concepts that are defined and then applied to the text. Typically a training corpus of documents is needed to test the model definitions, which are then tweaked based on how well they represent the documents. Boolean operators—like AND, OR, and NOT—detail the relationships among terms and control the processing order and importance of the inputs. Entity recognition and fact extraction

---

[3] An ancient Greek philosopher, circa early fifth century BC, Parmenides of Elea created one known work that has helped shaped Western philosophy. The poem, *On Nature*, can be referenced in English: http://www.davemckay.co.uk/philosophy/parmenides/parmenides.on.nature.php.

methods look up predefined lexicons using pattern-matching techniques and identify items such as names of people, companies, products, and places, as well as expressions such as e-mail addresses, phone numbers, and dates. Other notations can be used to examine term placement in the text (such as location in the paragraph or sentence), the order of terms preceding an element of interest, grammatical attributes of the term, multiword terms and phrases, symbolic links, concept sensitivity, and more. The ultimate goal is to define a model that can identify the text elements of interest well and easily generalize to new documents.

Once models are built and applied, knowledge is generated that describes the occurrence and relevance of concepts, entities, facts, and so on, found in any given document. Represented as linguistic scores, the results highlight the presence or absence of characteristics that describe the text. These characteristics of documents can be stored as metadata associated with each document, or be used as new variables in data mining.

The power of linguistic models is in their ability to very specifically mimic the nuances of language. Generally these nuances are not well defined by structured data. In fact, if we were to examine typical business processes, we may find that structured data elements used in data mining may not really reflect the business scenario at all—and it is only by analyzing the associated text data that we can be confident that the structured data represents event characteristics. This highlights one of the strong use cases for text analytics in business, to validate structured data, augmenting it with deeper understanding of *what* actually occurred and insight as to *why* it happened.

For example, as part of call center operations, agents are typically required to classify an incoming customer call, often from a pulldown menu of options, each of which denotes the conversation as belonging to a particular business category—billing, service, sales, or other something else. In some organizations, these classification options (also known as a controlled vocabulary) can be extensive—with tens and even hundreds of options presented to an agent who is instructed to select from them in order to define the call event. As you might imagine, if you are presented with a lot of options, you may be tempted to select something near the top of the list in order to get on to the business at hand; having the conversation with the customer. With human nature as it is, it is perhaps not surprising that this is often the case, but misclassification of calls occurs much more often than you might expect. And seldom is a conversation about only one thing, particularly when a customer takes the time to reach out to your business.

Call operation systems, like other transactional applications, were created by a developer who had semantic intent. Encoded into the system is the relationship between the event and language, even if that language is proprietary machine code, XML, Java, HTML5, and so on. As a result, the operational categories defined in systems, for example, may not adequately (and in our call center example, simply aren't) representing the business scenario at all. However, by analyzing the call center notes with linguistic models, the context of the call can be classified based on the conversation content itself—with identified categories, concepts, entities, and facts that are well defined and comprehensive. This knowledge is used to classify the call for reporting and operational processing as well as creating inputs to other models, like churn and acquisition models.

TEXT-MINING MODELS

While linguistic models focus on retrieving insights, text mining uses pattern-discovery methods to find knowledge contained in document collections. Similar to data mining, text mining involves statistical pattern learning—in this case to identify, extract, and assess terms and phrases. Also known as a *bag of words approach*, text mining can automatically count terms from parsed documents, examining which ones are more frequently used in conjunction with one another. However, unlike linguistic models, the context of word evaluations is limited, such as the order in which terms are mentioned. Text mining, however, can discover themes in document collections, even without context sensitivity, simply by the presence of co-occurring terms and concepts.

When presented with a set of documents it can be hard to know where to even start and to define what linguistic models might best describe the collection. Text mining is often used as a precursor to linguistic models simply because it can (often) automatically discover the popularity of words and phrases, giving the modeler an initial sense of what concepts are buried in the collection. In this unsupervised application, text mining holds great promise to cope with extensive collections and big text data.

Debate among text analysis professionals continues, espousing the merits of text-mining methods over that of linguistic modeling, and vice versa. Perhaps this isn't surprising, given that the methods were born from separate fields, like statistics and social science, respectively, but both with a heavy emphasis on computing science. What you will find are those that only use one particular method as an all-purpose tool to understand text documents. Examples of text-mining methods are beyond the purpose of this chapter, and are well described in existing volumes, such as *Practical Text Mining and Statistical Analysis for Non-structured Text Data.*[4] Suffice it to say that text-mining discovery can ease the burden of taxonomy development necessary for linguistic models, with automated generation of Boolean rules. Linguistic models in turn can add context-sensitive aspects to text knowledge discovery.[5] And in both cases, the model results constitute new structured knowledge about electronic text that is accessible to traditional applications.

Intelligence Revisited

The text analysis scores associated with the now structured categories, concepts and topics are in the required format for business intelligence applications. They can be directly read by these systems to interrogate the documents, to identify visual patterns, report on discovered events, and examine trends in business dashboards. Because these text-based variables describe the conditions and context of business scenarios, providing explanations of behavior they've also

---

[4] Miner, G. et al. *Practical Text Mining and Statistical Analysis for Non-structured Text Data Applications.* Whatham, MA: Elsevier Inc., 2012 describes text-mining methods and business applications.

[5] Albright, R., Punuru, J., and Surratt, L. "Relate, Retain, and Remodel: Creating and Using Context-Sensitive Linguistic Features in Text Mining Models," SAS Global Forum paper: 100-2013.

been known to better predict future outcomes traditional structured analysis. At a minimum these new structured variables can be used in conjunction with the structured data for predictive analysis, often improving model accuracy of acquisition, consumption termination, and insolvency models—simply because they include additional insights regarding behavior involved with the business event.

Text analysis results can be applied to all types of predictive models by extending customer knowledge with a bigger picture of the business scenario. For example, from a set of documents about a person, maybe their social network pages, incoming inquiries, service history, and so on, a broader sense of issues they've had, or preferences they've described can help define their interests and their social network relationships. Identified from the text, these new attributes become useful to complete the picture of customer behavior, and as such, often improve predictive model lift accuracy when inherently included in the calculations. Doing this would be difficult if there are only hard-coded lists in the background that you extract from. But with text analysis (and semantics), you can extract this type of information based on language. Perhaps even more relevant to customer applications is the ability to determine customer opinion from electronic text.

Sentiment Models

Deriving customer sentiment has become a popular application of text models for marketers, product developers, and customer service analysts. Sentiment models identify and differentiate positive and negative opinions. People have opinions, and often they can be relevant to a business that wants to deepen relationships and secure ongoing revenue throughout the customer lifecycle. Understanding that your camera product is enjoyed, except for the fuzziness of the lens focus when set on high zoom, can explain unrealized sales, identify product enhancement needs, and help better define the target audience for this particular type of camera. Social media sentiment for businesses is becoming a necessary attribute to broaden the overall customer picture and in particular the sentiment of influencers that can virally impact other social network members.

Outside of consumption behavior, public sentiment associated with policy, crises, and candidates is helping business leaders identify fundamental issues that matter to constituents, find trends that can augment intermittent national demographic statistics, and help identify the best use of words to convey messages so audiences are more receptive. Businesses assess the sentiment of their shareholders and their competitor's customers, human resource departments evaluate employee sentiment to evaluate satisfaction and turnover, the list goes on. And while the actual sentiment metric can be calculated, it is the relative ranking of sentiment scores across customer segments that can best direct new message strategy and targeting efforts. Moreover, trends in sentiment over time can illuminate the effectiveness of business actions like campaigns and other communications, informing success measures of tactical activities and forecasts of what could happen next.

Classification Models

Sentiment is a specialized type of classification model focused on identifying and categorizing individual opinion based on concepts, features, and attributes in a document. Polarity methodologies, such as sentiment, that rate documents on a scale of zero to one can extend to classifying author expertise, mood, and other target attributes. Classification for the purpose of this discussion extends to a broad suite of applications, practically described in *Text Mining and Analysis: Practical Methods, Examples and Case Studies Using SAS.*[6] All classification models are designed to organize text material using derived categories, concepts, themes, and taxonomies. Different from polarity models, however, a generalized set of classification models are used to make documents more accessible to information seekers.

Typically, search and retrieval systems are designed to access content based on criteria typed into a search box. Content Management Systems (CMS), with repositories that house the items to be retrieved,

---

[6] Chakraborty, G., Garla, S., and Pagolu, M. *Text Mining and Analysis: Practical Methods, Examples, and Case Studies Using SAS*, Cary, NC: SAS Institute Inc., Nov., 2013

also contain document attributes, such as title, author, date, and possibly tags to classify the document description into pre-defined categories (akin to our call center pulldown menu). In both search and CMS applications, a predefined set of words forms the basis of search terms that relate to the desired material. Within organizations, significant time is wasted because of ineffective searches. IDC has increased estimates of time wasted by information workers from $14,209 per worker per year in 2009[7] to $19,732 per worker per year in 2012,[8] an almost 40 percent increase per worker in just three years. With big data continuing to rise, the cost of not finding what is needed when it is needed is expected to continue to cut into business profits. What these systems lack, at least in part, is greater understanding of the content, so that only the most relevant material is presented to the seeker, naturally reducing the time spent continuing to look for it.

Classification models define elements associated with documents that are based on the content of the document itself. The concepts, facts, categories, and so on are identified from modeling efforts. All documents can then be scored with these models, tagging each document and classifying membership to these calculated attributes. These are then used by the search algorithm indexes as additional facets for pinpointing content. As with any kind of model, classification models can be embedded into operational and application systems, applying the knowledge scores, and in this case delivering organizational intelligence with the most relevant document being produced.

Sourcing text data from file systems and the web can also be improved with embedded classification models. Often, models are developed after data has been sourced. However, by embedding these models into the crawler procedures, sentiment can be defined, extraction for facts and entities completed, and membership to categories determined, storing these generated attributes along with sourced text. Moreover, extracting only desired content or text that meets preferred thresholds can be set, filtering out unwanted content from the sourcing process entirely.

---

[7] Feldman, S. *The Hidden Cost of Information*, IDC Update #217936, May 2009.

[8] Webster, M. "Bridging the Information Worker Productivity Gap: New Challenges and Opportunities for IT," *Sponsored by Adobe*, IDC White Paper, September 2012.

Classification results and determining the right membership of a document based on a model is a tradeoff that needs to be evaluated and decided by the analyst—a very heuristic process indeed. The best-fit criteria of text-based models consider the extent to which the model generalizes well enough to capture the desired outcomes (i.e., recall) with the accuracy of any particular specification (i.e., precision). Similar to structured data analysis, higher recall can lead to more false positives (assigning a document to a class that is doesn't belong to), whereas higher precision may miss some true positives (leaving some documents out of search results, for example). As was once coined *Fishing for Accuracy*,[9] the effectiveness of the model application should outweigh any metric used to assess model accuracy, for it is the application that will best define the model value.

Semantic Models

In both statistical and linguistic methods, the pattern and structure of language define models, and in the latter case can also be used to evaluate linguistic context (i.e., the combinations of units of a language). Different from these syntactic approaches, semantics goes a step further, examining the meaning of words. Context is core to understanding meaning. The phrase "do you have the time?" could mean "are you busy?" or "do you know what time it is?" depending on the conversation. Contextual clarification of concepts, entities, and facts is required to ascribe meaning. Ontologies are (typically) domain-specific models that specify the conditions under which relationships between entities and facts have meaning. So while sentiment analysis can provide some indication of the overall feeling about a particular topic, feature, or attribute, it tends to fail to detect things such as an author's sarcasm or innuendo. A semantic model would include additional information about the author, their general opinions for example, putting the expressed sentiment into a context for that individual, such as their beliefs—helping to decipher sarcasm.

---

[9] Foley, R. "Fishing for Accuracy in Text Analytics," Blog Post on the Text Frontier (www.blogs.sas.com/content/text-mining), Dec. 7, 2010.

To derive meaning, that is, semantics, we begin by mimicking the mind's interpretation and coding needed for computers to process with little or no human intervention. Semantics establishes the relationship between our language and what exists in the real world, designating objects and expressing the relationships between them. Online publishers may have been some of the earlier business application users of semantic models. By relating content found to the web based on reader profiles and online content clicks, web content offered new stories and topic suggestions based on the exhibited visitor behavior. Semantic technology links various forms of information in a cohesive way and, over the Web, semantic codification provides cost-efficient ways to publish information in distributed environments.

In knowledge-rich environments, an ontological layer that relates all content to all other content not only makes knowledge more accessible to an organization but helps to manage content by automating connections between content stores. A semantic model can be envisioned as an enrichment filter over all information, but with a scope mimicking that of existing IT infrastructure (with nodes of hardware connected by various networks). Similar to ideas presented in Chapter 7, graph databases are constructed with nodes (representing entities, concepts, etc.) and are linked together by edges and lines, which, in turn, describe the relationships between nodes. Graph databases are highly scalable and associate data with evolving schemas—and hold promise for semantically enabled information applications.

Experience Revisited

Recall that persisted intelligence leads to experience (as described in Chapter 4). A knowledge base is a maintained information store (machine readable, human accessible, or both) that is populated with content stemming from both structured and unstructured sources. For the unstructured aspects, text-analysis methods are used to isolate and organize text so that it is searchable and shared between members of an organization. There are experts working on specific problems in every organization and in order to retain that intellectual property (often from an aging specialist workforce), as well as make it accessible to aid similar problem solving, technical notes and diagnostics contained in disparate silos are classified for reuse using text models.

The development of knowledge bases requires effort. The Cycorp AI project has continued since its inception in 1984, working to assemble a comprehensive ontology and knowledge base of common, everyday ideas. And even if you buy or use a preexisting knowledge base, modifications will need to happen over time, since knowledge changes and grows as new experiences are had. Text discovery can greatly aid in the development of a knowledge base, or even fill in gaps when knowledge is not explicitly predetermined. For example, my daughter's recent school music project instructed the class to identify rhythmic similarities between two different pieces of music,—each from a different culture. She used the Rolling Stones song "Sympathy for the Devil," with its unique drum introduction,[10] and after searching site after site, no similar rhythmic signature could be found. A Japanese pop song on YouTube was discovered, but it simply reused the same Rolling Stone's intro. Nothing worth noting was found. If, however, the information had been related, say with tags that defined rhythmic signatures, than similar music should have easily been identified. It is this kind of relationship that is envisioned for all unstructured content, to maintain it as knowledge for reuse that is at the heart of this growing and evolving field.

In order to successfully code knowledge, it needs to be separate from the underlying application. As we learned from our Y2K experience, when system parameters are hard coded, they might not readily adapt to new conditions (like 1999 changing to 2000 in COBOL year fields). Experience is a learning construct, so by its very nature it will change over time.

SUMMARY

This chapter re-examined the customer-intelligence cycle (initially introduced in Chapter 4) as it relates to text data. Text retrieval using crawlers and other text import functions accumulates unstructured documents for input into the analysis process. Text processing is required to identify the elements contained in documents and is often automated, distinguishing native language features. Linguistic models

---

[10] http://www.youtube.com/watch?v=vBecM3CQVD8

that apply known sentence and grammatical lexicons were distinguished from text-mining models, which largely automate knowledge discovery. These methods identify facts, themes, and relationships of associated categories, concepts, and entities.

The output of text models is structured elements of the previous unstructured text. In the case of text mining, numeric representation of the discovered themes makes these results particularly amenable to other data-mining analysis. Applications of models for classification problems, including the special case of sentiment determination, were recognized to support a host of business scenarios. Semantic models focus on the meaning of the written word, requiring relationships between entities to be defined, in addition to any boundaries of when those relationships are valid to associated facts.

Linguistic models can benefit from text-mined inputs and may require domain experts who build syntactic rules to determine the text elements, including sentiment polarity. These methods use training data (e.g., documents that already have sentiment polarity assigned to them) to develop the model, classifying the sentiment of a document, feature, or attributes. Pattern discovery using text mining can help ease the burden with the high-level identification of training corpus elements. Similarly, text mining can be directed with linguistically defined entities for example, when discovery needs to include custom, desired constructs like a product table. In either case, predictive models such as decision trees, logistic regressions, or neural networks can use the outputs of text analysis, augmenting the structured data with variables that capture the knowledge often buried in text.

Semantics establishes the relationship between our language and what exists in the real world, designating objects and expressing the relationships between them. It is a key component to reliably understanding human-generated text given that language is still a primary means of communication. Heuristics is inherent in the analysis of language, with the implication of context on meaning as well as on model-accuracy assessment. Even still, machine analysis of text holds great potential, not only because it manages the burdensome reading for us but also because machines can connect with sources of information and historical data that are well beyond that of human capacity, extending collective experience.

Bibliography

Abbott, Dean W., Philip I. Matkovsky, and John F. Elder IV. *An Evaluation of High-end Data Mining Tools for Fraud Detection*, IEEE International Conference on Systems, Man, and Cybernetics." San Diego, California, pp. 12–14, October 1998.

Adelman, Sid, and Larissa Terpeluk Moss *Data Warehouse Project Management* Saddle River, New Jersey: Addison Wesley, 2000.

Backstrom, Lars, Dan Huttenlocher, Jon Kleinberg, et al. *"Group Formation in Large Social Networks: Membership, Growth, and Evolution."* KDD'06, Philadelphia, Pennsylvania, 2006.

Balakrishinan, Karthik, and Vasant Honavar. *"Intelligent Diagnosis Systems."* Journal of Intelligent Systems, v. 8, n. 3/4, pp. 239–290, 1998.

Berson, Alex, and Stephen J. Smith. *Data Warehousing, Data Mining and OLAP* New York: McGraw-Hill, 1997.

Borgatti, Stephen, Ajay Mehra, Daniel Brass, et al. *"Network analysis in the social sciences."* Science, 323(5916), pp. 892–895, 2009.

Boukerche, Azzedine, and Sechi, Mirela M., Notare, Annoni *"Behavior-Based Intrusion detection in Mobile Phone Systems."* Journal of Parallel and Distributed Computing v. 62, pp. 1476–1490, 2002.

Brause, R., T. Langsdorf, and M. Hepp. *"Credit Card Fraud Detection by Adaptive Neural Data Mining."* Interner Bericht - Fachbereicht Informatik, Robert-Mayer-Strasse, pp. 11–15, 1999a.

Brause, R., T. Langsdorf, and M. Hepp. *Neural Data Mining for Credit Card Fraud Detection.* 11th IEEE International Conference on Tools with Artificial Intelligence, 1999b.

Breiger, R.L. *"The Analysis of Social Network."* In Handbook of Data Analysis. London: SAGE Publications, pp. 505–526, 2004.

Burge, P., J. Shawe-Taylor, C. Cooke, Y. Moreau, B. Preneel, and C. Stoermann. *Fraud Detection and Management in Mobile Telecommunications Networks.* In Proceedings of the European Conference on Security and Detection ECOS 97, London, 1997.

209

Burge, Peter and John Shawe-Taylor. *"An Unsupervised Neural Network Approach to Profiling the Behavior of Mobile Phone Users for Use in Fraud Detection."* Journal of Parallel and Distributed Computing v. 61, pp. 915–925, 2001.

Carrington, Peter J., John Scott, and Stanley Wasserman. *Models and Methods in Social Network Analysis.* New York: Cambridge University Press, 2005.

Chakraborty, G., M. Pagolu, and S. Garla. *Text Mining and Analysis: Practical Methods, Examples, and Case Studies Using SAS(R).* SAS Institute Inc., Cary, 2013.

Culotta, Aron. *Maximizing Cascades in Social Networks: An Overview.* Amherst, MA: University of Massachusetts, 2003.

Dasgupta, Koustuv, Rahul Singh, Balaji Viswanathan, et al. *"Social Ties and their Relevance to Churn in Mobile Telecom Networks."* EDBT'08, Nantes, France, ACM, 2008.

Degenne, Alain, and Michel Forse. *Introducing Social Networks.* London: Sage Publications, 1999.

Calderon, Thomas G. and John J. Cheh. *"A roadmap for future neural networks research in auditing and risk management."* International Journal of Accounting Information Systems v. 3, pp. 203–236, 2002.

Chen Jie, and R. J. Patton. *Robust Model-Based Fault Diagnosys For Dinamic Systems.* Beijing, China: Kluwer Academics Publishers, 1999.

Chlapoutakis, George. *"The Use of Neural Networks in Telephone and Credit-Card Fraud Detection."* University of Sunderland, Department of Computer Science, 2002.

Davenport, Thomas H., and Jeanne G. Harris. *Competing on Analytics—The New Science of Winning.* Boston, MA: Harvard Business Scholl Press, 2007.

Davis, Jim, Gloria J., Miller, and Allan Russel. *Information Revolution – Using the Information Evolution Model to Grow your Business.* Hoboken, NJ: Wiley, 2006.

Derks, E. P. P. A., and L. M. C. Buydens. *"Aspects of network training and validation on noisy data - Part 2."* Validation aspects, Chemometrics and Intelligent Laboratory Systems, v. 41, n. 2, pp. 185–193, 1998.

Despagne, F., and D. L. Massart. *"Variable selection for neural networks in multivariate calibration,"* Chemometrics and Intelligent Laboratory Systems, v. 40, n. 2, pp. 145–163, 1998.

EmirBayer, Mustafa, and Jeff Goodwin. *"Network analysis, culture and the problem of agency."* American Journal of Sociology, v.99, n.6, pp. 1411–1454, 1994.

Estienne, F., L. Pasti, B. Walczak, F. Despagne, D. Jouan-Rimbaud, D. L., Massart, and O. E. de Noord, O.E. *"A comparison of multivariate calibration techniques applied to experimental NIR data sets. Part II: Predictive ability under extrapolation conditions."* Internet Journal of Chemistry, v. 2, n. 19, 1999.

Fayyad, U. E., G. Piatetsky-Shapiro, P. Smyth, and R.Uthurusamy. *Advances in Knowledge Discovery and Data Mining.* Menlo Park, CA: AAAI Press, 1996.

Fleming, Lee, Alexandra Marin, Jonathan McPhie, et al. *"Why the Valley went first: Aggregation and emergence in regional collaboration networks."* John Padgett and Walter Powell (eds.), Market Emergence and Transformation. Boston, MA: MIT Press, forthcoming.

Fletcher, R. *Practical Methods of Optimisation, v.1: Unconstrained Optimisation.* New York: John Wiley & Sons, 1980.

Goldberg, David E. *Genetic Algorithms in Search, Optimization and Machine Learning.* Indianapolis, Indiana: Addison-Wesley, 1989.

Groth, Robert. *Data Mining—Building Competitive Advantage.* Saddle River, NJ: Prentice Hall PTR, 2000.

Hastie, Trevor, Robert Tibshirani, and Jerome Friedman. *The Elements of Statistical Learning—Data Mining, Inference and Prediction.* Stanford, California: Springer, 2001.

Hawkins, D. M., D. Bradu, and G. V. Kass. *"Location of several outliers in multiple regression data using elemental sets."* Technometrics, v. 26, pp. 197–208, 1984.

Haykin, Simon. *Neural Networks – A Comprehensive Foundation.* Upper Saddle River, New Jersey: Macmillian College Publishing Company, 1994.

Hill, Shawndra, Foster Provost, and Chris Volinsky. *"Network-Based Marketing: Identifying Likely Adopters via Consumer Networks."* Statistical Science 2006, Vol. 21, No. 2, 256–276, 2006.

Hoerl, Roger D., and Ron Snee. *Statistical Thinking: Improving Business Performance.* Hoboken, NJ: Wiley, 2012.

Hollmen, Jaakko. *User profiling and classification for fraud detection in mobile communications networks.* Dissertation for the degree of Doctor of Science in Technology, University of Technology, Department of Computer Science and Engineering, Laboratory of Computer and Information Science, Helsinki, 2000

Hopkins, B. *"A new method for determining the type of distribution of plant individuals."* Annuals of Botany, v. 18, pp. 213–227, 1954.

Hush, D. R., and B. G. Horne. *"Progress in supervised neural networks: what's new since Lippmann."* IEEE Signal Processing Magazine, v. 1, pp. 8–37, 1993.

Isermann, R. "*Supervision, Fault-Detection and Fault-Diagnosis Methods—An Introdution.*" Control Engineering Practice, v. 5, n. 5, pp. 639–652, 1997.

Katz, J. Sylvan, and Ben R. Martin. "*What is Research Collaboration?*" Research Policy, v. 26, pp. 1–18, 1997.

Kempel, David, and Jon Kleinberg. "*Maximizing the Spread of Influence through a Social Network.*" SIGKDD '03, Washington, DC, 2003.

Kempel, David, Jon Kleinberg, and Eva Tardos, Eva. "*Influential Nodes in a Diffusion Model for Social Networks.*" L. Caires et al. (Eds.): ICALP'05 Proceedings of the 32nd International Conference on Automata, Languages and Programming, pp. 1127–1138, 2005. Berlin Heidelberg: Springer-Verlag, 2005.

Kimball, Ralph. *Data Warehouse Toolkit.* São Paulo, Brazil: Makron Books, 1998.

Kimball, Ralph, Laura Reeves, Margy Ross, and Warren Thornthwaite. *The Data Warehouse Lifecycle Toolkit.* Danvers, MA: Wiley, 1998.

Kimball, Ralph, and Richard Merz. *The Data Webhouse Toolkit—Building the Web-Enable Data Warehouse.* Danvers, MA: Wiley, 2000.

Knoke, David, and Song Yank. *Social Network Analysis.* London: Sage Publications, 2007.

Kohonen, T. *Self-Organization and Associative Memory,* 3rd Edition. Berlin: Springer-Verlag, 1989.

Kretschmer, Hildrun. "*Author productivity and geodesic distance in bibliographic co-authorship networks, and visibility on the Web.*" Scientometrics, v. 60, n. 3, pp. 409–420, 2004.

Leskovec, J., L. A. Adamic, and B. A. Huberman, B. A. "*The dynamics of viral marketing.*" ACM Transactions on the Web, 2007.

Lippmann, R. P. "*An introduction to computing with neural nets.*" IEEE Computer Society, v. 3, pp. 4–22, 1987.

Looney, C. G. *Pattern Recognition Using Neural Networks: Theory and Algorithms for Engineers and Scientists.* New York: Oxford University Press, 1997.

Mahlck, Paula, and Olle Persson. "*Socio-bibliometric mapping of intradepartamental networks.*" Scientometrics, v. 49, n. 1, pp. 81–91, 2000.

Masters, T. *Practical Neural Network Recipes in C++.* Boston: Academic Press, 1993.

Mattison, Rob. *Web Warehousing and Knowledge Management.* New York: McGraw-Hill, 1999.

Miller, Gloria J., Dagmar Bräutigam, and Stefanie V. Gerlach. *Business Intelligence Competence Centers—A Team Approach to Maximizing Competitive Advantage.* Hoboken, NJ: Wiley, 2006.

Mitchell, Melanie. *An Introduction to Genetic Algorithms*. Cambridge, Massachusetts: Bradford Book - MIT Press, 1998.

Moeller, R. A. *"Distributed Data Warehousing using Web Technology."* AMACOM, 2000.

Nanavati, Amit, Rahul Singh, Dipanjan Chakraborty, et al. *"Analyzing the Structure and Evolution of Massive Telecom Graphs."* IEEE Transactions on Knowledge and Data Engineering, 2008.

Newman, M. E. J. *"From the Cover: The structure of scientific collaboration networks."* Proceedings of the National Academy of Sciences of the United States of America, v. 98, pp. 404–409, 2001.

Olla, Phillip, and Nandish V. Patel. *"A value chain model for mobile data service providers."* Telecommunications Policy, v. 26, n. 9-10, pp. 551–571, 2002.

Onnela, J.-P., J. Saramäki, J. Hyvönen, et al. *"Structure and tie strengths in mobile communication networks."* Proceedings of the National Academy of Sciences of the United States of America, 2007.

Otte, Evelien, and Ronald Rousseau. *"Social network analysis: a powerful strategy, also for information sciences."* Journal of Information Science, Thousand Oaks, v. 28, n. 6, pp. 441–453, 2002.

Pandit, Vinayaka, Natwar Modani, and Sougata Mukherjea. *"Extracting Dense Communities from Telecom Call Graphs.* Proceedings of the Third International Conference on Communication Systems Software and Middleware, pp. 82–89, 2008.

Pinheiro, Carlos A. R. *Social Network Analysis in Telecommunications*. Hoboken, NJ: Wiley, 2011.

Pinheiro, Carlos A. R. *"Community Detection to Identify Fraud Events in Telecommunications Networks."* SAS Global Forum Proceedings, p. 106, Orlando, Florida, 2012.

Pinheiro, Carlos A. R. *"Highlighting Unusual Behavior in Insurance Based on Social Network Analysis."* SAS Global Forum Proceedings, p. 130, Las Vegas, Nevada, 2100.

Pinheiro, Carlos A. R. *"Revenue Assurance through Data Mining and Business Analytics."* SAS Global Forum Proceedings, p. 119, San Antonio, Texas, 2008.

Pinheiro, Carlos A. R. *"Competitive Intelligence through Business Analytic and Data Mining Environments."* SAS Global Forum Proceedings, p. 326, Orlando, Florida, 2007.

Pinheiro, Carlos A. R. *"Revenue Recovering with Insolvency Prevention on a Brazilian Telecom Operator."* SIGKDD Explorations special issue on Successful Real-World DataMining Applications, United States, 2006.

Pinheiro, Carlos A. R. *"Neural Network to identify and prevent bad debt in Telephone Companies,* Proceedings of the First International Workshop on Data Mining Case Studies" IEEE International Conference on Data Mining, pp. 125–139, Louisiana, United States, 2005.

Pinheiro, Carlos A. R., Nelson F. F. Ebecken, and Alexandre G. Evsukoff. *Identifying Insolvency Profile in a Telephony Operator Database,* Data Mining 2003, pp. 351–366, Rio de Janeiro, Brazil, 2003.

Pinheiro, Carlos A. R., and Markus Helfert. *"Social Network Analysis Combined to Neural Networks to Predict Churn in Mobile Carriers."* Journal of Communication and Computer (JCC), 2012, vol. 9, no. 2, pp.155–158, David Publishing (ISSN: 1548-7709).

Pinheiro, Carlos A. R., and Markus Helfert. *"Social Network Analysis Evaluating the Customers Influence Factor Over Business Events in Telco."* International Journal of Artificial Intelligence & Applications (IJAIA), 2010, vol. 1, no. 4, pp. 122–131, AIRCC.

Pinheiro, Carlos A. R., and Markus Helfert. *"Neural Network and Social Network to Enhance the Customer Loyalty Process."* Innovations and Advances in Computer Sciences and Engineering, 2010, pp. 91–96, Springer.

Pinheiro, Carlos A. R., and Marksu Helfert. *"Customer's Relationship Segmentation Driving the Predict Modeling for Bad Debt Events,* User Modeling, Adaptation and Personalization." Lecture Notes in Computer Science, 2009, vol. 5535, pp. 319–324, Springer.

Pinheiro, Carlos A. R., and Markus Helfert. *"Creating a Customer Influence Factor to Decrease the Impact of Churn and to Enhance the Bundle Diffusion in Telecommunications Based on Social Network Analysis."* SAS Global Forum Proceedings, p. 111, Seattle, Washington, 2010.

Pinheiro, Carlos A. R., and Markus Helfert. *"Social Network Analysis to Improve the Customer Loyalty."* Statistical Methods for the Analysis of Network Data, 2009, Dublin, Ireland.

Pinheiro, Carlos A. R., and Markus Helfert. *"Mixing Scores from Artificial Neural Network and Social Network Analysis to Improve the Customer Loyalty."* Proceedings of Advanced Information Networking and Applications Workshops, 2009, pp. 954–959, IEEE Computer Society.

Pinheiro, Carlos A. R., and Markus Helfert. *"Using Distinct Aspects of Social Network Analysis to Improve the Customer Loyalty Process."* Conference on Applied Statistics in Ireland, 2009, Mullingar, Ireland.

Rich, Elaine, and Kevin Knight. *Artificial Intelligence.* São Paulo: Makron Books, 1994.

Ritter, Helge, Thomas Martinetz, and Klaus Schulten. *Neural Computation and Self-Organizing Maps.* New York: Addison-Wesley New York, 1992.

Rosenblatt, F. *"The Perceptron: A Probabilistic Model for Information Storage and Organization in the Brain."* Psychology Review, v. 65, pp. 386–408, 1958.

Rud, Olivia Parr. *Data Mining Cookbook.* Denvers, MA: John Wiley & Sons, 2001.

Rumelhart, D. E., and J. L. McClelland. *Parallel Distributed Processing,* v.1. Cambridge, Massachusetts: MIT Press, 1986.

Russell, Stuart, and Peter Norvig. *Artificial Intelligence—A Modern Approach.* Berkeley: Prentice Hall PTR, 1995.

Saito, Kazumi, Ryohei Nakano, and Masahiro Kimura. *"Prediction of Information Diffusion Probabilities for Independent Cascade Model."* I. Lovrek, R. J. Howlett, and L. C. Jain (Eds.): KES 2008, Part III, LNAI 5179, pp. 67–75, 2008. Berlin Heidelberg: Springer-Verlag, 2008.

Savant, Marilyn von, "Ask Marilyn," *Parade* magazine, Parade Publications Inc., September 9, pp. 16, 1990Seshadri, Mukund, Sridhar Machiraju, and Sridharan Ashwin. *"Mobile Call Graphs: Beyond Power-Law and Lognormal Distributions."* KDD'08, ACM SIGKDD, pp. 596–604, 2008.

Selvin, Steven, "Letters to the Editor: A Problem in Probability," *The American Statistican,* American Statistical Society, Vol. 29, No. 1, pp. 67, 1975

Shawe-Taylor, John, Keith Howker, and Peter Burge. *"Detection of Fraud in Mobile Telecommunications."* Information Security Technical Report, v. 4, n. 1, pp. 16–28, 1999.

Simon, Phil. *Too Big to Ignore: The Business Case for Big Data.* Wiley, Hoboken, 2013.

Stubbs, Evan. *Delivering Business Analytics: Practical Guidelines for Best Practice.* Wiley, Hoboken, 2013.

Wasserman, Stanley,and Katherine Faust. *Social Network Analysis: methods and applications.* Cambridge: Cambridge University Press, 1994.

Watts, Duncan. *Small Worlds.* Princeton, New Jersey: Princeton University Press, 1999.

Watts, Duncan. *Six Degrees.* New York: Norton, 2003.

Watts, Duncan, Peter Dodds, and Mark Newman, Mark. *"Identity and search in social networks."* Science, 296: 1302–1305, 2002.

Weiss, Sholom M.,and Nitin Indurkhya. *Predictive Data Mining—A pratical guide.* San Francisco, CA: Morgan Kaufmann Publishers, 1998.

Wellman, Barry. *"Structural analysis."* Barry Wellman and S. D. Berkowitz (eds.), Social Structures, pp. 19-61. Cambridge, Massachusetts: Cambridge University Press, 1988.

Wellman, Barry, and Scott Wortley. *"Different strokes from different folks."* American Journal of Sociology, 96(3):558-588, 1990.

Wellman, Barry. "*The community question.*" American Journal of Sociology, 84:12011231, 1979.

Wellman, Barry and Kenneth Frank. "*Network capital in a multi-level world.*" Nan Lin, Karen Cook, and Ronald Burt (eds.), Social Capital, pp. 233-73. Chicago: Aldine Transaction, 2001.

Wellman, Barry, Bernie Hogan, Kristen Berg, et al. "*Connected Lives: The project.*" Patrick Purcell (eds.), Networked Neighborhoods, pp. 157–211, Guilford, UK: Springer, 2006.

Wortman, Jennifer. "*Viral Marketing and the Diffusion of Trends on Social Networks.*" University of Pennsylvania Department of Computer and Information Science, Technical Report No. MS-CIS-08-19, 2008.

Yoshikane, Fuyuki, and Kyo Kageura. "*Comparative analysis of co-authorship networks of different domains: The growth and change of networks.*" Scientometrics, v. 60, n. 3, pp. 435–446, 2004.

Index

Printed and bound by CPI Group (UK) Ltd, Croydon, CR0 4YY

16/04/2025

14658516-0002